I0094341

POLITICAL AUTHORITY AND
THE NIGERIAN CIVIL SERVICE

POLTICAL AUTHORITY AND THE NIGERIAN CIVIL SERVICE

by
HUMPHERY N. NWOSU

Fourth Dimension Publishing Co., Ltd.

First Published 1977 by
FOURTH DIMENSION PUBLISHING CO., LTD
16 Fifth Avenue, City Layout. PMB. 01164, Enugu, Nigeria.
Tel+234-42-459969. Fax+234-42-456904.
email: fdpbooks/a;aol.com, fdpbooks;a;yahoo.com
Web site: http://www.fdpbooks.com.

Reprinted 1985, 2002

© Humphrey N. Nwosu 1977

ISBN 978-156-006-1

CONDITIONS OF SALE

All rights reserved. No part of this publication may be reproduced, stored in
a retrieval system, or transmitted in any form or by any means, electronic,
mechanical, photocopying, recording, or otherwise without the prior
permission of the publisher.

Photoset and printed in Nigeria by
Fourth Dimension Publishers, Enugu.

CONTENTS

AUTHOR'S NOTE

The general purpose of this book is to investigate how successive regimes in Nigeria sought to create and develop legitimated political authority and structures which have in turn shaped and influenced the development and role of the Nigerian civil service and its capacity to induce economic development through national planning.

The danger in Nigeria seems to be less that the federal government and the civil service possess more authority and power to overawe the society, than the fear that they do not have enough legitimated authority to carry out their increasing economic and social functions and thereby earn the support of the powerful interests groups and local authorities which constitute the society.

Consequently, creation as well as development of legitimated central political authority and structures such as the civil service have been a primary concern to all regimes in Nigeria, since she became a unified country in 1914. The book focuses attention on the various plural independent clusters of powers in Nigeria's heterogeneous social environment, primarily because their "capture" of public authority and institutions determines the degree of legitimacy grants to the incumbents of authority roles at national and regional levels of society. Second, they shaped and determined the constitutional and political processes which in 1954 turned Nigeria into an unbalanced federation.

As Nigeria's federal constitution did not grow out of the needs of the wider environment, it failed to serve as a dependable source of legitimacy grant to the federal authorities and civil service. Besides, experiences of Nigeria between 1954 and 1966 have shown that "loose" federal arrangements which involve dispersal rather than consolidation of power are hardly appropriate devices for the creation and development of legitimated central political authority and institutions in fragmented societies.

In an effort to secure *willing* compliance with and support of their decision choices, successive regimes in Nigeria relied upon such techniques and mechanisms as power sharing, leadership coalition, constitution making, ideologies, ethnic appeals, political parties and civil service, but none of these instruments has served as a reservoir of legitimacy grant to the central political authority.

In the absence of legitimating ideology, rules, political institutions and structures, all claims by Nigerian national and regional leaders to legitimate title to rule, are dependent on performance and their ability to grant "payoffs" and positive inducements to the various individuals, groups and sectors in the society. Various regimes in Nigeria have, therefore relied upon the federal and state civil services to formulate national development plans as a means of earning legitimacy. But as our study has shown the implementation of planned objectives in Nigeria is constrained by such factors as corruption, lack of high level manpower, poor management and inadequate organizational and physical infrastructures. Nevertheless, given Nigeria's windfall resources, she stands a better chance than most other poor African states to demonstrate effectiveness by achieving economic development.

ACKNOWLEDGEMENTS

This book was completed with the help, assistance and advice of a number of people. Above all, the many fellow Nigerians, officials and non officials who were willing to help me locate research materials and documents and who patiently answered my questions. Without their cooperation, none of what follows would have been possible. I wish also to acknowledge my gratitude to the Institute of International Studies, University of California at Berkeley, and the James Grubb Foundation for the generous financial assistance which enabled the field research and subsequent analysis to be carried out.

I also take this opportunity to express my gratitude and indebtedness to Professors C. G. Rosberg, Jr., M. Landau, J. Ogbu, whose comments, advice, and encouragement at every stage of this work were invaluable. I am especially indebted and thankful to Professor C. G. Rosberg, who has proved to be more than a teacher, and has made my graduate study at Berkeley so much easier and more rewarding. I also wish to express my gratitude to my generation of graduate students at Berkeley, paticularly Russell Stout, Jeremy Curtoys and Ernest Wilson for their friendship and stimulating discussions in graduate seminars.

Above all, I owe an enormous debt to my wife Stella and my children, Ogechukwu and Nnaemeka, for their patience, understanding and encouragement throughout the period of preparing this work. They alone know the cost of writing this book.

However, all the errors in judgment and facts are entirely my own.

CHAPTER ONE

INTRODUCTION

With a heterogenous social environment characterized by powerful contenders of state authority, Nigeria perhaps more than any other country in Africa faces greater challenges to development and rational allocation of societal resources. In the absence of a strong sense of national unity, successive regimes in Nigeria have to deal with such problems as redefinition of 'new' socio-political order emerging out of a diverse set of "traditional societies"[1] and establishment of national political authority acceptable to the various historic groups that constitute the state. Second, the state and the administrative machinery—the civil service—are increasingly looked upon by the wider society to implement developmental goals such as the creation of new economic and political structures and infusing them with values and purposes, adaptation and reconstruction of old ones, and the acceleration of economic and social changes that will reduce unemployment, increase social products and ensure a more equitable redistribution of income. Despite the increases in the responsibilities and the problems of the national state, there are no corresponding increases in the legitimacy and support granted by the wider society to the national political authorities, because most Nigerians still retain strong ties to and identify their primary loyalties with their immediate local authorities.

This study investigates how successive regimes in Nigeria sought to create and maintain political authority and structures which in turn have shaped and influenced the development and role of the Nigerian civil service and its capacity to induce economic development through national planning.

The crux of the development problem in Nigeria lies not in the absence of political authority but in the existence of several legitimated "authorities" in the wider society which in various ways constrain the exercise of national political authority, as well as threaten the existence of political community.[2] First, there are several dozens of legitimated traditional authorities scattered all over Nigeria. Each traditional authority derives legitimacy from the institutions and structures which have acquired values and special sanctity as a result of their successful survival and adaptation to the changes and vicissitudes of time. As the state and society are poorly integrated, the various historic and particularistic groups in the wider society develop close ties and loyalties with their immediate traditional authorities (*emirs, obas, obis,* and *obongs*) and thereby deprive the central political authority of the legitimacy and support it needs in order to carry out its policies. Besides there

1

are no shared common and stable expectations among the different traditional authorities about behaviours appropriate for incumbents of various authority roles at the national level. Rather each 'traditional system' has its own normative and structural mechanisms for granting and withdrawing legitimacy and allegiance to the central and regional political authorities.

The second form of 'legitimated' authorities which have constrained the emergence of a centralized and legitimated national political authority in Nigeria are the 'regional' authorities. From 1946 to 1966, Nigeria had three powerful regions[3] of which one was bigger in size and population than the other two put together. The regional governments and authorities did not derive their legitimacy from rules and structures based primarily on 'rational legal order'[4] but mainly from three dominant regional oriented political parties which in turn drew their support from three powerful ethnic groups. Our study will show that the structuring of Nigeria into three regional authorities between 1946 and 1966 contributed immensely to constraining the legitimacy and authority of the central government and the capacity of the central civil service to induce economic and social changes through national planning.

The third authority pattern in the Nigerian social environment is the ethnic groups. Though Nigeria like several other African countries has several ethnic groups which are at varying degrees of 'social mobilization', three of these Hausa/Fulani, Yorubas, and Igbos, are so large in population that each of them is bigger than such small African countries as Gabon, Gambia, Niger, Senegal, and Ivory Coast. Our study will show that these ethnic groups through generation of independent resources and powerful cultural organizations exercised such influence on their members that the movement of Nigerian society towards a "rational legal system" of authority was slowed down particularly between 1954 and 1966. Besides the ethnic groups granted legitimacy to the regional governments and parties and denied the same to the Federal government.

The fourth type of authority pattern in Nigeria is 'personal authority'. For a period, the Nigerian political processes revolved around the "personal authority" of three individuals—Alhaji Bello, the Sardauna of Sokoto, Dr. Nnamdi Azikiwe and Chief Awolowo. Although each of the three leaders for a while headed a regional government and was able to engender some form of 'personal' legitimacy none of them had such charisma as to engender legitimacy to the central political authority in the same way that Nkrumah did in Ghana, Nasser in Egypt, and Sukarno in Indonesia. Our study will show that the struggle amongst the three leaders for dominance, and the population's affection constrained rather than enhanced the legitimacy of the federal authority.

2

Fifthly, there is the "military authority" which became a significant factor when the Nigerian armed forces intervened in the political process in January 1966. Since then, the military has formed the government of Nigeria with the help of the civil service and 'hand picked' civilians. At the same time, the armed forces also constitute a powerful institutional interest group whose activities more than that of any other "authority" within the wider environment have helped to shape and determine the structure of the present Nigerian government and the capacity of the central and regional civil service to induce economic and social changes.

The Nigerian military authorities have their external and internal legitimacy problems. First, there is the problem of their continually justifying their rule to Nigerians, because they cannot always secure compliance through coercion or the threat of it. This problem relates to the need of creating structures and mechanisms which can engender legitimacy to the military rule and thereby help in the consolidation of the central authority. Our study will highlight what steps the military regime has taken to create structures to link the state and the society so as to engender legitimacy for its rule. Second, the military rulers face the additional problem of earning the legitimacy of the armed forces which form the "core" of its support. To be sure, the allegiance of the men and the rank in the army and other services is not and cannot under the Nigerian circumstances be taken for granted. As the strength of the army grew from a paltry figure of 10,000 in 1966 to a sprawling one of 250,000[5] in 1970, there is a staggering problem of maintaining order and discipline within its organization, so that its internal conflicts will not perpetually threaten the existence of the political community. The coups and counter-coups that have marked the military regime in the past ten years, do not only deplete its stock of legitimacy, but also release passions of rivalry, ambition, and vindictiveness which have negative consequences not only for the internal cohesion of military organization but for consolidating the federal government authority and its capacity to induce development through national planning.

The central issue that arises out of our discussion so far is the problem of legitimacy. There are many "authorities" in Nigeria which are competing with the central authority for the grant of legitimacy and allegiance by the wider society. If the question is addressed: To whom should the primary loyalty and sense of identification and commitment be given in Nigeria? To an outsider who is unfamiliar with the central problem of a developing country such as Nigeria, the question may seem uncalled for because the answer in the circumstances of several 'older' states is quite obvious. For instance, a typical American citizen has been 'socialized' to give his primary loyalty and affection to the American nation; then he can defer to his particular state, county, city

3

and so on. This claim can also be made for a typical citizen in Britain or the Soviet Union. While all the citizens in the older states may not give their primary loyalty to the state, the majority of them do. Let us now find out what the answer to our question will be in Nigeria. To be sure, the state as our Table I below illustrates is not the recipient of the primary loyalty and identification in Nigeria.

Most Nigerians retain very strong ties and affection for their primary groups, families, kinships, villages, clans, town communities; and thereby easily grant legitimacy to the local authorities out of sheer habit and custom. They equally have very close identification with their ethnic groups, which became highly mobilized with the introduction of western education and cash economy. As the ethnic groups and cultural associations served as dependable vehicles and platforms for mediating the discontinuities which generally accompanied the process of "modernization", the majority of Nigerians identify closely with their ethnic groups and easily grant them legitimacy for both cultural, economic and political activities. Identification with individual authorities was more of a phenomenon before than after the attainment of independence. It has been so transitory that none of the three Nigerian dominant civilian leaders—Bello, Azikiwe, and Awolowo—had enough of it at any one time to transpose it to the central government. Nigerians so far have not seen enough "charisma" in any single leader —military or civilian—to allow him to generate personal legitimacy in choice of policy or structures of government. The regional (state) governments are recipients of greater legitimacy and identification than the national state and its agencies. Invariably a particular ethnic group views a given region or state's government as its "own" and other regions and states as "their own". Undoubtedly, "our own" states or regions are entitled to a high degree of legitimacy even when their performance may be quite below expected standards, while "their own" states or regions are not entitled to legitimacy even when their performance is above average. Consequently, each region or state derives its legitimacy from a particular dominant ethnic group which, because of what is generally considered as "ethnic interest" grants its support without giving much consideration to the performance of the state government. Invariably it is only those who consider themselves 'minorities' within a given state or region that constantly require a regional or state government to "earn" its legitimacy through systems of "payoffs".

In the scheme of things in Nigeria, the national state is considered last, even though its increased responsibilities and position warrant that it should be placed first. As the central regime is viewed largely in terms of governmental outcomes, each group in the wider society sees representation in the state authority structure as a zero sum game. Those who consider themselves unrepresented in the state authority

4

TABLE 1. AUTHORITIES IN NIGERIA AND LEVELS OF LEGITIMACY AND IDENTIFICATION

Types of Authority		Levels of Legitimacy and Intensity of Loyalty and Identification
Nigerian state including the military regime and the civil service		Legitimacy is low, loyalty and identification are "latent". Legitimacy is reluctantly given—easily withdrawn. Sustenance of legitimacy entails greater positive inducements.
The regions (now known as states). This includes regional civil services		Legitimacy is higher, but generally not as high as in most older states. Identification is strong but not primary. Legitimacy is easily given, but sustained more by "payoffs".
Personal authorities		Legitimacy and identification fluctuate according to different groups' perception. No single person has had enough charisma to transpose it to the national state. Legitimacy is very temporary.
Ethnic groups and cultural associations		Legitimacy is high. Identification and loyalty are strong and "manifest". Ethnic groups and cultural associations earn the greatest legitimacy when they operate in "alien" lands.
Traditional political systems		Legitimacy is very high. Loyalty and identification are stronger than at ethnic group level.
Primary groups, town communities, villages	Families, Kinship groups	At these two levels, legitimacy is primary. Loyalty and identification are strongest. Legitimacy is instantly granted, even at periods of severe deprivation.

5

structure generally may withdraw their support from the state or at least remain indifferent to its activities. In a sense, withdrawal of support implies denial of legitimacy or the belief in the right of a regime to make decisions and choices on behalf of the society. As the granting and withdrawal of legitimacy is crucial to problems of consolidating the national authority and inducing social and economic changes in Nigeria through the civil service, we will in the following section elaborate the concept in greater detail.

Legitimacy: What is legitimacy? Why is it considered necessary for a central regime in Nigeria to acquire it? Why is it considered important for the national civil service to be viewed as legitimate in order to perform its functions effectively? What are the sources of legitimacy to regimes in developing countries such as Nigeria? When can a regime be said to be having a legitimacy crisis? To be sure, answers to these questions are necessary in tackling our research problem.

First, the concept of legitimacy. When legitimacy is viewed from the perspective of the member of a political system it refers to a strong belief that it is proper and right to comply with policy choices and other requirements of a regime and political system. It is therefore a quality endowed by the citizens which facilitates the exercise of authority. It principally accrues from the subjects to the political authorities and their agencies. Viewed from the perspective of the political authorities, legitimacy refers to the sentiment and feelings that if the activities and decision choices of the authorities come within some definable "zones", they, the authorities, can expect compliance on the part of the members of the society.

Legitimacy is a quality which rulers cannot secure from the population through the use of coercion or threat of it. Granting and withdrawal of legitimacy to political authorities, regime, institutions and rules are entirely the prerogative of the wider society. Groups, individuals and sectors of the society can grant or withdraw their legitimacy to a regime according to their perception and evaluation about what activities and policy choices the regime ought to be pursuing. Legitimacy is not therefore permanently granted to a regime. All regimes, particularly those of the emergent states are primarily concerned with seeking and sustaining legitimacy of their populations. While it is possible for new regimes such as the military regimes in Africa to come into existence through the use of force, no regime, no matter the scale of instruments of violence at its disposal, can endure for a long time without legitimacy. Undoubtedly, political authorities seek legitimacy for themselves and their regimes as it constitutes the most dependable means of securing compliance with and support of their policy decisions. The acquisition and exercise of political authority are made easier and more effective if the majority of the population

6

consider the incumbents of authority roles and authority structures legitimate.[7] On the other hand, the exercise of political authority by a regime as well as its agencies, is made difficult in a social environment such as that of Nigeria where several independent contenders of state power constantly challenge the legitimacy of incumbents of authority roles. Consequently, a belief in the legitimacy of political authorities provides a basis for stabilizing the day to day activities of a political system.[8] Furthermore, legitimacy guarantees the authorities compliance as they seek to mobilize resources, regulate behaviour, carry out administrative reforms or induce economic and social changes through national planning. Attainment of compliance through a "reservoir of good will" of the population makes it possible for a regime to invest societal resources in other goals and objectives which will later increase its legitimacy. The "older" states such as the United States of America and the emergent states as Nigeria can be compared in terms of legitimacy that stems from the population to the national political authorities. While the "older" states are marked by a high degree of legitimacy because of greater "institutionalization" of their institutions and structures; the "newer" states are characterized by low degree of legitimacy, because the central institutions and structures have not been popularly accepted by their wider societies.[9] However, some older states such as Portugal and Italy from time to time drift from high to low legitimacy continuum.

Legitimacy and Compliance: As we pointed out earlier, legitimacy is the 'cheapest' and most dependable means of securing compliance. The other two sources are coercion and "payoffs" (benefits and rewards). Coercion involves threat or use of force in order to induce a "reluctant" compliance with government decision choices. Because of fear of punishment, reprisal and deprivation, groups and individuals comply with coercion or threat of it. But this method of attaining compliance is very expensive and requires heavy investment of scarce societal resources in the mechanisms of the police state. Given the low legitimacy that marks several emergent states, their regimes ars usually tempted to rely on coercion as a primary means of attaining compliance. For instance, Mobutu used coercion to eliminate powerful contenders of state authority who were accused of "conspiring" against his regime.[10] Milton Obote used force to consolidate national authority in Uganda. He forcefully eliminated the independent power enjoyed by Uganda's historic kingdoms. Obote himself was later a victim of coercion. He was ousted by General Idi Amin who did not only remove all his supporters from position of influence but eliminated all his real and potential enemies.[11] Perhaps the most chilling and terrifying use of coercion to secure compliance is illustrated by the violence prone regime of Micombero of Burundi. He used force to eliminate thousands of Hutu leaders who challenged the dominance of the central authority by Tutsi, who constitute only 15 per cent of the population.[12] The extensive use of coercion erodes the sense of legitimacy and thereby depletes the effectiveness of national political authority. It reduces the reliance on formal structures as a means of conflict resolution and decision making. It alienates people against the government and thus may lead to what Parsons refers to as "power deflation". It encourages the opponents of incumbents of government to rely on violence as a means of attaining their goals. Again, the spate of military coups that characterizes African politics illustrates that extreme reliance on coercion has not helped much in consolidation of national authority. As Zolberg put it:

The coups is normal consequence of the show down between a government and its opponents who use force against each other in a situation where the force at the disposal of government is very limited.[13]

The third means of securing complience with policy choices is payoffs. In fragmented polities which are deficient in affective ties toward government, regimes elicit compliance by positive inducements or reciprocal exchanges. Regimes thus use rewards and benefits to engender compliance by engaging in a form of specific bargaining. For instance, securing of compliance from a number of groups, individuals, or some sectors in the society may be subject to the imperatives of good performance in the economic sector, lowering taxes, increasing unemployment benefits, modernizing agriculture, carrying out land and administrative reforms, providing universal and free education. Generation of compliance through a system of payoffs has obvious disadvantages. It is very costly and involves extensive investment of scarce resources to satiate specific demands. It is highly utilitarian, because it works only whenever a regime is able to deliver the goods. Regimes that earn their right to govern by virtue of their performance run the risk of repudiation as a result of non-performance.[14] Consequently most of the African regimes which earn compliance with their policies through payoffs are highly vulnerable as they often lack enough resources to redeem all their promises. In the final analysis, legitimacy remains the cheapest means of securing compliance.

Legitimacy, Authority, and Power: Authority at any level in the society presumes a superior-subordinate relationship. At the level of the polity, authority, refers to the right to speak on behalf of the state, and make binding decisions that control the behaviour of individuals and groups in the society. Every polity has authority structures such as the executive, legislature, the courts, civil service, statutory boards, agencies, political parties, electoral commissions, through which authority roles are acquired and exercised. In many 'developed' polities, the authority structures are more integrated and 'rooted' with the wider society, but several 'developing' states are marked by more atomized and fragmented authority structures of which the ones at national level are generally "transfer institutions". On the other hand, power is the capacity to enforce decisions. Power possession invariably involves the ability to do something, to act, enforce, sometimes to reward the compliant, persuade the recalcitrant, punish the offender, mediate over conflict and coerce the intransigent. Besides exercise of power can be reflected in demonstration of confidence and quality of leadership. The substance of power is always contingent on the available societal resources. These resources which are categorized by social scientists in various ways, usually include material resources such as means of production, physical infrastructure and intangible resources, such as quality of leadership, esteem, prestige, information, influence, status and coercion. The possession of these resources confers a regime potential power to exercise authority. But this is not enough, for it is possible for occupants of authority roles to have resources of power and yet lack legitimacy. Consequently, possesion of power resources and acquisition of authority roles are not by themselves enough to make the exercise of authority effective. A regime must in addition earn the legitimacy of the wider society in order to secure compliance with and support of policy choices. The central problem that confronts the emergent states of Africa is how to create a legitimate authority. Given their slim resource base, they are faced with the critical choice of investing their scarce resources among such competing and pressing goals as creation, retention, and maintenance of legitimated authority, inducing economic and social change and carrying out administrative reforms. As each choice has an opportunity cost, the African leaders are generally guided first by what is politically feasible and secondly by what is technically sound. African leaders make their choices in reference to the objective situation rather than on the basis of "universal desiderata". Often self interests, the need to survive, are played off against the needs for economic development and administrative reforms. In several circumstances, national planning or administrative development is undertaken to the extent that it enhances the securing of compliance and induces a sense of legitimacy. They seek solutions to legitimacy problems which accommodate the congeries of independent 'authorities' that constitute the wider society.

Sources of Legitimacy: Ideologies are means of securing legitimacy. Ideologies espouse belief in the rightness of a regime. They articulate sets of ideals, ends, and purposes which interpret the past, explain the present and offer a vision of the future. An ideology is a type of "political religion" which is directed to "capture" the imagination of all the members of the wider society and thereby mobilize their sup-

9

port. A legitimating ideology consists of two main components—the 'consummatory' which is future oriented and the 'instrumental', which emphasizes the immediate and practical advantages of supporting a regime. An ideology has several uses. Apart from legitimating a regime, it calls for sacrifices and individual discipline, thrift and savings. It 'solicits' ruthless capital accumulation in order to facilitate industrialization.[15] The plural nature of the emergent states of Africa has inhibited the use of ideology as a means of legitimating political authority.

Structural Legitimacy: This accrues to a regime from the institutions and structures of a political system such as the executives, the courts, the legislatures, the political parties, and the bureaucracies. In order for political structures to serve as a source of legitimacy they must be perceived by individuals and groups in the wider society as valuable and beneficial. Members of a regime may be 'legitimated' by reason that they acquire power and exercise public authority via structures and institutions which have been legitimated. The more a given set of institutions and structures survive and adjust to changes and vicissitudes of time, the more they are able to build up reserves of legitimacy. Such structures provide dependable and convenient source of legitimacy so long as the rules and spirit of the institutions are not tampered with. In several 'older' states such as the United States, Britain and Japan, the constitutional political structures such as the congress, the monarchy, and the emperor generate good reservoir of legitimacy to the incumbents of authority roles. However, structural legitimacy as experiences of Italy and recently Ethiopia have shown may wane and cease to provide a dependable means of ensuring political stability. The constitutions and political structures of the new states are lacking in this type of legitimacy, because they are not 'legitimated' by the wider society. These structures are so 'recent' and contain such 'alien' provisions that the several 'legitimated' traditional authorities in the wider environment do not perceive them as valuable and beneficial.

Personal Legitimacy: Occupants of authority roles may generate personal or 'charismatic' legitimacy if they are perceived by individuals and groups in the society as being endowed with special leadership qualities such as the "gift of grace". Consequently, a wide variety of personal attributes such as heroism, selflessness, oratorical skill, devotion, confidence and style of government, help to determine the extent of deference a leader may earn from the wider society. However, it is possible for some leaders who lack 'charismatic' appeal, but who are able to manipulate large numbers of people to believe in qualities which in fact they do not possess, to engender personal legitimacy.[16]

Personal legitimacy is viewed as a temporary substitute for ideological and institutional legitimacy and it can be transferred to each. The demise of Nkrumah and Sukarno illustrates that personal legitimacy vanishes as soon as a leader appears to be devoid of his "magical power" or to be "forsaken by his god".

Creation and development of a legitimated central authority remains the crux of institution building problems in a developing state such as Nigeria. The problem is accentuated as the new states lack institutions and structures which can provide normative sources of compliance with their decision choices. Besides several of them cannot secure compliance through positive inducements as they are severely constrained by lack of resources. Under the circumstances, most of the new states in spite of the rhetoric, cannot accelerate the pace of economic development through national planning, nor implement far-reaching administrative reforms. Their objective situation compels them to adopt a policy of "muddling through" in a continued search for solutions to their legitimacy and authority problems.

From the above discussions we will now develop further propositions that will form the basis of our study.

(i)   The Nigerian pre and post independent federal constitutions and structures did not serve as dependable means for legitimating the authorities of federal government and the civil service.

The study argues that Nigerian federal constitution, with adequate provisions for federal and state jurisdiction, as well as formal structures such as House of Representatives and Senate, and Supreme Court, did not grow out of the needs and interests of the wider environment. Rather the constitution emerged as a result of a series of negotiations, bargainings, and compromises, first, among the leading Nigerian politicians, and secondly between them and the British colonial officials in London.

From the onset, the Federal constitution did not derive much legitimacy from the wider society which scarcely knew the implications of its provisions. Given the failure of federal arrangements in several emergent states—West Indies, Malaysia, Central Africa, and Mali— its appropriateness as a means of creating, maintaining, and consolidating a legitimated political authority in environment characterized by plural groups with long and differing roots has been questioned by several scholars of African politics.[17] As federalism entails dispersal of authority and power between two sets of governments which are each within a sphere coordinate and independent, it hardly serves as means of building legitimated authority in environment marked with strong centrifugal forces as that of Nigeria. As the Nigerian federal constitution between 1954 and 1966 hardly drew any legitimacy from

11

the wider society the exercise of central political authority was premised on the "politician's agreement" between the dominant political leaders and their parties—the Northern People's Congress (NPC) which espoused communalist principles and the National Council of Nigerian Citizens (NCNC) which espoused a type of populist nationalism. The exclusion of another regional party, the Action Group (AG), which had a powerful regional base support, constantly posed a threat to the legitimacy of the federal government. Had the Nigerian leaders combined skilful leadership with other societal resources, perhaps Nigeria would have been saved from a bloody three-year civil war which in effect stemmed from a legitimacy crisis. However, they did not, and their excesses not only eroded the legitimacy of the political structure, but constrained the effectiveness of the federal and state civil services.

(ii) In a federation marked by a weak central political authority and powerful and legitimated regional governments, which have independent resource base, the regional civil services tend to be more effective than the central one.

Our study will show that between 1954 and 1966, the Nigerian regional civil services were more effective in implementing moderate economic and social policies as they derived normative inducements from the regional governments. The regional governments had considerable independent resource base and derived their legitimacy from highly mobilized ethnic groups and dominant regional parties. On the other hand, the federal civil service was less effective as the exercise of the federal authority rested more on the agreement and consent of the regional overlords than on the legitimacy granted to it by the wider society.

(iii) Administrative reforms which are directed to improve performance can only be carried out by a regime which has a dependable source of legitimated authority.

Until recently all talks about administrative and organizational reforms in Nigeria did not yield much result, because the federal government lacked a reservoir of good will which is necessary to implement reforms. However, the successful conclusion of the Nigerian civil war and the strengthening of federal authority which have been made possible by unity of military command and increases in federal government oil wealth had enabled the federal authorities to implement some structural and administrative reforms which no civilian regime before 1966 would have been capable of implementing. The impact of these reforms is yet to be assessed. Moreover, the federal government in

12

Nigeria still has to earn a reservoir of legitimacy from the new institutions and structures which it is trying to create as well as from its other policy choices and actions.

The rest of the study is arranged as follows: Chapter two focuses on the various plural independent clusters of power in the Nigerian social environment primarily because the degree of legitimacy they grant to the central political authorities and the civil service help to determine the effectiveness of their policy choices and actions. Chapter three discusses events and processes that led to the emergence of the federal and state governments in Nigeria and their administrative machines. It analyzes the authority relationships between the federal and state governments and how this has affected the development, functions, and performances of the federal and state civil services. Furthermore, it discusses how the weakening of the authority of the federal government by strong centrifugal forces led to the collapse of Nigerian federation in 1966. It concludes by discussing the features of the "new federalism" which is marked by some 'increments' in the legitimacy of the federal government as well as increases in the functions of the federal civil service. Chapters four and five which deal with planning and problems of implementation, illustrate that planning is undertaken in Nigeria primarily to build legitimacy for central and regional political authorities and second to induce moderate economic and social changes. Attainment of these goals are severely constrained by such problems as those of infrastructure, organizational and management constraints, and corruption. Successful planning and implementation in the final analysis can only be undertaken in normal circumstances by a regime with a legitimated political authority having a sound resource base. Chapter six is the conclusion and re-examines the various techniques which Nigeria and other African states have used in creating and maintaining legitimated authority.

FOOTNOTES

1. The concept of tradition is used here as a residual concept. It is a category which covers a number of different social systems which are at varying stages of "social mobilization". These social systems become similar only when they are contrasted with "modernity". In a sense, there is no longer a 'pure' traditional society as each 'old' Nigerian society incorporates some elements of "modernity". However, these social systems are 'traditional' to the extent that the predominant principles that regulate their behaviour are determined more by 'ascriptive' rather than 'universal' considerations.

2. The concept of "political community" is used here to refer to the entire political system. Its usage corresponds to the way David Easton has used the concept. See David Easton, *A System Analysis of Political Life,* New York, John Wiley and Sons, Inc.; 1965, pp. 171-189.

3. A fourth region—Mid West was carved out of the Western region in January 1964. The existence of Midwest did not alter the dominance of Nigerian political life by the three regions—North, East, and West—from 1964 to 1966.

4. Max Weber distinguishes three ways in which political authorities could be legitimated—tradition—obedience is based on custom or sheer habit; "rational legal order" is considered legitimate because authority is exercised according to the stated rules and because it is to the subjects advantage to abide by these. The third is through charisma. Here the exercise of authority derives from the supposedly special quality of the person "Hence charismatic authority" shall refer to a rule over men, whether predominantly external or predominantly internal, to which the governed submit because of their belief in the extraordinary quality of the specific person". See H. H. Gerth and C. Wright Mills, eds. *From Max Weber: Essays in Sociology,* New York: Oxford University Press, 1958, pp. 295-296.

5. Colin Legum, *Africa Contemporary Records: Annual Survey and Documents 1970/71.* London: Lex Collings, 1971, P.B416.

6. A sector of the society may for instance deny legitimacy to a regime if it feels that the regime is spending more resources on foreign policy when it ought to be paying greater attention to domestic problems; while a different sector may grant its legitimacy to the regime, because of what it considers to be "great" achievements in foreign policy. In effect, no regime can ever hope to secure the legitimacy of all the members of the population. For the elaboration of the opportunity costs involved in investing resources on acquiring legitimacy see Warren F. Ilchman and Norman T. Uphoff, *Political Economy of Change,* Berkeley and Los Angeles, University of California Press, 1969, pp 73-80.

7. Our view here is also held by Henry Bretton who argues that: Legitimacy derives from proven, verified popular acceptance of basic principles of government, of the broad outlines of a constitution and of the principal personages associated with their implementation. See Henry Bretton, *Power and Politics in Africa,* Chicago: Aldine Publishing Co., 1973, p. 162.

8. David Easton, Op. Cit., p. 279.

9. Samuel P. Huntington makes the same point when he compares the 'developed' and 'underdeveloped' states in terms of degrees of authority. See S. P. Huntington, *Political Order in Changing Societies.* New Haven: Yale University Press, 1968. p. 1.

10. Jean-Claude Williams, *Patrimonialism and Political Change in the Congo,* Stanford, Stanford University Press, 1972. p. 141.

11. Colin Legum, Op. Cit., pp. B 187-192.

12. Ibid., See 1972-73 ed. pp. B 125-132. See also the 1973-74 ed. pp. B 141-147.

13. Anstride Zolberg, "The Structure of Political Conflict in the New States of Tropical Africa" in Frankle and Gable, eds., *Political Development and Social Change,* New York: John Wiley, and Sons, Inc. 1970, p. 631.

14. Norman H. Keehn, "Building Authority: A Return to Fundamentals" *World Politics,* Vol. XXVI, No. 3, April, 1974, p. 337.

15. Commenting on the social function of 'consensual' idealogy, David Apter states: "With the addition of political religion, the mobilization system becomes a prototype for what ought to obtain in other systems. The state is not only the teacher and guide for its own citizens it is a religious heartland for the conversion of infidels abroad. The translation of political morals into political religion becomes a practical art." See David Apter, *The Politics of Modernization.* Chicago: The University of Chicago Press, 1965, p. 366.
16. David Easton in contrast to Weber argues that a leader who lacks "charismatic" quality, under some circumstances can generate personal legitimacy. See David Easton, *Op. Cit.,* pp. 303-304
17. See, for instance, the work of Uma Eleazu, "Federalism and Nation Building for Nigeria", unpublished doctoral dissertation, University of California, Los Angeles, 1969.

15

CHAPTER TWO

THE NIGERIAN SOCIAL ENVIRONMENT

The Nigerian social environment is characterised by several traditional societies with ethnic homelands. The societies vary considerably
in terms of their cultural heritage, language, patterns of western contact
and population. Acording to the 1963 census, the population of the
ten largest ethnic groups are as follows:

TABLE 2. THE POPULATION OF TEN LARGEST
ETHNIC GROUPS IN NIGERIA (1963 CENSUS)

	MALE	FEMALE	TOTAL
Hausa	5,936,424	5,716,321	11,652,745
Yoruba	5,767,978	5,552,531	11,320,509
Igbo	4,684,849	4,561,539	9,246,388
Fulani	2,448,537	2,335,829	4,784,366
Kanuri	1,149,473	1,109,618	2,259,091
Ibibio	982,010	1,024,479	2,006,486
Tiv	711,481	682,168	1,393,649
Ijaw	522,661	566,224	1,088,885
Edo	473,002	481,968	954,970
Annang	332,173	342,831	675,004

Source: Nigeria Handbook, 1973, Lagos. Federal Ministry of Information,
April 1973, p. 131.

In order to come to grips with the problems posed to state authority
by cultural pluralism in Nigeria, we shall briefly analyze three
dominant traditional societies: Hausa, Igbo and Yoruba. Though the
social, political and economic organization principles upon which these
societies were premised differed considerably, yet as traditional
societies they shared some common features. Before the British contact,
each of them had a degree of occupational differentiation. Roles such
as those of craftsmen, hunters, traders, farmers, workers of metal,
wood and leather existed in each of the three societies. To a certain
extent each of them practiced slavery and engaged in active slave trade
during the nineteenth century. Though entry into their elitist groups
was not as open as it is in those of several industrialized and modern
societies, yet each, in a way allowed an upward mobility among the
less privileged but talented citizens.[1]

16

THE HAUSA

The Hausas are the largest ethnic group in Nigeria. They are mainly Islamic people and are quite spread out in many parts of Northern Nigeria. Their principal cities and towns include Kano, Katsina, Sokoto and Zaria. Before the Fulani invasion in 1804, the Hausa established flourishing kingdoms, and states whose fame and importance extended to the North Africa. Following the Fulani religious wars of 1804, most of the Hausa polities were conquered by Fulani Islamic lords. While the new Fulani overlords introduced Fulani dynasties, they incorporated the Hausa language, economic, social and political institutions. LeVine describes this enmeshing of the Hausa and Fulani kingdoms succinctly: "The Hausa language, Islamic religion and slavery provided a framework for the rapid assimilation of large numbers of alien persons into the traditional Hausa culture as modified by the Fulani conquerors".[2] The Hausa traditional political system was highly centralized.[3] Unlike the Igbo system, it had more elaborate structures and organs for performance of societal roles. There was a central bureaucracy, having linkages with several peripheral communities within an Hausa emirate. There were also structures for law enforcement, tax collection, articulation and processing of demands and external defense. At the head of an Hausa political system is an *Emir* who was in many respects a political sovereign. Though he was surrounded with a number of political elites as palace advisers, he exercised substantial authority and influence throughout his domain. The position and prestige of the *Emir* were enhanced by the enormous resources he commanded. He presided over an extensive patronage system; and used his resources not only to reward supporters, but also to punish those who challenged him or dared exercise independent political power. Hence, the principal means of rising to the top political hierarchy in an Hausa system is through "patron-client relations". Attainment of political office became the main instrument of acquiring wealth and social position. Besides, the clientage system was widely practised in the population and was a common feature in all the sub-systems of the society.[4]

In summary, the Hausa traditional political system "was a status system which strongly favoured qualities of servility, respect for authority, allegiance to the powerful and rejected qualities of independence, achievement, self-reliant action and initiative".[5]

IGBO

The Igbo political, social and economic institutions come under the variant usually referred to as "segmented system",[6] although there are isolated kingdoms such as those of Arochuku, Onitsha and Oguta. The segmented social system is characterized by several communities enjoying relative degrees of political authority with complex linkages with

17

the periphery. The commonest unit of social organization is the extended family—*umunna*. Members of the family are bound by kinship ties, and its eldest member exercises considerable power and authority over other members. Several groups of families make up an Igbo village. A number of villages will constitute a political community; hence there are several independent political communities in Igboland before the British contact.

TABLE 3. THE STRUCTURE OF AN IGBO
POLITICAL COMMUNITY

POLITICAL COMMUNITY

|

Villages

These political communities existed as independent and sovereign states and had only minimal and tenuous relationships with one another. The emergence of Igbo as an ethnic group is therefore a modern phenomenon.

The Igbo had scarcely urban organization or islamic influence in the pre-colonial days.[7] Before the British established its presence in Igboland, contact with Europe was maintained mainly through the *Aros,* a sub-Igbo group who lived on the South Eastern fringe of Igbo territory. The *Aros* gradually penetrated the Igbo heartland and established flourishing trading and religious centres. Despite the absence of centralized and consolidated political authority, the Igbos had several similarities in matters of structures, norms and customs.

Every Igbo community in a sense, could be described as an open society. Invariably each community was administered by a council of elders.[8] The Council was made up of titled men, some heads of families, warlords, heads of secret societies and age-grades; men of wealth and outstanding talents. Political decisions were reached not by a single leader, but by collective effort of the members of the council. Often issues were fully discussed, alternative courses and their consequences were considered. Talented and informed members led discussions and exercised greater influence in decisional outcomes.

18

Another common feature of Igbo political system is the existence of titled and secret societies. Membership of these societies entailed payment of fees, feasting of the old members, and performance of ritual ceremonies.[9] Though the membership was usually open to free born, yet the rich and the successful in trades and professions, the religious and oracle leaders often had an easier access to it than the poor and lowly placed. In several communities the titled and secret societies constituted the ruling elites or the dominant power group. Most titles were not inherited. They reverted to the community once their holders died. As the societies became more "institutionalized", they became mechanisms through which men of wealth and war heroes could attain high social status. Achievement rather than ascription constituted the main route of attaining upward mobility in Igbo society. In comparing the Igbo and Hausa societies in terms of their achievement orientation LeVine points out that:

"The over-all picture which emerges of the traditional Ibo status system is not only of an open system in which any free man could attain high status, but of one that placed a premium on occupational skill, enterprise and initiative. The man more likely to rise socially is the one who was sufficiently self motivated to work hard and cleverly marshall available resources in the cause of increasing his wealth . . . As a large centralized and highly differentiated hierarchy of ranks, the Hausa status system entailed much greater differences in wealth, power and prestige between the top and bottom statuses than the Ibo system . . . The ideal successful Hausa man seems to have been the office holder who faithfully supported his superior and rewarded his followers; the Ibo ideal appears to have been the energetic and industrious farmer or trader who aggrandized himself personally through productive or distributive activity. By Ibo standards the Hausa ideal was overdependent and confining to the individual; by Hausa standards, the Ibo ideal was dangerously selfish and anarchic".[10]

THE YORUBA

The Yorubas are by far the largest ethnic group in both Western Nigeria and the Federal territory of Lagos. They are made up of several sub-cultural groups and clans, the most important of which are: Ife, Egba, Ijebu, Owo, Ilesha, Ekiti, Ondo and Ibadan.[11] The Yorubas have myth of common descent from Oduduwa who was supposed to have 'descended' from heaven. As the Yorubas regarded Oduduwa as their progenitor, their rulers often claimed to be direct lineal descendants of Oduduwa[12]. It was from the ancestral home of Ile-Ife that the "children" of Oduduwa went forth to become the founders of kingdoms and dynasties in all parts of Yorubaland.[13] Ile-Ife has since remained an important cultural and religious center for all the Yorubas.[24] Before the penetration of the British into the Yoruba heartland, the various Yoruba kingdoms were often warring against each

19

other; thereby making their political communities vulnerable to outside attack and invasion.[15] As a result of their internal feuds and conflicts the Yorubas lost Ilorin, one of the most important sub-cultural groups to the Fulani invaders.[16] However, the Yorubas learned their lesson after the Fulani invasion of Ilorin, closed ranks and prevented further penetration by the Fulanis of the Yoruba heartland.

Though the Yorubas lacked common leadership and were divided into several political kingdoms, their traditional political systems can be classified as "centralized chiefdom".[17] Similarity of political culture and behavior of these chiefdoms stems from the myth of common descent and conquest. The Community's Chief, the *Oba*, had greater legitimacy in the eyes of his people and secured greater compliance from them if his claim to rulership was solid and he was able to trace his lineage to Oduduwa. As Oduduwa was regarded as the founder of the Yorubas, the *Oba* was regarded as the founder of his political community.[18] As an *Oba*—King—his power and authority were highly circumscribed. His prestige and ritual status far exceeded his political power.[19] Immediately below an *Oba* were lesser provincial and village chieftains who exercised some measure of military, administrative and ritual powers. The chief's titles were often hereditary and they are representative of major territorial and associational groups in the community.[20] The congregation of the community's chiefs constituted the *Oba's* council. Unlike his Hausa counterpart, a Yoruba monarch was not a free agent. Fundamental and many "routine" decisions were made by the *Oba's* council. Apart from the council, there were other checks and balances that tended to make him a constitutional rather than an absolute ruler. These include various differentiated occupational groups, and secret societies such as *Ogboni* society.[21] The Yoruba Monarch could be dethroned or replaced by his council. Summarizing the constraints surrounding the institution of *Obaship* Peter Lloyd states:

> There has always been a delicate balance of power between the chiefs who made the policy and the Obas whose sacred status commanded such authority as will ensure obedience. If the Oba misused his power he might be deposed by his Chiefs who will ask him to die.[22]

In spite of the constraints that limit the power of a Yoruba monarch, he could still, as a patron of his political community, distribute many favors to his favorites and clients. The patronage system which was part of the Yoruba social traditions sometimes made the monarch acquire influence and importance higher than those of his chief and titled men. This resembled the Hausa clientage system, but the Yoruba kings did not control and dispense such wealth as Hausa governing elites.[23] When also compared with the Igbo social structure, the

20

Yoruba society was "intermediate" between the Igbo which was segmented and achievement oriented and the Hausa system which was highly centralized and premised on extensive clientage principles.

The establishment of British administration in Nigeria diluted to varying degrees, the nature of the various traditional societies in Nigeria. Western patterns of schools, roads, communication and transportation were established. Cash economy followed almost immediately, and this led to the emergence of economic institutions such as mining manufacture, commerce, and chambers of commerce. The new market economy drew young men and women into new urban communities for paid labor. Within the urban communities emerged new social groups such as "nationalists", merchants, petty traders, small shopkeepers, professional men such as lawyers, doctors, engineers, architects, senior civil servants, company managers, transport owners, and teachers. The number of these groups which instituted the new economic, political, social elites varied from one ethnic group to another. These new groups competed among themselves and with the traditional elites for whatever scarce goods and services the colonial administration could offer.

The new social groups did not shed their varied traditional values and belief systems, rather they accommodated them with adopted western values and belief system. Depending on where they were and what they wanted, their actions and behavior were guided by both belief systems and values. They formed ethnic and cultural associations in the urban centers to mediate the discontinuities arising from the encompassing process of "modernization", and to advance their claims and competition against other groups in the society. The emergence of the new urban groups did not lead to their enmeshing with their traditional elites, but increased the plural nature of the Nigerian societies as well as it aggravated competition for roles in both the traditional and the modern sectors of the economy. This competition for the "limited good" and factors that led to them will be described in detail below.

The existence of several heterogeneous societies as discussed above, implies that Nigerians, currently have no common political culture and belief system. Their absence inhibit the exercise of national authority. Political mobilization and participation which are necessary steps towards the achievement of a legitimated national authority are aided in such communities as Britain, Japan, France with relatively homogeneous political culture, national language and religion. But in societies such as Nigeria and Zaire, there is a fundamental problem of evolving national political authority out of the various historic groups that constitute the state. Consequently, the existence of several legitmated authorities with conflicting values, norms, traditions, structures and visions of the world, attenuates the emergence of

21

a strong national political center. Instead of transference of the main focus of loyalty and identity from peripheral areas to the national state, individuals attach themselves closely to their primary and kinship groups. It is argued that individual loyalty and identification are not permanently fixed, that the nature of issues and conflicts in a society help to determine the intensity and levels of loyalty and identification. This observation holds more for integrated and industrialized states than fragmented societies. As Ken Post recent study on Nigeria shows, individuals in a plural society are more likely always to identify with their ethnic groups on many national issues, than with the central political authority of their common political system.[24] This implies that their loyalty on several issues is attached to their primary and ethnic groups.

Another factor which constrains the creation of legitimated national authority in Nigeria is the varied impact of colonial policies on the traditional institutions and structures. Lord Lugard, the first colonial Governor General of a unified Nigeria was much impressed by the elaborate political, social and economic infrastructure of the emirate system of the northern Nigeria, and less so with the southern institutions especially those of the Igbos. He wanted to adapt the same to the purposes of British colonial administration. He therefore adopted a colonial policy which is generally referred as "indirect rule".[25] The policy aimed at not only rationalizing the British administration, considering the meagre human and material resources available to Lugard, but at preserving the traditional institutions and patterns of the emirate system. To achieve these dual objectives, colonial officials were carefully inducted and instructed in their roles. Fundamental changes, penetration of western missionaries and schools were prohibited. In effect the Northern Nigerian was sealed off against the revolutionary impact of "modernization".[26]

The policy of indirect rule was applied to the Southern Nigeria with hardly any deference to its traditional institutions and patterns. As the policy only tolerated incremental changes, it suited the traditional political elites of the Northern Nigeria. It left their traditional institutions and patterns almost intact at a time when their Southern counterparts were undergoing transformation. The indirect rule failed in the South, especially among the Igbos who detested the "hand picked" warrant Chiefs.

The differential effects of the colonial policy led to imbalances in the process of "social mobilization" and exposure to western education, between Northern and Southern Nigeria. Generally the peoples of the South embraced western education more than their Northern counterparts. This led to the conversion of many people into Christian faith and their abandonment of traditional religion. As all instructions at higher level was given in English, "the Nigerian who acquired a knowledge of English had access· to a vast new world of literature and of ideas and his contact with it awakened new aspirations, quickened the urge toward emulation and provided the notions and the medium for the expression of grievances. Moreover, the English language (and its corrupted form, pidgin English) served as a lingua franca for communication among the educted elements of all tribes, a bond of decisive importance in the development of a pan-Nigerian or even a regional, nationalist movement".[27]

Exposure to western education imparted several skills and knowledge which became invaluable assets in the newly introduced cash economy of Nigeria. Educated Southern Nigerians were employed in several positions as clerks, and artisans in the civil service and commercial firms, and in the ranks and files of the police force and the army.

Educational expansion in the South led to the emergence of a new group of Nigerians as political elites. Most of these people were sons of peasants who had no connections with the traditional political elites. The emergence of the new political elites resulted into reversal of status for the traditional elites in the South, as they yielded power and authority to the western educated elements.

Noting the educational gap between North and South, Coleman observed that: "of the total population over seven years of age 8.5 per cent were literate in roman script in all Nigeria, 16 per cent in the Eastern Nigeria, 18 per cent in the Western Nigeria and 2 per cent in the Northern Nigeria".[28]

The differences can be explained partly as we noted earlier by the policy of the colonial Administration which shielded Northern Nigeria from Christian evangelization and western education. There were also reasons of geography and historical sequence of impact[29] and the rate of ethnic group receptivity to the encompassing process of "modernization". The disparity in western education was not only discernable between North and South but also existed in the South. The Yorubas because of their nearness to the coast and their early contact with the British had an early lead over other ethnic groups in the Southern Nigeria. Schwarz points out that

Yorubas had been exposed to western education at a much earlier date than any other group in Nigeria. They were the wealthiest Nigerians with a substantial middle class based on cocoa farming and their cities, Lagos, Abeokuta and Ibadan were Nigeria's intellectual and political centers.[30]

As early as in 1920's the Yorubas had 12 practising barristers, and 8 medical doctors, while the Igbos their present competitors had none.[31] This early differential in the impact of western education in the South explains why in order to catch up some ethnic groups mainly Igbos

23

and the Ibibios formed cultural associations. These cultural associations speeded the expansion of western education by founding schools and colleges and by sponsoring students overseas. This process of "catching up" in the South created more tensions and violent competition between the Yorubas and Igbos. This led to stock taking and accusation of domination by some Yoruba and Igbo leaders.[32] The competition between the Igbos and the Yorubas to maintain an educational lead resulted into distrust, lack of moderation, blurred communication and the vision of each other through unfavorable stereotypes.[33] Clashes between the Igbos and the Yorubas became common. It led to the removal of an Igbo Vice-Chancellor by the Yoruba dominated Council of Lagos University. O'Connell also states that the "Clashes were decisive factors in preventing a Southern alliance to form a federal cabinet after the 1959 Federal election".[34] Abernethy notes that the Yoruba cool response to the news that Igbos had been massacred in the North and the isolation of the Igbo military leaders in the delicate negotiations following the July (1966) coup can be explained partly as a result of cleavage which was based in part on patterns of educational expansion dating back several decades.[35]

The impact of western education has so far not resulted into emergence of national consciousness among Nigerians that transcend communal and primary identification and loyalties. It has not led into enmeshing of Nigeria's numerous ethnic groups which still have several diffuse cultural associations and loose sense of political community. Rather, it has resulted into their mobilization and consolidation. Most Nigerians in spite of their periodic geographical mobility, change of urban residence, exposure to mass media, and desire for greater national integration, still have ethnic homeland and are greatly attached to them.

The growth of several urban centers such as Kaduna, Kano, Zaria, Jos, Ibadan, Lagos, Benin, Onitsha, Enugu, Calabar and Port Harcourt had not led into coalescence of many mobilized and differentiated groups living and working in these urban areas. The urban centers are usually stratified into areas for the indigenes who are referred to as "sons of the soil" and areas for the other Nigerians who constitute the various categories of stranger elements. For instance, in Hausa cities, there are special quarters—*sabongaris*—where mostly other Nigerians live. This is equally a phenomenon of Igbo and Yoruba cities which have enclaves for the stranger elements. Several years of occupation of the other Nigerians in "foreign cities" do not qualify them for full assimilation and acceptance into their host's culture and institutions rather it carries the notion of domination, especially when the economic achievements of the other Nigerians had become very pronounced. Cultural assimilation is made more difficult because "immigrant community" brings along not only its language but also its religion. For example, the Igbos, Ibibios the Efiks and to some extent the Yorubas who migrated to Northern Nigeria are differentiated from the Hausa Majority not only by their linguistic identities but by their Christianity, in contrast to Hausa Islamism. Hence, the cultural clusters in Nigerian urban centers emphasize group solidarity in religion, language and occupational differentiation.

The communal stratification and segregation of urban centers helped to politicize the cultural associations whose initial objectives were mainly welfare functions. As political organs, their new goals became protection of economic and political interests of their ethnic groups. The existence and competition of several cultural associations led to increased tensions and conflicts.[36]

Imbalances in the level of social mobilization amongst the various ethnic groups also led to imbalances in the distribution of societal resources commonly referred to by Nigerians as the "national cake". The "national cake" in Nigerian context will at once include a variety of economic goods and services, location of federal institutions and industries, federal and state employment positions such as ambassadorial appointments, senior academic and administrative positions, chairmanship of statutory corporations and boards; status, authority, power esteem and prestige.

TABLE 4. REVENUE THROUGH STATUTORY ALLOCATIONS FROM FEDERAL GOVERNMENT BY STATE GOVERNMENTS (1970-71, 1973-75)

States	1973 Estimated Population (M)	N'000 Actual Amount 1970-71	N'000 Estimated Amount 1974-75	Percentage change from 1970-1971 to 1974-75
Mid-West	3.2	19,241	139,864	626.9
Rivers	1.9	18,880	101,073	435.3
East Central	9.2	25,714	58,349	126.9
Western	11.5	55,424	47,385	14.5
North Eastern	9.9	25,142	41,687	65.8
Kano	7.3	24,246	34,951	44.2
North Western	7.3	19,258	34,879	81.1
Benue Plateau	5.1	16,022	30,077	87.7
North Central	5.2	16,508	29,117	76.4
South Eastern	4.6	21,652	28,147	30.0
Kwara	3.0	14,112	23,926	69.5
Lagos	1.8	12,272	20,705	68.7

Sources. Budget estimates and New Nigeria April 10, 1974, quoted in *West Africa*, No. 2976, July 1st, 1974; pp. 790-791.

As in all countries of late development, the central and regional civil services in Nigeria grew and expanded at a faster pace than the economic sector. They, therefore, acquired prestige and importance over and above other organizations in the private sector. This partly explains why key administrative positions in the public services and universities became subject to violent competition among the mobilized and differentiated members of the various ethnic groups.

In several respects the competition for the scarce societal resources became a zero sum game in which the various ethnic groups had high stakes. Each ethnic group alone or in coalition with others aspired to control the federal and state governments, as such control resulted into acquisition of more "national cake". Those who lost and were not incorporated into the national and state executive councils often developed relative sense of deprivation and insecurity. They demonstrated their disgust and frustration not only by withdrawing their support from the "unrepresentative" government, but also by directing their contempt, anger and antagonism against the dominant ethnic groups.

One of the main causes of ethnic conflicts between the Yorubas and the Igbos was their stiff competition for control of the scarce national resources. The Igbos who arrived late both in exposure to western education and cash economy speeded their process of "catching up" with the Yorubas in the 1950's and 1960's. Thus "catching up" with the Yorubas exacerbated the Yorubas alienation and distrust against the "intruding and aggressive" Igbos.[37] Melson and Wolpe state this succinctly.

> In a real sense it is their equality rather than their inequality which is at the heart of contemporary Igbo/Yoruba communal conflict. In short, communal (ethnic) mobility rather than producing a sense of competitive gain and satisfaction, may lead to a deepening sense of relative deprivation and communal insecurity.[38]

The scarcity of goods and services apparently generates the value of *"the limited good"* hence, the competition for what are peceived as limited supply: jobs, contracts, scholarships, revenue, political seats, industries, opportunities and means of access to all these. The perceived scarcity of these goods arises also from the value attached to them in the country's stratification system.

While the Igbos and the Yorubas competed for dominance in the federal public service, the North which controlled the federal government politically used its power to ensure that most of the vital expenditure in the 1962-66 development plan, was carried out in the North. Some of these vital programs include the Niger Dam (£68.1 million), the Defence item of £29.7 million, £39.2 million for Health and Education, £12 million for the Bornu Railway Extension and £35.3 million for roads mainly in the North.[39]

26

Gradually the Hausas, Yorubas and the Igbos emerged as the three dominant groups competing for the control of the societal resources. Each saw the control of the Federal and State governments as an important strategy for acquiring greater share of the national resources. In a sense, the state and the national elections in Nigeria, especially the Federal election of 1964, the Western Nigerian regional election of 1965, which generated violent conflicts and threatened the existence of the political community could be seen as part of the struggle by the three dominant ethnic groups to control the means of access to power and wealth.[40]

In each of the former three regions of Nigeria, the leadership also controlled a political party, which was the main machinery for patron-client relationships. Noting the role of the political party in the Nigerian clientage system Sklar states "In every region, the party waxed fat in its house of patronage. It had money, favors, jobs, honors to distribute among those who support it".[41] Below we shall analyze the patterns of party and regional alliances in a bid to control the regional and federal governments.

The competition to control the State and the Federal government and thereby control the societal resources also affected the patterns and sequences of constitutional development in Nigeria. Northern and Southern Nigeria developed separately, in spite of Lugard's amalgamation of Southern and Northern protectorates of Nigeria in 1914. Nigeria, until 1946 did not evolve common institutions, norms and understandings that would have aided National consciousness and confer legitimacy to the nationalists from both South and North of the country. The policy of separate development not only insulated Northern Nigeria from the main stream of Nigerian nationalist movement, but also created suspicion in the minds of the emerging Northern Nigerian political elites about the intensions of Southern nationalists.

The opportunity for accelerating National integration was missed in 1922 when a Legislative Council was established in Lagos. While Southern Nigeria had representatives in the Legislature, the North had none.[42] Because Nigeria contained several traditional societies, there was no doubts in the minds of many colonial Governors that Nigeria did not constitute a single 'nation' hence their pursuit of exclusive and divisive policies which tended to favor the relatively dormant North and alienate the more articulate South. This observation stood out clearly in Clifford's dismissal of the concept of a single Nigerian nation:

Assuming the impossible were feasible . . . that this collection of self contained and mutually independent native states, separated from one another . . . by great distances, by differences of history, and tradition and by ethnological, racial, tribal, political, social religious

27

barriers were indeed capable of being welded into a single homo-geneous nation ... a deadly blow would thereby be struck at the root of national self government in Nigeria which secures to each separate people the right to maintain its identity, its individuality and its nationality, its own chosen form of government and the peculiar political and social institutions which have been evolved for it by the wisdom and accumulated experience of generations of its forbears.[43]

It was therefore not surprising that the official policy towards those nationalists who thought in terms of a single and unified Nigerian nation was both hostile and isolative. The political and administrative as well as local government machineries became closed systems to University educated Nigerians. While they viewed services in the "native administration" with disdain, the colonial public bureaucracy did not provide for them. Before 1943, no Nigerian had participated directly in policy formulation at the executive level. Furthermore, with few exceptions, Africans were excluded from the various functional councils and boards appointed by the government to advise on specific problems.[44] As we noted earlier, the British pursued exclusive policy for Northern Nigeria. It shielded it from the influences of western missionaries and education, and limited the contact between the Northern people and highly politicized Southerners living in the North.[45] The sons of the traditional elites and few other Northerners who had benefit of formal and higher education were absorbed in the native administration system of the North. So far as the colonial officials were concerned, the North as a region remained a placid and predictable administrative environment, while the South constituted a problem area.

The conclusion of the Second World War, the increase in the num-ber of nationalists and their demands for participation, the change of attitude in London, all helped to bring about a constitutional advance in 1946; known as Richard's Constitution. The greatest innovation in the 1946 Constitution was the bringing together of the Northern and Southern political leaders into a single legislative body.[46] In several other respects the constitution had little to commend it; for it laid foundation for regional exclusiveness which was to mark Nigerian post independent politics. As Schwarz noted:

"Native authorities, the traditional tribal instruments of indirect rule, were given crucial roles. They selected the numbers of the regional Houses, who in turn selected from their ranks the numbers of the legislative Council".[47]

The Richard Constitution provided for a central legislature, three three regional Houses of Assemblies at Kaduna, Ibadan, and Enugu; and a regional House of Chief for Northern Nigeria. The members of the regional Houses of Assemblies were not elected directly by the elec-torates, but were selected from the native authorities. In turn the

Regional Assemblies from their memberships selected five members as representatives to the central legislative council in Lagos.[48] Many nationalists also objected to the Richard's Constitution, on the grounds that Nigerians were not sufficiently consulted in policy formulation, that it did not provide for greater national integration and "responsible" government.[49]

The party which led criticisms against the Richard's Constitution was the National Council of Nigeria and Cameroon (N.C.N.C.) which had grown out of the unrest of Kings College students in 1944. The N.C.N.C. at its inception enjoyed the support of many Yorubas and Igbos and attracted the support of professional associations, labor unions, literary and social clubs, several ethnic and communal organizations. It was the only party that came close to being a national party, before regionalism and ethnic cleavages became entrenched in Nigeria.

The N.C.N.C. carried widespread campaign against the Richard's Constitution both in Nigeria and in Britain. As a result of the N.C.N.C. insistence of having more changes and constitutional advance, John MacPherson who replaced Richard in 1948, ordered a review of the Richard's Constitution. In order to avoid his predecessor's mistakes, MacPherson set up a constitutional machinery which garnered opinions from every level of the Nigerian community. Constitutional conferences were organized on village, divisional provincial and state levels. Much should not be attributed to the so called "grass root" consultation undertaken by MacPherson, because the majority of Nigerians who live in the rural areas did not understand what the real constitutional issues were. The recommendations of the state conferences were worked upon by the National Conference.[50] The outcome of these series of conferences was the MacPherson's Constitution of 1951, which provided for central legislature. It also provided for a central executive known as Council of Ministers, a national public service commission. It formalized the tripartite divison of the country, by providing for three regions—Northern, Western and Eastern. The Northern and Western regions had two Chambers known as House of Chiefs and House of Assembly. Eastern region had only a regional House of Assembly. Each region had an Executive Council of which membership was drawn from the Regional legislature. While the Regional legislature had enumerated powers, the Central legislature covered all subjects, including those on which the regions had power.[51]

One immediate effect of MacPherson Constitution was the entrenchment of regional nationalism in Nigeria, as well as founding and institutionalization of regional political parties. The Action Group (A.G.) was founded in 1951 by Chief Obafemi Awolowo and other leading Yoruba nationalists to take advantage of the provisions of Macpherson's Constitution. While N.C.N.C. decried the new constitution on the grounds that it compromised the emergence of a strong

29

and united Nigeria; the Action Group and the political party representing the Hausa/Fulani interests in the North—the Northern People's Congress (N.P.C.) welcomed it. The N.P.C. leaders accepted the new constitution, not only because it ensured their effective control of the Northern region, but it adequately provided for their representation in the Central legislature. The A.G. on the other hand, saw in the new constitution an opportunity to gain power in Western Nigeria and thereby limit the spreading influence of N.C.N.C.

The N.P.C. and A.G., were therefore prepared to give the MacPherson's Constitution a trial. The A.G.'s strategy for attaining power was opposition to Dr. Nnamdi Azikiwe the leader of N.C.N.C.; and the exposition of threat of Igbo domination. The A.G. had some advantages over N.C.N.C. It had a disciplined leadership. Besides, its organizational structure was modern. It allowed for free flow of communication and information between leadership and membership. While the N.C.N.C. was restrained in adoption of ethnic appeal as a strategy of winning support because of its national outlook and organization, the A.G. and N.P.C. deployed sub-nationalism and regionalism to their greatest advantages. It was not surprising that A.G. riding on ethnic and regional "horses" comfortably won the elections to the Western House of Assembly in 1951, thereby defeating the older party N.C.N.C. In the North and East, the N.P.C. and N.C.N.C. also won elections to the Northern and Eastern Houses of Assembly respectively. With each of the three dominant parties representing mainly Hausa, Yoruba and Igbo interests entrenched in North, West and East respectively, the stage was set for sub-cultural nationalism and extreme regionalism which marked the Nigeria political processes from 1952 to 1962, and which constrained the emergence of strong political center. Summarizing the extent of MacPherson's 1951 Constitution, helped to bring about sub-cultural nationalism, Coleman states:

> There can be little doubt that the implementation of the constitution of 1951 accelerated the drift toward sub-group nationalism and tribalism. Educated Nigerians who aspired to fill the new positions of power and status opened up to Nigerians by that constitution realized that their most secure base of support would be the people of their own groups. The indirect electoral system strengthened this realization . . . In the struggle that ensued tribalism was the dominant note; but when appealing to the people for support, the competing parties strove to out-do each other in the use of nationalist slogans.[52]

The subsequent events and processes between 1952 and 1962 were characterized by regional and ethnic interests rather than those of the nation. First, there was the 1954 constitution which formally transformed the Nigerian political system into a federation of three regions, of which one of the regions North was greater in size and population than the other two regions put together.[53] The 1954 Constitution brought about the regionalization of Civil Service and judiciary as well as the autonomy of Southern Cameroon which was until then administered as part of Eastern Nigeria. Second, there was the minority question which loomed large between 1954-1960. The minorities in each of the regions demanded separate regions of their own. They accused the regional governments of maladministration, of entrenching the interests of the dominant ethnic groups.[54] The regional governments, in order to avoid carving new states out of their domain, used several strategies such as formal cooptation of minority leadership into the power structure, minor territorial and administrative adjustments to appease the minorities. But these strategies did not allay their fears. This compelled the British to set a commission to look into the problems of the minorities. The commission did not ease the situation. While it recognized the unproportionate size of the Federal units and the substantial power of the Regions as against those of the center, it recommended against creation of new states. It argued that the demands of the minorities could be met within the framework of the existing regions.[55]

Perhaps if the British terminal administration had allowed the creation of more states, alternative centers of power other than Kaduna, Ibadan and Enugu would have been established. The dominance of the Hausas, Yorubas and Igbos in the political processes would be reduced, the authority of the federal government would have been strengthened while those of the peripheries would have been weakened. Nigeria perhaps, would have been saved from the violent crises and civil war which characterized her paths to development from 1962-1970.

But Britain acted on the basis of her interest. It was said that the Commission's reluctance to recommend the creation of new states stemmed from the belief that the existing systems of three regions dominated by the North, helped the conservative forces within Nigeria, the forces, Britain hoped would rule Nigeria.[56] Northern Nigerian rulers, since the inauguration of the Nigerian Federation, had consistently opposed the creation of new states, particularly within their own territory. Alhaji Ahmadu Bello, speaking for Northern regional government states:

> The Northern Region, as it is today, is the product of geography, history and the character of the people. The overwhelming majority of its people are vehemently opposed to the creation of a new region or at any revision of regional boundaries. The Regional government shares their feelings.[57]

In a sense, the terminal British administration contributed to the weakening of Nigeria's political center by its policy of deference

toward Northern Nigeria, and before its departure, deliberately ensured the dominance of the North over the more politicized and
mobilized peoples of the South. Noting this view, Mackintosh states:

> The British officials serving in the North may have wished not only
> to preserve the unity of Nigeria. They may have regarded Northern
> leaders as the best hope for the country, men with whom it was pos-
> sible to deal on a frank and realistic basis.[58]

Besides the minority problem, the constitution by which Nigeria
attained political independence in 1960, reflected both regional and
sectional interests. The provisions of that constitution were the result
of compromises between the British Government officials and Nigerian
politicians. The Nigerian politicians were more concerned with the
fact of independence and inheritance of power than the problem posed
to state authority of having a Federation in which one state by its
size and number dominated all the others.[59] The functions assigned
to the regional governments such as education, health, agriculture,
industrial development, public works, tended to emphasize the strength
and autonomy of the regions at the expense of the central authority.
Consequently, the leaders of the two major parties Ahmadu Bello and
Michael Okpara preferred their roles as premiers of North and East
respectively, rather than to serve as national leaders of their parties.[60]
The authority of the federal government did not stem from the inherent power of the constitution nor from the legitimacy of its institutions, but from a politicians' agreement between the N.P.C. and
N.C.N.C., the two parties which formed the Federal Executive Council
following the 1959 Federal elections. In time the Federal coalition
became unworkable not only as a result of exclusion of the A.G., the
party which mainly served Yoruba interest, but as a result of increased
differences between N.P.C. the Senior partner in the coalition and
N.C.N.C. The situation not only weakened the authority of the
Federal government, but made the Nigerian state a victim of forces
emanating from a highly politicized society. Gradually the two forces
regrouped into two major ideological camps—communalism and
nationalism. They differed on how best Nigerian interest and unity
could be served. The cummunalists supported the existing units and
structure of Nigerian Federation which guaranteed a weak federal
government and strong regional governments at Kaduna, Ibadan and
Enugu. They advocated that each regional government should be an
exclusive domain of each of the three dominant political party in
Nigeria, hence an "outside" interference should not be tolerated. On
the other hand, the nationalists had a 'vision' of new and integrated
Nigerian society made up of several constituent states. They advocated
the splitting of the existing regions, strengthening of the federal
government power, greater state intervention in the economy, enlarged

and strengthened linkages between the center and the peripheries. By 1964 the two groups crystallized into alliances: the Nigerian National Alliance (NNA) and United Progressive Grand Alliance (UPGA). The N.N.A. which was communalist in orientation was made up of N.P.C.—dominant party of the North; dissident members of A.G. led by Samuel Akintola, and two minority parties in the East and Mid-west—Niger Delta Congress (NDC) and Mid-west Democratic Party (NWDP).

The U.P.G.A., the alliance of the nationalists, was made up of N.C.N.C. and the members of the A.G. loyal to Chief Awolowo, the Northern People's Progressive Union (NEPU), and the United Middle Belt Congress (NMBC). The last two parties were based in Northern Nigeria.

The two forces—Communalism and Nationalism as represented by N.N.A. and U.P.G.A. fought against each other in events and processes in Nigeria between 1962 and 1966. The issues and events in conflict included the A.G. crisis, the 1962-63 census controversy, the declaration of emergency in Western Nigeria, the trial and imprisonment of Awolowo, the 1964 Federal elections, and 1965 regional election in the West.[61] In each conflict, the forces of communalism, because of their control of the resources of the center won over the forces of nationalism. As a result, Nigerian central institutions—the courts, the bureaucratic structures and agencies, the electoral commission, the census board, the police commission were manipulated to serve partisan and communal interests. As their behaviours were not always guided by the prescribed impartial norms they ceased to serve as integrative institutions. This 'raping' of central constitution and structures eroded the federal government authority and legitimacy. Consequently, it had to rely on coersion to gain compliance with and support for its policies.

In a sense, reliance on force represents an attempt to overcome deteriorating legitimacy and authority. Constant use of coercion by any government stimulates employment of violence on the part of its citizens as a means of expressing their lack of support for their government.[62] The forces of communalism used the military for internal, security operations, notably in pacifying the Tiv in 1960 and 1964, maintaining essential services during the 1964 general strikes, as well as for policing the Western Nigeria after the regional elections of October 1965.[63] This contributed to the politicization of the army, especially among the junior officers, and consequently resulted in the demise of the Nigerian political system when the military intervened in the political process in January 1966.

There was little doubt that the organizers of the January 1966 Coup had the sympathy of the forces which advocated nationalism, for Ahmadu Bello, Premier of Northern Nigeria, Abubakar Belewa the

33

Federal Prime Minister, and Samuel Akintola Premier of Western Nigeria all lost their lives in the first military intervention.[64] The second military coup in July of the same year, organized and executed by the Northern non-commissioned officers, was an attempt to re-assert the political control by the North. Gowon was coopted by the organizers of the second coup into assuming power as the most senior Northern officer in the army.[65]

The two coups and their aftermath generated much violence and conflicts which resulted in a three year civil war (1967-70).[66] As the Nigerian Civil War, is not the subject of our study, it will not be appropriate to discuss the processes of the war here. Of greater interest to our study is the conclusion of the war, and the fact there are new factors in the wider environment, which could facilitate the creation of a legitimated central political authority. These factors include the new structures of the Federal and the State Governments, and in-creased "windfall" resources from the Nigeria's oil industry.

Whenever the Nigerian military rule is fully assessed, the splitting of Nigeria into smaller states would be counted as a major contribution to the strengthening of the central authority in Nigeria. The military rulers accomplished this by abolishing the previous four regions, dividing that unbalanced division into a twelve and later into a nine-teen state structure.

As we noted earlier the demands for creation of states had been articulated by the minorities before Nigeria's attainment of political independence in 1960. The minorities argued that their interests were not effectively served by the existing regions. The two of the three major political parties—N.C.N.C. and the A.G. had at one time or the other supported the demands for creation of more states. But owing to the politician's love for power and intransigence of Northern Nigeria rulers, the creation of more states was forestalled. It is in this sense that the creation of states by the military could be regarded as a major achievement. The existence of more states brought new factors into Nigerian politics. It strengthened the relationship between the center and its peripheries; and ensured effective representation of minority interests. The minorities now share in the Federal largesse, and sometimes some of them such as Mid-West and Rivers States which are oil rich, get more money from the Federal government than some of the larger states such as the West which is not so endowed. Because of their new gains, the minorities have developed a new sense of identity and acknowledge greater commitment and loyalty to the Nigerian nation.

Another factor which affects the consolidation of national authority in Nigeria is the structure of the Federal military government. At the head of the present regime is the Commander in Chief of the Nigerian Armed Forces, who also is the Head of State of Nigeria. The Head of State presides over the supreme military council which is the highest policy organ in Nigeria. He appoints the military governors who owe direct allegiance to him. He also appoints the members of the Federal executive council, judges of Federal Supreme Courts and State High Courts, ambassadors and other senior government officials. By directly appointing the state governors and Federal Commissioners, his powers exceeded those of the civilian president and Prime Minister of Nigeria. His leadership of the armed forces, and the unity of command which characterizes military organizations not only facilitates coordination of government activities, but aids decision making.

Under the military rule, the executive and legislative powers are vested in the federal military government which is made up of a supreme military council, National Council of State and a Federal Executive Council.

The Supreme Military Council consists of all the heads of Nigerian Armed Forces: The Commander in Chief, Chief of Naval Staff, Commandant of Nigerian Defence Academy, Chief of Staff, Nigerian Army, Head of the Air Force, Deputy Chief of Naval Staff, Inspector General of Police and his Deputy. On the other hand the National Council of State consists mainly of all the State Governors and the leading members of the Armed Forces.

TABLE 5. THE STRUCTURE OF THE NIGERIAN FEDERAL MILITARY GOVERNMENT

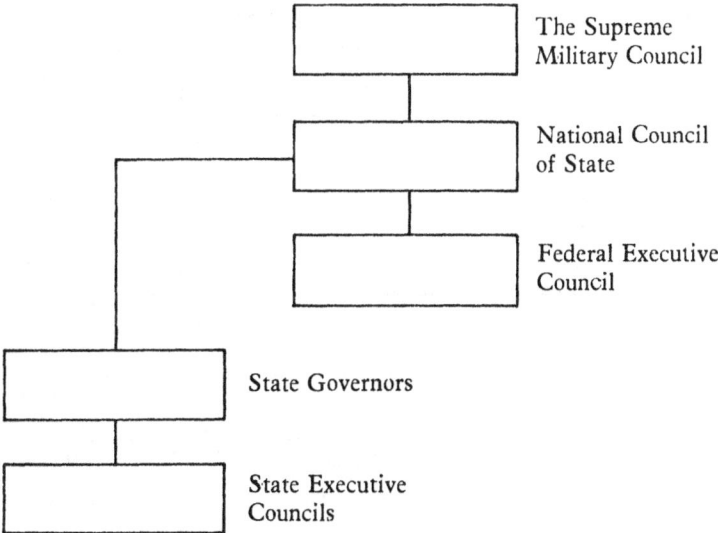

	The Supreme Military Council
	National Council of State
	Federal Executive Council
	State Governors
	State Executive Councils

The Federal Executive consists of the military leadership, the Inspector General of Police and his Deputy, and civilian appointed Commissioners. The civilians are appointed by the Head of State and they hold office at his pleasure. They have no popular political base. The Federal Executive Council deliberates on those subjects delegated to it by the Supreme Military Council. In a sense it constitutes the Federal Cabinet and executes decisions and policies on a national level.

The State Governors are appointees of the Head of State. They are members of the National Council of State, the second highest policy making body in Nigeria. In this sense, they are national officers, owing no accountability to the people of their States. On the other hand the State Governors act as linkages between their States and the Federal Government. They transmit to the Central Government the peculiar problems and the needs of their States.

Finally, the State Executive Councils are the main legislative and executive organs in the States. The members are appointed by and owe allegiance to the State Governors. With the State Governors, they formulate policies on subjects which are within the State competence.

Another new factor in the social environment in Nigeria is the increased resources available for payoffs to the various groups and sectors in the society. This had been made possible by substantial increases in Nigerian oil production and the current world energy crisis which has more than doubled the price of crude oil.

TABLE 6. OIL INDUSTRY STATISTICS—AUGUST 1974

Oil Production	B/D	August 1973 B/D
Shell BP/NNDC	1,423,000*	1,285,663
Gulf	387,156	381,612
Mobil	238,793	226,643
Agip/Phillips	165,922	111,591
Elf	84,000*	61,411
Texaco	–	8,615
	2,298,871	2,075,535

*Estimated

	Net tons	B/D	August 1973 B/D
Oil exports	9,051,026	2,186,921	2,004,496

Source: Oil Producer's Trade Section, Lagos Chamber of Commerce and Industry, September 18, 1974.

In 1965, Nigeria's total recurrent revenue was £200m, of which oil accounted for £13m; but in 1973 (before the oil price increases) total revenue had risen to £1,100m with oil revenue reaching £600m. The oil revenue alone in 1974-75 financial year was expected to total no less than £3,500m. Again, when compared with the traditional foreign exchange earners such as palm produce, cocoa, and groundnut, revenue from oil is witnessing astronomical growth while the revenue from cash crops is on the decline.

TABLE 7. OIL AND NON OIL EXPORTS (MILLION NAIRA)

Non Oil Trade	1970	1971	1972*
Cocoa	133.0	143.2	101.2
Groundnuts	43.4	24.4	19.2
Palm Kernels	21.8	26.0	15.6
Palm Oil	1.2	3.4	0.2
Rubber	17.6	12.4	7.4
Raw Cotton	13.2	11.0	'0.6
Timber, Logs & Swan	6.2	5.3	6.3
Tin Metal	33.2	24.8	19.3
Re Exports	8.4	12.6	13.0
Total Non Oil	**375.6**	**340.4**	**258.6**
Crude Petroleum	509.8	953.0	1,156.9
Total Exports	**885.4**	**1,293.4**	**1,415.5**

*Provisional

Source: Federal Office of Statistics, Lagos: quoted in Colin Legum, ed. *Africa Contemporary Records*. Rex Collings, London, 1974 p. 747.

The revenue figures in Table 7 show that Nigeria, unlike some other African countries such as Dahomey, Togo, Ghana, Somalia, Tanzania is blessed with resources to pursue her development objectives.

As it will be shown in Chapter five the mere existence of abundant material resources does not mean that development is automatic. Much depends upon the orientation of the leadership and the extent it wishes to deploy the societal resources for the benefit of all. Sometimes, the resources might be stored away in foreign banks, or may be utilized to ensure the survival of an unpopular regime.[67]

FOOTNOTES

1. Robert LeVine, "Dreams and Deeds: Achievement Motivation in Nigeria" in Melson and Wolpe, (eds.) *Nigeria: Modernization and the Politics of Communalism*, Michigan State University Press, 1971, p. 171.
2. *Ibid.* p. 173. For detailed description of the Hausa social institutions see the following works: M. G. Smith, *Government in Zazau*, London: Oxford University Press, 1960.
3. James S. Coleman, "The Politics of Sub-Saharan African" in Coleman and Almond eds. *Politics of Developing Areas*, Princeton, Princeton University Press, 1960. p. 254.
4. Robert LeVine, *Op. Cit.*, p. 175.
5. *Ibid.* p. 178.
6. See Coleman, *Op. Cit.*, p. 255.
7. Robert LeVine, *Op. Cit.*, p. 181.
8. The exceptions to this general feature of council of elders are a number of kingdoms such as those of Aro, Onitsha, and Oguta. Dr. Nzimiro carried out an enthnographic study of Igbo Kingdoms situated along the Niger River—see Ikenna Nzimiro, *Studies in Igbo Political Systems*, Berkeley and Los Angeles, University of California Press, 1971.
9. Robert LeVine, *Op. Cit.*, p. 182.
10. *Ibid.* pp. 184 and 185.
11. Hugh H. Smythe and Mabel M. Smythe: *The New Nigerian Elite*, Stanford: Stanford University Press, 1960; p. 17.
12. Victor Olorunsola; "Nigeria" in V. A. Olorunsola; ed. *The Politics of Cultural Sub-Nationalism in Africa*, New York: Anchor Books: Doubleday and Co. Inc., 1972, p. 9.
13. Smythe and Smythe, *Op. Cit.*, p. 11.
14. *Ibid.* p. 17.
15. *Ibid.* See also: J. F. A. Ajayi and R. S. Smith, *Yoruba Welfare in the Nineteenth Century*. Cambridge: Cambridge University Press, 1964. S. Johnson, *History of the Yorubas*, Lagos 1921 and Michael Crowder, *Story of Nigeria*, London: Faber and Faber Ltd. 1962. Each of this work gives a fairly detailed account of the warfare among the Yoruba kingdoms.
16. Frederick A. O. Schwarz, Nigeria: *the Tribe the Nation or the Race, The Politics of Independence*. Cambridge M.I.T. Press, 1965, p.14.
17. James S. Coleman, *Op. Cit;* pp. 254-255.
18. Victor Olorunsola, *Op. Cit.*, pp. 9-10.
19. LeVine, *Op. Cit.*, p. 186.
20. *Ibid.*
21. *Ibid.*
22. Peter C. Lloyd, *Yorubaland Law*, London: Oxford University Press, 1962, p. 46.
23. LeVine, *Op. Cit.*, p. 189.
24. Ken Post and Vickers, *The Structure and Conflict in Nigeria 1960-1966*. London: Heinemann 1973, pp 11-16.
25. For detailed exposition of the concept of Indirect Rule and its application in the Northern Nigeria. See the following works:
   Margery F. Perham, *Lord Lugard Vol. II: The Years of Authority*, 1898-1945, London: Collins 1960.
   —*Native Administration in Nigeria*. London: Oxford University Press, 1937.
   Sir Frederick Lugard, *The Dual Mandate in the British Tropical Africa* 4th ed. London: William Blackwood, 1929.

Lord Hailey, *Native Administration and Political Development in British Tropical Africa*. London: Colonial Office, 1940.

C. S. Whitaker, *The Politics of Tradition Continuity and Change in Northern Nigeria*, 1946-1966. New Jersey Princeton University Press, 1970.

26. *Ibid.* p. 27.
27. James S. Coleman, *Nigeria: Background to Nationalism*. Berkeley and Los Angeles. University of California Press, 1958, p. 114.
28. *Ibid.* p. 133.
29. *Ibid.*
30. Frederick A. O. Schwarz, *Op. Cit.*, p. 66.
31. Coleman, *Op. Cit.*, p. 142.
32. David B. Abernethy. "Education and Integration" in Melson and Wolpe, *Op. Cit.*, p. 409.
33. James O'Connell, "Authority and Community in Nigeria" in Melson and Wolpe, *Op. Cit.*, p. 632.
34. *Ibid.*
35. David Abernethy, *Op. Cit.*, p. 417.
36. Melson and Wolpe, *Op. Cit.*, p. 15.
37. *Ibid.* p. 10.
38. *Ibid.*
39. B. J. Dudley. "Federalism and the Balance of Political Power in Nigeria" *Journal of Commonwealth Political Studies*, Vol. IV, March 1966, pp. 21-22.
40. R. L. Sklar, "Contradictions in the Nigerian Political System" *The Journal of Modern African Studies*, 3, 1965, quoted in Melson and Wolpe *Op. Cit.*, p. 516.
41. *Ibid.* p. 517.
42. Kalu Ezera, *Constitutional Development in Nigeria*. Cambridge, Cambridge University Press, 1960, p. 28.
43. Address by the Governor, Nigerian Council, Government Records of Proceedings of the Council, Lagos—December 29, 1920, quoted in Kalu Ezera, *Ibid.* pp. 25-26.
44. Coleman, *Op. Cit.*, p. 154.
45. *Ibid.* p. 322.
46. Ezera, *Op. Cit.*, p. 80.
47. Schwarz, *Op. Cit.*, p. 63.
48. Coleman, *Op. Cit.*, p. 276.
49. *Ibid.* pp. 279-280. See also Ezera *Op. Cit.*, pp. 76-81.
50. Eme O. Awa, *Federal Government in Nigeria*, Berkeley and Los Angeles, University of California Press, 1964. pp. 29-36.
51. Ezera, *Op. Cit.*, pp. 124-125.
52. Coleman, *Op. Cit.*, p. 352.
53. The N.C.N.C. leadership crisis of 1953, which started when Azikiwe could not gain entry to the Central Legislature in Lagos through the Western House of Assembly was one of the most important factors that led to the demise of the 1951 constitution. Besides, under this constitution the African ministers did not have full responsibilities over matters within their ministries and departments. Hence, the 1954 constitution was an attempt to make up for some of the weaknesses of the 1951 Constitution. See Ezera *Op. Cit.*, pp. 153-199.
54. Awa, *Op. Cit.*, p. 64.
55. *Ibid.* p. 66.
56. Schwarz, *Op. Cit.*, p. 87.

57. Memorandum to the Minorities Commission of Northern Nigeria, Kaduna 1957, quoted in MacKintosh, *Nigerian Government and Politics*, (London: Allen & Unwin Ltd., 1966, p. 34.)
58. *Ibid.*
59. *Ibid.* p. 22.
60. *Ibid.* p. 64.
61. H. N. Nwosu, *Politics in Western Nigeria*, 1962-66. A study in Crisis of Leadership. M. A. Essay, University of California, Berkeley 1973. The study focused on the crisis of leadership in Western Nigeria within the period, and also highlighted the events and issues in conflicts, which had wider implications to Nigeria as a whole. These events and processes gradually contributed to the demise of the Nigerian political system in 1966.
62. Aristride Zolberg, "The Structure of Political Conflicts in the New States of Tropical Africa" *American Political Science Review* Vol. LXI; March, 1968, p. 67.
63. Rubin Luckham, *The Nigerian Military*, Cambridge: Harvard University Press, 1971, p. 17.
64. *Ibid.* p. 34.
65. *Ibid.* p. 71.
66. For some of the works on the Nigerian Civil War see the following: Robert Collins, *Nigeria in Conflict*, London: Seeker and Warburg, 1970. Ralph Uwechue, *Reflections on the Nigerian Civil War*, Paris: Jenne Afrique, 1971.
Frederick Forsyth, *The Biafra Story*, Baltimore, Penguin Books, 1969. *Nigerian Handbook*, 1973, *Op. Cit.*, p. 30.
67. The deposed emperor of Ethiopia was alleged to have stored away in a Swiss bank account an estimated amount of from US $1 billion to US $15 billion. *African Confidential*, Vol. 15, No. 24, December 6, 1974, p. 2.

CHAPTER THREE

THE EMERGENCE, GROWTH AND THE CHANGING PHASES OF THE FEDERAL AND STATE GOVERNMENTS AND THEIR CIVIL SERVICES

The environmental factors which we discussed in the last chapter, combined in various ways to shape the growth, structure, functions and the changing phases of the Nigerian Federal and State's authorities and civil services. This chapter briefly examines the Nigerian civil service from the time Nigeria became a unified state in 1914 to the present. Our analysis is divided into four sections. The first covers the period from 1914 when the Northern and Southern protectorates of Nigeria were amalgamated into a single administrative system, to 1946, when the British colonial administration built a "federalist principle" into the Nigeran constitution. It discusses the structure, and the limited functions of the unitary service which was dominated by the expatriate civil servants. In addition, it seeks to explain why the 'centralist' principle of administration failed.

The second section covers the period 1946-1966, an era which corresponds with the decentralization of political and administrative authorities in Nigeria. This section analyzes the centrifugal forces which led to the creation of the Nigerian federation and the emergence of the federal and state civil services. It also highlights why the regional (state) civil services rather than the federal one were dominant within this period. The third section discusses the emergence after 1966 of what we have described as the "New Federalism". The "new federalism" is marked by substantial growth in the powers and functions of the federal government and civil service and the reduction of the autonomy of the state governments and civil services. The last section analyzes some of the implications of the "new federalism" in terms of consolidation of central authority as well as the problems and complexities it poses.

The term "civil service" is used here to cover those public servants who are direct employees of the federal and state governments, other than the police, the armed forces personnel, the judicial personnel and the teachers. Its usage excludes also employees of statutory corporations and boards such as railways or Ports Authority. The civil service is therefore a component of public bureaucracy.[1]

The Civil Service 1914-1946—An era of experimentation in unitary civil service.

In 1900, Britain formally established its authority in a number of traditional political communities which together had come to be known as Nigeria.[2] For the purposes of administration, Nigeria was divided into three administrative units:—the colony of Lagos and the protectorates of Northern and Southern Nigeria. In 1906, the colony of Lagos was merged with the protectorate of Southern Nigeria. In 1914, the two protectorates were amalgamated into a single administrative unit called the colony and the protectorate of Nigeria. The British imposed a unified alien civil service on its newly integrated territories without giving much thought to its impact on the Nigerian traditional communities with their conflicting values, interests, norms and authority structure.[3] In spite of the unification of the civil services of Northern and Southern Nigeria the two areas developed separately. The higher echelon of the civil service was from the onset staffed with British officials. Like many colonial bureaucracies, its goals were limited; and the most critical one was maintenance of law and order,[4] as well as mobilization of enough local resources in order to make colonial administration financially self-sufficient. Transportation and communication activities were embarked upon to the extent that they aided achievement of the primary objectives.

Hence, the colonial civil service was structured in such a way as to achieve efficiency with least cost. Its main "technical core" which was based at Lagos was isolated from the constraints and the contingencies of the environment. At the head of the public service was the Governor-General, who was accountable to the Colonial Secretary in London. The Colonial Secretary was himself accountable to the British Cabinet and the Parliament. The Governor-General delegated his authority to the Chief Secretary, who was the effective head of the service.

The Chief Secretary coordinated the entire service which was divided into two major parts—the Departmental and the Political administrations.

The Departmental administration covered the technical and professional functions of the colonial regime.[5] It was organized along functional lines such as Education, Health, Agriculture, Treasury, Forestry, Public Works and Audit.[6] Assisting the Chief Secretary were the various departmental heads.[7] In the absence of elected representatives of the people, they not only advised the Governor, but initiated policies, participated in legislation, and supervised the execution of enacted bills and approved policies.[8] While the heads of technical departments operated from the central secretariat in Lagos their subordinates were in charge of field offices.[9] Considering the "authoritarian" nature of colonial regimes and given the limited scope of colonial policies, the technical and professional heads of departments carried their duties without any deference to any organized clientele or public; the constraints and contingencies that stemmed from the wider environments were tackled by the field administrators.

TABLE 8.   CIVIL SERVICE IN NIGERIA–
COLONIAL STRUCTURE

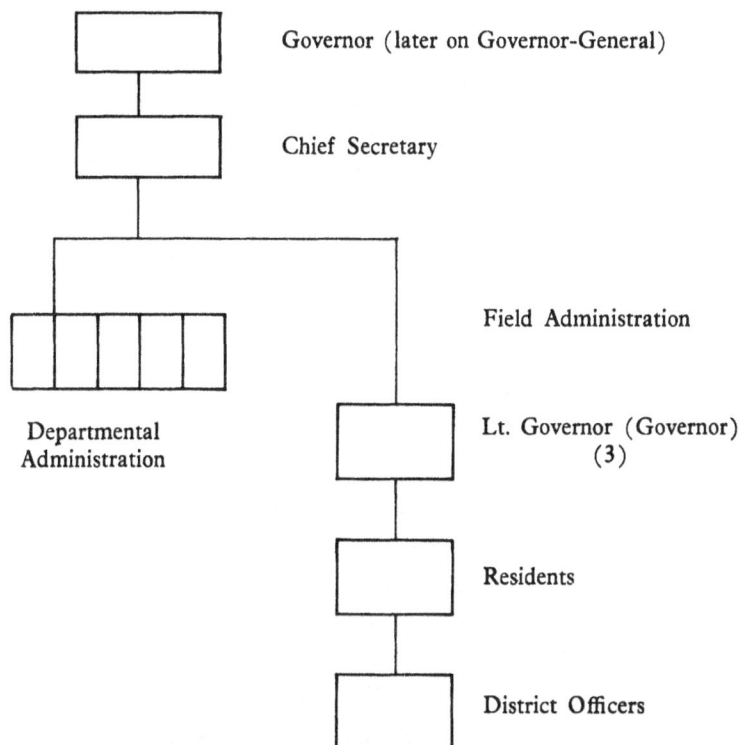

Governor (later on Governor-General)	
Chief Secretary	
Field Administration	
Departmental Administration	Lt. Governor (Governor) (3)
	Residents
	District Officers

Sources: E. O. Awa, "High Level Administration in the Public Services of Nigeria," *The Nigerian Journal of Economic and Social Studies,* Vol. 6, No. 1, March 1964, p. 43. Also H. O. Davies, *Nigeria, the Prospects for Democracy,* London: Weidenfeld and Nicolson, 1961, p. 76. Ladipo Adamolekun, "High Level Ministerial Organization in Nigeria and the Ivory Coast", in D. J. Murray (ed.), *Studies in Nigerian Administration,* London: Hutchinson Educational, Ltd., 1970, p. 12.

The pillars of colonial administration were by far the field officers —the Lieutenant Governor, the residents and the district officers. It was through them that the principal goals of colonial administration— maintenance of law and order and resource mobilization—were achieved. The residents and the district officers enjoyed much discre-

43

tion in the exercise of their power and responsibilities. As Donald Kingsley aptly observed,

> The Resident and the Governor, each in his geographical area, was the government, so far as the governed was concerned. And more often than not, in the more remote areas, a strong administrative officer was the government in fact.[10]

Apart from ensuring the maintenance of law and order, the field officers also supervised the activities of the departmental administration located within their areas of jurisdiction. As if the above functions were not enough the field officers performed police and judicial duties. They issued warrants for arrests, heard and reviewed cases.[11] The field officers were not accountable to the people they served; rather they were only answerable to their superiors who "hardly interfered with their routine activities".[12]

Given the nature of the environment which was at best non-cooperative—how did the field officers cope with the constraints and contingencies?

They carried out their functions usually through recognizable intermediaries. They utilized the traditional political authorities as mediators. In the Northern part of the country the traditional rulers—*emirs*, *sultans*, and *shehus*—had well developed but "fused" channels of decision-making, authority and information gathering. This was also the position in Western Nigeria, where the *obas* and *alafins* provided formidable institutions for local administration. In Eastern Nigeria, with the exception of a few areas such as Calabar, Arochuku, Onitsha, Oguta, such elaborate traditional structures were not in existence. The field officers made up for the deficiency by imposing their own created structures—the warranted chiefs—on unwilling people. The traditional institutions at once provided ready means for the administration of the entire country by a few field officers. Stating the need for governance through local intermediary which has been referred to as "system of indirect rule", Kautsky notes that the colonial authorities can achieve their purposes much more effectively by imposing themselves on top of the native aristocratic hierarchy, rather than by replacing it. Merely influencing, manipulating and controlling it, they leave it in charge of the government of the great bulk of the population for whom therefore little is changed politically by the advent of colonialism.[73]

The political officers, in order to avoid the problems of "system overload", used the traditional institutions—the *emirs*, *obas*, the warranted chiefs—as "gate-keepers" to regulate the flow of input activities. In order to reduce the contingencies and constraints from the wider environment, they learned to segment and ignore some aspects of the environment. By not establishing many educational institutions, primary and secondary, the rate of social mobilization was slowed and

44

thereby challenges from the educated but unassimilated for a long time was very minimal.

Gradually, symbiotic relationships developed between the colonial officers and their local intermediaries. The traditional rulers helped the colonial field officers to achieve their main objective of maintenance of law and order. In return the colonial officers allowed these traditional rulers to exercise some administrative and judicial authority over their people with minimal supervision.

In several respects the structure of colonial administration in Nigeria corresponded to Fred Riggs' description of the pattern of role differentiation in a transitional society:

> We find, then, in the transitional society a dualistic situation. Formally superimposed institutions patterned after Western models coexist with earlier indigenous institutions of a traditional type in a complex pattern of heterogeneous overlapping. The new patterns thrive best at the center in the higher levels of society; the older patterns persist most vigorously at the periphery, in the rural hinterlands and the lower levels of society, but the mixture is everywhere present and produces new forms characteristic of neither the Western nor the traditional institutional systems.[14]

Where the symbiotic relationship were fully developed as in Northern Nigeria; the influences of "modernization" were most limited. The colonial officers governed through the *emirs*. While they were responsible for formulation of policies, the *emirs* and their traditional institutions provided the main instrument through which policies were executed. In return the colonial officers restrained the missionaries and commercial houses from "interfering" with the patterns of normative relationship in parts of Northern Nigeria.[15]

While the alien colonial administrative structure absorbed some of the products of the primary and secondary institutions into the clerical cadre, it effectively remained a closed system for the few Nigerians who had acquired higher education and Western "democratic" values. To the colonial administrators, this group of Nigerians constituted a major threat to an otherwise placid social environment; hence a non-recruitment of Nigerians into senior administrative positions was pursued with vigor. For instance,

> Before 1943, no African had participated directly in policy formulation at the central executive level. Furthermore, with few exceptions, Africans were excluded from the various councils and boards appointed by the government to advise on specific problems ... As late as 1938 provincial committees were created to advise on pay rate for employees but it was not until 1941, that an African was named to one of these committees.[16]

The exclusion of Nigerians from positions of administrative responsibility was based on an earlier principle enunciated by Lord Lugard (the architect of the Nigerian state) in 1920:

> It is a cardinal principle of British policy that the interest of a large active population shall not be subject to the will· of a small minority of educated and Europeanized natives who have nothing in common with them and whose interests are often opposed to theirs.[17]

With the increased number of qualified Nigerians barred from the senior administrative positions which had been the exclusive domain of British officers, there was a "sudden burst of organizational activity among the educated Nigerians in the early 1930s".[18] The future of Nigeria was of such concern to the colonial administration, that it became a subject of special investigation in the 1930s and 1940s. The most notable of such special investigations was that undertaken by Lord Hailey in 1940-42. His recommendations included: that there should be increased employment of educated Nigerians in positions of responsibility; that the economic life of the North was bound with that of the South, and hence there was no need for a separate legislative council for the North; that the development of Regional Councils should be approached with caution. Local authorities should not be sole units of representation in regional councils and legislatures.[19]

Between the two World Wars, Britain did little to advance the course of political and administrative development in Nigeria. It carried out a minor reform in 1923. In that year, it reorganized the Advisory Legislative Council which was established in 1861 to advise the governor in the forming of legislation for Lagos Colony only. The reorganization provided for the election into the Council of four Africans from Southern Nigeria, but Northern Nigeria was not represented in the Council. These minor reforms did not appease the educated Nigerians who wanted increased participation in the administration of their country. In 1939, Britain further divided Southern Nigeria into Western and Eastern groups of provinces. This "reform" further polarized the people of the South and left the large territory of the North and its inhabitants unaffected. The size of the North as we shall see later constituted a major threat to the ambitions of the Nigerian nationalists. Towards the end of the Second World War it became obvious to the British Colonial Administration that its policy of unified civil service had neither integrated the Nigerian diverse communities nor advanced the course of Nigeria's political development. It therefore needed to carry out a series of incremental political reforms, as well as decentralize administrative authority in order to appease the nationalists, as well as to contain the centrifugal forces which had become dominant in the northern and western parts of the country. Before we discuss the series of steps the British took to decentralize political and administrative power, it is in order to analyze why its policy of a unified administration failed.

One main reason was the ambivalence of colonial policy. The unevenness of the British colonial policy in Nigeria contributed immensely to the failure of unitary administrative service between 1914 and 1946. In spite of the amalgamation of 1914, Northern and Southern Nigeria continued to be administered separately. The administrative units of the former protectorates were retained.

Despite the existence of a unified civil service, each of the two groups of provinces was administered by a Lieutenant Governor who reported directly to the Governor General. Amalgamation did not in fact mesh the two separate civil services. For instance, departments like education, police and prisons in the north were separated in policy and control from their southern counterparts.[20] Besides, the Colony of Lagos had a separate legal status which it continued to enjoy until the inauguration of MacPherson's 1951 constitution.

During this period most of the interior areas in Northern Nigeria remained 'unexplored' and thereby unaffected by the colonial policies. On the surface, the amalgamation of the two territories in 1914 was directed to strengthen national unity and integration, but in practice the colonial policy was aimed at strengthening local administrative institutions and structures, especially in the North, and at the expense of central government and principles of unitary civil service administration.

A second reason is the plurality of Nigerian society. Nigeria, as we made the point earlier is inhabited by diverse ethnic groups which have varied and conflicting cultural heritages. There are differences in customs, religion, political institutions and world view. At the time amalgamation was effected in 1914, Nigeria "basically remained a collection of separate communities linked together by nothing more substantial than the British rule".[21] There was no common language used in the administration of the country, for while English was used as the official language in the South, Hausa was used as the official language in the North.

Thirdly, as the different communities in Nigeria did not have equal opportunity for exposure to Western forms of education, there were imbalances on the level of social mobilization. The imbalance was more prominent between North and South. It meant that the North could not compete with the South in whatever opportunities the central civil service offered. The lower echelon of the central civil service was staffed with clerks recruited mainly from Southern Nigeria, and this created fear and suspicions in the minds of the Northern leaders. They began to equate the unified civil service with "Southern domination"; they hoped that their own interests would be better served not by a 'distant' administration based in Lagos but by a regional administration which they could control. This fear of Southern domination based on the technological and educational backwardness of the North (as we shall see below) compelled the Northern leaders to embark on an extreme regional policy known as "Northernization". The implementation of this policy constituted a major constraint in attaining greater national integration between 1954 and 1966.

Lastly, one of the reasons why the bond of unity failed to grow among Nigerians after 35 years of 'centralist' administration by the British, was due to the lack of common sets of national institutions. There was no forum in which the various peoples of Nigeria could discuss their common problems, reconcile their differences or develop bonds of friendship. The higher civil service did not offer that opportunity as it was dominated by the expatriate officials. The 1923 Clifford's Legislative Council did not serve to foster a unified Nigeria because Northern Nigeria was not represented in its deliberation. As John Ostheimer succinctly argued:

> The involvement of Northern politicians in the activities of the central legislative Council would have stimulated northern political awareness and organization and would have prevented some of the fears of the northern leaders against the threat of Southern domination.[22]

Besides the lack of political institutions, there were no common economic and social institutions in which both the Southern and Northern elites participated. The Nigerian economy was essentially a peasant economy. Within the period, Britain did not execute any program that either induced economic development or established common social institutions in which the northern and southern leaders participated. While the few educated northerners were assimilated in the 'native' administration of their areas and found job satisfaction in this, their southern counterparts had contempt for native administration because it held little or no career opportunities for them. As they were shut off from the 'centralized' civil service, they formed political movements and coalesced with the various centrifugal forces to make demands for political reforms and the devolution of administrative power.

The Civil Service 1946-1966: The Era of Decentralization
The emergence of federal and state civil services:

Though the colonial administration in Nigeria between 1914 and 1946 was premised on a unified administrative system, with headquarters in Lagos, in reality Nigeria was administered along "federalist principles".

Given the vastness of Nigeria and the heterogeneity of its people, it was therefore not surprising that under conditions of ambivalent

48

colonial policies, and separate development schemes, centrifugal forces in both northern and southern parts of the country could gain enough strength and compel the British to accelerate the process of political and administrative decentralization. The conclusion of the Second World War and the agitations of the Southern Nationalists contributed to the devolution of administrative and political powers to Nigerians. In order to contend with centrifugal as well as nationalist forces the British embarked on a series of incremental political and administrative reforms. In 1946, the first post-war governor, Arthur Richards, inaugurated a new constitution which more or less formalized the separate developments which had been going on in the different areas of the country since 1914. The constitution represented a guideline for the new British policy in Nigeria. It reflected a change of policy from political and administrative centralization, to political devolution and administrative decentralization. The constitution provided for a legislative council for the whole of Nigeria which consisted of an unofficial majority. It also provided for Regional Councils for the Northern, Western and Eastern provinces. The Regional Council for the North had two chambers—a House of Chiefs and a House of Assembly. The Eastern and Western Regional Councils each had a House of Assembly only. The Regional Houses of Assembly were meant to establish linkages between the various Native Authorities and the Legislative Council. They had advisory powers. They were to advise the Regional governors on matters which they referred to them, the governors were not, however, bound to accept their recommendations.

Commenting on the need for developing political and administrative structures which allowed for unity in diversity, Governor Richards, the author of the 1946 Constitution claimed that his objective was to:

> create a political system which is itself a present advance and contains the living possibility of further orderly advance—a system within which the diverse elements may progress at varying speeds amicably and smoothly towards a more closely integrated economic, social and political unity without sacrificing the principles and ideals inherent in their divergent ways of life.[23]

Though the nationalist forces led by the National Council of Nigeria and Cameroon (N.C.N.C.) opposed the Richards' Constitution, because of its implied decentralization of political and administrative powers and gave no real executive powers to Nigerians, the centrifugal forces in the northern and western parts of the country welcomed it. For them the constitution offered an opportunity of having their own political and administrative institutions, as well as reducing the competition from educated Igbos who at this time constituted a force in Northern and Western Nigeria.

It was not surprising that it was the N.C.N.C. leadership that led the opposition against the Richards' Constitution. It demanded more political control of Nigeria by Nigerians. The centrifugal forces in both north and west could only go along with the demand for more political and administrative powers to the extent that those powers were distributed to Nigerians along regional boundaries. The Richards' Constitution was short-lived. It was replaced by the 1951 Constitution which was initiated by a Governor MacPherson. This Constitution did not reverse the 'regional principle' which had been formalized by the Richards' Constitution. In several respects the MacPherson Constitution fortified regional institutions and foreshadowed the emergence of a federal constitution. From this period up to 1966 when the military intervened in the political process, two forces—communalist and nationalists—crystallized and all the major administrative, political and economic questions were viewed from regional and 'centralist' perspectives. In 1953, the northern leaders passed in the Northern House of Assembly an 8-point program in which among other things they demanded complete legislative and administrative autonomy with respect to all matters with the exception of customs, external affairs and defense, the abolition of central legislative council and its replacement with a Common Services Organization, and the existence of a 'neutral' territory for the activities of the Common Services Organization.[24] On the other hand the N.C.N.C. and other nationalists demanded more central authority, and the weakening of regional administration.

These conflicting demands of the Regionalists and Nationalists led to another constitutional conference in London in 1953, which continued in Lagos in 1954. The compromise reached by the Regionalists and the Nationalists resulted in the birth of the 1954 federal constitution. The 1954 Constitution for the first time established a truly federal structure by delimiting spheres of activity between the Federal and Regional governments. There were three legislative lists. The Federal government had enumerated legislative list. Its jurisdiction included such subjects as external affairs, customs, banking, excise duties, and internal and external security. The Regional governments had residual power just as the states do in the USA. The constitution also provided for a concurrent legislative list which included such subjects as agriculture, health, education and economic development. The units of the federation were the federal government, the federal territory of Lagos, the Northern, Western and Eastern regions; the Midwest region was later, in 1964, carved out of the Western region.[25] It is pertinent to remark that the northern region which was larger than all the other regions and the federal territory put together was left intact. This unbalanced structure of the newly established federation was to affect the effectiveness of both the federal government and its administrative machinery because it made it possible for one of the constituent states—the Northern Region—to hold the federal government to 'ransom' for most of the period (1954-1966).

The constitution also provided for the existence of federal and regional civil services. As most of the able and experienced civil servants who served in the former unitary service, returned to their regions to start the new regional civil services, the 'new' federal civil service started its existence under less favorable conditions. As Nicolson succinctly states:

> (The Federal Civil Service) was pieced together from what was left after Regional Public Services, Statutory boards, Federal corporations had been amputated from the old unitary service. All the new bodies had fresh starts; each region with a clear cut party majority, could make a clear cut policies for its public service, and could and did adopt a policy of staffing posts with men of regional origin. There was a rapid advancement in each of the new services. In the federal government, on the other hand, there has been government by coalition in which clear-cut policies are not so readily decided. Many of the ablest Nigerians were lost on promotion of the new Eastern and Western Public Services, to the New Foreign Service and to the staffs of the new legislatures and the new public corporation. The anomaly of an almost complete absence of Northerners on the Federal service was recognized but not so easily cured.[26]

From 1954 when the federal constitution was inaugurated, to 1966 when the 'old federal system' was destroyed by the emergence of the Military in the Nigerian political process, the federal and state civil services were marked by a number of important features which included the devolution of administrative power from the expatriate to indigenous personnel, the increased dominance of the Regional civil services and the institutionalization of the communal and nationalist forces.

The process of devolution of administrative power to the indigenous civil servants (a process which has been referred to as "Nigerianization") was quickened, especially in the eastern and western civil services which inherited more able and experienced administrative officers from the defunct unitary service. Each of the three regional governments was anxious to earn legitimacy of its own people through positive inducements and payoffs. One of the easiest ways of doing this was to 'Nigerianize' the Regional Civil Service.

In 1955 the Eastern House of Assembly passed an appropriation bill which deliberately froze the expatriate allowances for six permanent secretaries and two assistant secretaries attached to the Governor's office.[27] This act triggered off a 'crisis' which was only averted through the use of the governor's veto and the intervention of the colonial Secretary in London. The Eastern Regional government used all the available indigenous personnel to fill up most of the vacant senior administrative positions in its service. The more experienced indigenous administrative officers were promoted to be heads of departments, positions which some years earlier were . exclusively reserved for the expatriate officials. The rate of Nigerianization in the East Nigerian civil service was ultimately contingent on the available trained personnel. However, by 1963, almost all the administrative positions had been Nigerianized. All the expatriate staff that remained in the service served in advisory capacity.

The western Nigerian government was also very eager to 'Nigerianize' its civil service. The government of the Western region under the leadership of the Action Group, a highly organized and disciplined party, passed a number of 'anti-expatriate' resolutions which included provisions that expatriation pay votes of all vacant posts in the state civil service would be frozen and would not be released in respect of any particular vacancy except with the approval of the Regional Executive Council, and that non-Nigerians should not be appointed to a vacant position by promotion, if a suitable Nigerian was available.[28] The Western Nigerian government had earlier reserved certain positions to indigenes of Western Nigeria. The reserved positions included all posts in the recruitment branch of the Public Service Commission; all those in the office of the commissioner for western Nigeria in London; Secretary to the Cabinet and his staff; Crown Counsel; and magistrates.[29] Furthermore, in 1960 the western government decided to reserve for Nigerians the posts of head of the civil service, all permanent secretaries, all heads of professional divisions in every Ministry.[30] Under the experienced administrative leadership of Simeon Adebo who was the first indigenous head of the Western civil service, the "Nigerianization" process furthered most in the Western region. The western Nigerian lead was understandable, given the early contact that part of Nigeria had with Western education and colonial administration. The point has been made in Chapter Two that the Yorubas, the dominant ethnic group in Western Nigeria, as early as 1928 had 12 practising lawyers and 8 medical doctors while the Igbos, their immediate competitors, had none.

On the other hand, because of the educational backwardness of the North and the lack of qualified personnel the 'Nigerianization' process was pursued with great caution by the northern regional government. We made the point earlier of how the exclusive policy of Lord Lugard shut off the muslim areas of northern Nigeria from the influences of Christian educational activities. Part of the price the north had to pay when the federal system was inaugurated in 1954 was to contend with 'aliens' from the south who dominated its civil service. The 'dominance' of the southern administrative officers and clerks in the northern civil service was intolerable to the northern leaders, who were determined to use their newly acquired political and administrative power to solve the "Southern question". The northern regional government initiated an exclusive policy known as "Northernization" as an answer to the grave lack of its own people in its service. The "Northernization" policy—a product of educational imbalance and real fear of Southern domination—initially took the form of harassing the Southerners in the northern civil service and a five-year plan for filling the junior positions in the civil service of the region, where there were no fewer than 1400 vacancies.[31]

Further declaration of the northernization policy stipulates that:

If a qualified Northerner is available, he is given priority in recruitment, and if no Northerner is available, an expatriate may be recruited or a non-Northerner on contract terms.[32]

Thus, in the actual implementation of 'Nigerianization' policy in the north preference was given to northern Nigerians, followed by the expatriate personnel. The non-northerners—mainly the Southern Nigerians—were hired on a contract basis where the first two categories of personnel were not available. The table 9 below shows the plan for the Northernization of senior positions in the Northern Nigerian civil service between 1956 and 1960. There is no doubt that the consequences of the 'Northernization policy' exacerbated the conflicts between the northern leaders and the southern nationalists and contributed to the destruction of the old federation in 1966.

'Nigerianization policy' proceeded cautiously in the federal civil service for two main reasons. The federal civil service had lost a number of senior and able civil servants to the eastern and western civil services and as a result there were few qualified and experienced Nigerians who could replace the expatriate heads of departments and ministries. Secondly, there was the anomaly of an almost complete absence of northerners in the federal civil service.[33] As the northerners were the senior partners in the federal coalition government, they were not in a hurry to replace the more preferred expatriates with the 'ambitious' southern administrative officers. The northern members of the Nigerian federal government therefore saw the southerners as the main beneficiaries of the 'Nigerianization' policy of the federal government.

Consequently, despite the declared intention of the federal government to quicken the process of Nigerianization, a legislative report issued in 1959 indicated slow progress. The report showed that out of 73 super-scale positions in the Federal Service only 10 were held by Nigerians or other West Africans, while 63 were held by expatriate officers; that Nigerians held only 1 of 14 posts of permanent secretaries; 2 of 20 posts of deputy permanent secretaries; and 6 out of 34 posts of deputy permanent secretaries.[34] As a result of these findings,

TABLE 9. NORTHERNIZATION PLAN FOR SENIOR PROFESSIONAL & ADMINISTRATIVE POSITIONS IN THE NORTHERN NIGERIAN CIVIL SERVICE 1956-1960

Professional & Administrative Position	New Appointments					Promotions					Transfer from Native Authorities				
	1956	1957	1958	1959	1960	1956	1957	1958	1959	1960	1956	1957	1958	1959	1960
Northerners	35	13	11	19	51	44	9	17	3	46	–	3	9	2	–
Nigerians— Pensionable	–	2	–	–	–	52	1	1	–	2	–	–	–	–	–
Nigerians— Contract	1	–	–	2	–	–	–	–	2	–	–	–	–	–	–
Expatriates— Pensionable	171	17	42	1	–	93	56	90	30	69	–	–	–	–	–
Expatriates— Contract	213	106	123	138	142	25	10	1	32	2	–	–	–	–	–
Total	420	138	176	160	193	214	76	109	67	119	–	3	9	2	–

Source: A.H.M. Kirk Greene, "The Higher Public Service", in Frank Blitz, ed., *The Politics and Administration of Nigerian Government*, London: Sweet & Maxwell, 1965, p.231.

the government demanded that all higher posts should be filled by Nigerians at independence, even if it involved deterioration of standards.[35] In effect the Federal Government, because of the pressures of the nationalists, was prepared to achieve greater 'Nigerianization' of its civil service at the cost of efficiency and increased output. This partly explains why regional services as those of the West and East at this period proved to be better administrative institutions. As the Federal government accelerated the Nigerianization process each region and each of the three major Nigerian ethnic groups—Hausa, Yoruba and the Igbo—saw the federal positions as 'national cakes' to be shared.

It is important to note that two administrative concepts—representativeness and efficiency—were in conflict here. While the northern members of the federal government generally favored recruitment into the federal civil service on a quota (representative) basis, the eastern and western members, because they had more educated and qualified personnel, argued that recruitment into federal civil service should be based on merit. In practice, in pursuit of 'Nigerianization' the principle of merit was diluted into the one of representativeness and this obviously affected the quality and output of the Federal Civil Service between 1954 and 1966.

TABLE 10. NIGERIANIZATION OF THE HIGHER RANKS OF THE FEDERAL PUBLIC SERVICE, 1958-1963

Year	Posts held by Nigerians (%)
1958	48.1
1959	49.3
1960	64.0
1961	74.0
1962	78.0
1963	87.0

Source: A. Kirk Greene, "The Higher Public Service", in Frank Blitz, ed., The Politics and Administration of Nigerian Government, London: Sweet & Maxwell, 1965, p. 225.

Moreover, the federal civil servants were viewed by the regional leaders as the representatives of regional interests, rather than as national civil servants, owing allegiance to federal authority. They were often faced with the conflicting demands of serving as national officers and the expectations of their ethnic groups and friends, who pressurized them to use their public positions to serve their interests.[36]

The other issue relating to Nigerianization which was tackled by the federal government before the attainment of independence in 1960 was that of integration of technical departments with the newly created ministries. The legislative committee which investigated the problem recommended "Organization" and adaptation of the public service in Nigeria along the British Model. The departments were to be "integrated" in the ministries, the permanent secretaries of the ministries were to act as official liaison between the minister and the heads of divisions, which in most cases were to replace the departments, as well as serve as the general administrative heads of the ministries. The former departmental heads who were professionals—engineers, agriculturalists —became directors of divisions such as in Ministries of Works and Agriculture. Others were given titles of "advisors" as in ministries of Education and Health. New ministries created shortly before the attainment of independence included Establishment, which incorporated the former federal establishment office, the pension and Nigerianization offices; Economic Development and Defence.[37]

In spite of the accelerated pace of the Nigerianization of the civil service between 1954 and 1966 the structure of both the federal and state civil services remains essentially a British class oriented system. The class structure was based on the recommendation of the Gorsuch Report of 1954 which prescribed the division into four broad classes corresponding to the general education standards of the time. The four main classes in the state and federal civil services are:

(1) sub-clerical and technical
(2) clerical and technical
(3) executive and higher technical
(4) administrative and professional[38]

Each of the four classes is divided into several groups, known as cadres. For instance, the professional class includes the following cadres: engineering, architecture, education, law, agriculture, accountancy and medicine.[39] A typical state or federal ministry will at once contain the four main classes of civil servants mentioned above. Within the period the political head of a ministry and the official head was the permanent secretary. The permanent secretary under the direction of a minister was responsible for the execution of a program of activities assigned to his ministry.

With the firm entrenchment of the concept of "Regionalism" and the consolidation of the regional Civil Services between 1954 and 1966, each of the three Nigerian regional governments pursued varied schemes of economic and social development that limited the influence of the federal government and civil service within its area of jurisdiction.

The western region, under the disciplined leadership of the Action Group government embarked upon large-scale economic schemes[40] which included road and bridge construction. In addition, a number of statutory corporations and commercial companies such as the Nido

Gas, Nigersol, Nigerian Water Resources Development, Nigerian Textile, West African Portland Cement Co., and Asbestor Cement Products were established. It also pursued vigorous social welfare programs which included universal free primary education, hospitals, a TV station and the University of Ife. It equally expanded the regional Civil Service and thereby created more jobs for the Secondary School leavers and the University graduates. It secured the support of the natural rulers by giving them positions in the government and the statutory boards.

The Eastern Nigerian government under the leadership of N.C.N.C. which was the most nationalist of the three Nigerian political parties, also settled down to cultivation of regional and ethnic support by pursuing a moderate program of economic and social development.[41] It established a number of statutory boards and commercial companies which included printing, tourist, textile, beer and ceramic industries, iron and steel works, asbestos products and a cement factory. It also executed a number of social schemes such as the award of scholarships, construction of roads and bridges, hospitals. It founded the University of Nigeria in 1960. It also expanded its civil service and thereby improved available job opportunities. With more jobs, contracts, scholarships and improved output of the regional civil service, the government of eastern Nigeria consolidated its regional support.

The northern regional government which had executed the 'Northernization' policy with vigor, also carried out a modest social and economic program. It carried out local government reforms and expanded facilities for primary education. It also founded the Ahmadu Bello University.

There is no doubt that in terms of social and economic performance, and mobilization of the support of the majority of Nigerians, the three regional governments and their administrative machineries 'stole' the show from the federal government and its civil service. The important question that arises is: Why should the state governments and civil services dominate the federal government between 1954 and 1966? Three principal reasons—the pattern of political leadership, the ethnic foundation and dominance of the three main Nigerian political parties and the resources at the disposal of the states—shed some light on the question.

During this period the exercise of effective political power lay with the Regional premiers rather than with the federal prime minister and his ministerial colleagues. The most powerful man in Nigeria at that time was Alhaji Ahmadu Bello, the chairman of the Northern Peoples Congress (N.P.C.) and the Regional premier of northern Nigeria, rather than the federal prime minister, Alhaji Abubakar who was only deputy chairman of N.P.C. For most of the period, the authority of the Federal government did not derive from the inherent powers of the Federal constitution (which were considerable) or from the legitimacy of its institutions, rather it was premised on a "politicians" agreement between the leaders of N.P.C. and N.C.N.C.—the two parties which formed the federal coalition. It was inconceivable for the federal government to embark on any fundamental decision which the leaders of the two parties opposed. For instance, the Federal government would not have declared the State of Emergency in Western Nigeria in 1962 and created the State of Midwest in January 1964 (the two most important federal acts within the period) without the consent and support of the Northern and Eastern Regional governments. Moreover, the State governments in several other respects derided federal leadership and acted independently. For instance, up to the early 1960s the regional governments had in London diplomatic representatives known as Agents General. As most of the powerful Nigerian leaders at this time preferred to operate from the regional bases rather than from the national level, the regional governments and the civil services appropriated more power and importance than the federal government.

Another reason for the dominance of the Regional governments and the civil services is that the three Regional premiers who constituted the commanding political actors in Nigeria derived their support from their regionally based parties. The premier of northern Nigeria derived his support from the Hausa and the N.P.C.; while the premier of the West derived his support mainly from the Yorubas and the A.G. The core of support for the premier of the Eastern region came from the Igbos and the N.C.N.C.

Reciprocal patterns of relationships developed between each party and the major ethnic group. While the ethnic group gave its unflinching support, especially during the regional and federal elections, the party in return distributed favors, money, contracts and jobs to the members of its ethnic group. As the parties and their ethnic supporters competed for control of the societal resources, the federal government and the federal civil service were regarded as part of the 'national cake' to be divided between them. The ethnic groups did not see the federal government and its administrative machineries as the national institutions requiring their primary loyalty. Throughout the period the federal government and federal civil service were denied the legitimacy and support which the ethnic groups and the regionally oriented parties gave to the regional governments.

The third explanation for the dominance of the state civil service at this period was due to human and material resources available to the states. The point has been made earlier as to how the most able senior civil servants from the defunct unitary service joined the civil services of their own regions. With the exception of the northern civil service, each of the civil services in the east and west started off in

58

1954 with more experienced indigenous civil servants than the federal civil service had. The states were also able to execute impressive programs of social and economic schemes because of the monetary reserves accumulated by the Nigerian Produce Marketing Board. The Board accumulated reserves as ample cushion against fluctuations of world prices of cocoa, cotton, groundnuts and palm produce. At the end of the 1953-54 crop season the reserve of the Board amounted to £82,771,000.[42] With the federalization of Nigeria in 1954 the produce market system was reorganized and the existing national crop boards were replaced by regional (State) boards and a central marketing board. Consequently, the western, northern and eastern regional governments inherited large sums of money, part of which was deployed in executing schemes of economic and social development.

As our analysis has shown the problem of 'regionalism' and 'centralism' remained a thorny question throughout the duration of the old federalism 1954-1966. The regional forces were generally stronger in the North and West than in the East. As the North was much less advanced educationally and economically, it feared the domination of the South. It naturally favoured a slower evolution to independence with more complete guarantees for regionalism. It opposed the creation of states or the readjustment of regional boundaries, as this would entail its losing its grip on the peoples of northern Nigeria, which provided it with the broad premise for its continued domination of the Nigerian political scene.

The west under the leadership of the Action Group supported regionalism for the first two years of independence. It saw it as a means of checking the Igbo competition, and stopping the leadership of Azikiwe who was gradually emerging as the leader of Nigerian nationalism. Secondly, the west was the wealthiest region of the federation, primarily because of the high prices for cocoa of which it was the heaviest producer in Nigeria; as a result, she did not want to share her wealth with the poorer regions of the federation. She persistently advocated a method of revenue sharing based on derivation.

On the other hand, although the East was less financially strong than the other regions, it advocated a more centralist political philosophy. This was partly so because the Igbos which constituted the major ethnic group in the east were more 'outgoing' and had their economic assets scattered in all parts of the Federation, and thus their interests would be better served by a stronger and more national government, than by a weak central government dependent on powerful regions. Besides, the Igbos had special pride that the N.C.N.C. which enjoyed their support started as a national movement, rather than as a cultural organization as was the case with N.P.C. and A.G.

With the exception of the North, where the concept of "Regionalism" was adhered to with some religious flavor, the western and eastern leaders and their political parties were more pragmatic in their espousal of regionalist and centralist philosophies. They modified their stance when it suited their interest. The understanding of this point is vital to the appreciation of the reason why N.C.N.C. and A.G. finally emerged as the champions of 'centralist' philosophy, and why the N.P.C. and the dissidents of A.G. became the principal advocates of regionalist doctrine.

The aftermath of the federal election of 1959, the Action Group crises of 1962 and the controversial censuses of 1962 and 1963 brought the regionalists and centralists conflict to a head. It led to a major realignment of the Nigerian political parties and their supporters into two forces: Communalists and Nationalists. The Communal forces formed the Nigerian National Alliance (N.N.A.) and was supported principally by the N.P.C. and the Akintola's Nigerian National Democratic Party (N.N.D.P.), while the Nationalists formed the United Progressive Grand Alliance (U.P.G.A.) which comprised mainly of A.G. and the N.C.N.C. and other splinter parties in the North.

From 1964 to 1966 all events and issues such as the controversial 1964 federal election and the 1965 regional election in the West were fought by the two forces along communal and nationalist lines. Given the extent of institutionalization of the communal forces which was made possible, by their control of the federal government; the nationalists lost in all the major contests. The struggles between the two forces generated such ill feelings and conflicts that it not only attenuated the legitimacy of the federal government and its administrative machinery but led to the military intervention in the political process on January 15, 1966.

The Civil Services and the "New Federalism" 1966—Onwards: the Era of increased Centralization

The establishment of a military regime in Nigeria on January 15, 1966 saw the end of the "old Federalism" and the shaky beginning of a new one. As we pointed out earlier the organizers of the January 15, 1966 coup d'etat were ideologically motivated.[43] They had the sympathy of the forces in Nigerian politics who advocated nationalism; and the leading proponents of communalism—Ahmadu Bello, Abubakar Balewa and Samuel Akintola lost their lives in the coup. The "New federalism" was not destined to grow and mature in a placid social environment, for it had to surmount thorny problems and processes before its existence could be assured. The new military regime was headed by General Ironsi who espoused and pursued a centralist political philosophy. In pursuit of integrative policies, he de-emphasized Nigeria's longstanding regional divisions.[44] The most singular act that set the communalist forces against him and his centralist supporters was his Decree 34 of May 24, 1966, which was directed towards the unification of all the Nigerian civil services. In effect the "Unification Decree" implied a centralized political authority and a return to the pre-1954 unitary civil service. The reaction to this act was immediate and violent. It initiated a chain of events that not only threatened the territorial integrity of the country, but also plunged Nigeria into a three-year bloody civil war. The communalists who had been alienated by the loss of their leadership and who feared the Igbo domination, unleased such violence on the Igbos that several thousands of them were killed.[45] The northern elements in the Nigerian army who shared communalist ideology staged a counter coup on July 29, 1966 which ousted Ironsi's regime and enthroned Yakubu Gowon who was then a lieutenant colonel. For a while Gowon pursued a regionalist and communalist policy. It appeared that the 'new federal system' was heading backwards to the pre-1966 situation, if not worse. Gowon in his August 1, 1966 broadcast claimed among other things that there was no basis for Nigeria's unity and included a confederal system as one of the options of governmental arrangement Nigerians could choose. He abolished the unification decree and even agreed for a while to regionalize the army. The events and processes that followed the ousting of Ironsi's regime in July 1966 up to January 1970 when the "new federalism' was firmly established are so complex that they lie outside the purview of our study.[46] However, the important event that ensured the survival of a "new federalism" was Gowon's reversal of policy. From 1967 onwards, Gowon started to espouse nationalist policies and abandoned his communalist stance. He ruled out secession and the confederal system as options for consideration. He split the unbalanced federal structure into a 12-state structure on May 27, 1967, partly as a strategy for forestalling the Biafran secession.

The "new federalism" is marked by a number of factors which include increased centralization of political authority, ascendancy of centripetal forces, greater structural differentiation of the constituent states, increases in the federal government largesse and increases in the functions of the federal and state civil services.

One significant fact of the "new Nigerian federalism" is the greater centralization of national political authority. This has been made possible by the existence of a military regime and the banning of the three Nigerian dominant and ethnic oriented political parties which in several respects captured the authority of the federal government in the pre-1966 federation. With the conclusion of the Nigerian civil war in 1970, General Gowon and his military aids firmly established the federal authority in all parts of the Nigerian federation. Through the enactment of a series of legislative decrees the federal military government suspended some aspects of the old Nigerian constitution that limited its authority.[47] The most powerful man in Nigeria today is the head of the federal government rather than the head of a state government as was the case in the old federation. The constituent states now look up to the federal government for direction and support in all important decisions and programs. Although a new Nigerian constitution still has to define the spheres of power and authority between the federal and state governments, there is no doubt that the balance of power has tilted in favour of the federal government. In terms of present power sharing and the exercise of it, the trend so far suggests that the Nigerians do not want a return to the pre-1966 federation.

Perhaps, the greatest turnover of events that has strengthened the centripetal course, and thereby helped in the emergence of the 'new federalism' is the 'conversion' of the Northern leadership of emirs and military officers into advocates of centralist principles. Faced with the threats of Biafran secession and the disintegration of Nigeria, the Northern leadership abandoned their longstanding opposition to re-structuring the unbalanced federal structure into smaller constituent states.[48] The reversal of policy by Northern leadership is so remark-able, especially when it is remembered that the Northern leadership had earlier in a conference convened in Lagos in September 1966 to settle the Nigerian crisis advocated a confederal system with "virtual political autonomy for the regions, including the right to secede, but with a common services organization".[49]

Besides, the centripetal forces had earlier gained more strength when Gowon released Chief Obafemi Awolowo from prison. Chief Awolowo, the chairman of the proscribed Action Group and the leader of the Yoruba is a firm believer in a stronger federation based on small constituent states. He therefore helped to rally the Yorubas in support of the "new federalism".

The most singular event that weakened the regional forces and ensured the survival of the New federation was the restructuring of the former four regions into a 12-state structure on May 27, 1967. We have earlier made the point that the largest Nigerian ethnic groups—Hausa, Yoruba and Igbo—dominated Nigerian politics at the expense of the minorities. However, the restructuring of the state system and the abolition of the former four unequal regions had strengthened the center-periphery relationships and assured effective representation of the interests of the minorities. These minority ethnic groups now share in the federal largesse and they have developed a new sense of identity and acknowledge greater commitment and loyalty to the new Nigerian federalism. It is necessary to point out that Gowon comes from a minority ethnic group—Anga—in the Benue Plateau area of Nigeria. His people, as well as others in the Nigerian Middle Belt area, detested the hagemony of the Hausa-Fulani group in the pre-1966 federation. It is sometimes argued that Gowon over-

62

represented minority interests in his Cabinet, for the following officers belong to minority ethnic groups.

TABLE 11. MINORITY MEMBERS OF GOWON'S CABINET[50]

Officer	Position Held	Minority Ethnic Group
Yakubu Gowon	Head of the Federal Govt. and Commander-in-Chief of the Nigerian Armed Forces	Anga
O. Arikpo	Commissioner for External Affairs	Ekoi
T. S. Tarka	Commission for Communication	Tiv
Anthony Enahoro	Commissioner for Information and Labor	Edo
N. Douglas	Attorney General	Ijaw
H. Briggs	Commissioner for Trade	Ijaw
A. Y. Eke	Commissioner for Education	Edo

The important point is that the state creation has weakened the regional forces. More states now look to the federal government for help, rather than the reverse, which was the situation in the old federal system.

A major commanding factor that has significantly helped to shape and strengthen federal-state relationships in the new federation is the dramatic increases in the federal largesse. The present federal government commands enormously more financial and human resources than its pre-1966 predecessor. This is most readily seen in great increases in the proceeds from Nigerian oil. For instance, while the gross proceeds from the oil sector was N66 million in 1964[51] the gross proceeds from the sector in 1975 were N5,320 million.[52] As the Federal Government retains most of the proceeds from the oil sector, the states are now financially dependent on the federal government, not only to supplement their recurrent expenditure but to finance their capital programs. Perhaps the financial dependence more than any other factor has acted drastically to alter the federal state relations. For instance, out of the federal government's gross revenue of N5,252 million for the 1975-76 financial year, an estimated sum of N1,300 million has been earmarked for statutory and non-statutory appropriations to the states.[53] Although, a new principle of revenue sharing between the federal and state government is yet to be worked out in the future, at present the federal government on its own determines how much money the states can get. This confers to the federal government more political control in all parts of the federation.[54] The authority that holds the purse strings is automatically the new Nigerian boss, and not the dependent recipients.

Perhaps the most remarkable feature of the "new federalism" in Nigeria is the substantial increases in the policymaking and execution functions of the federal and state civil services. Because of the availability of more financial resources, both services are increasingly involved in drawing up a complex program of economic and social activities for both the federal and state governments. As the federal government increasingly overshadows the state governments through its retention of bulk of national financial resources, the federal civil service equally through centralized planning institutions dominate the state civil services in evolving national development plans. The states can no longer as they did in the pre-1966 federation evolve independent programs of activities. In effect the scope and magnitude of state planning activities are at present determined by the federal government through the Federal Ministry of Economic Development. In the next chapter we shall discuss in detail the role of both federal and state civil services in development planning.

Here we shall discuss in general terms the changes in the policymaking and implementation roles of the federal and state civil services. Their role in policymaking has increased rapidly since the conclusion of the Nigerian Civil War in 1970.

In the absence of a legislature, and the elected representatives of the people, such as ministers or commissioners, with popular political base, the federal civil servants have acquired wide legislative functions. They play a major part in the formulation of social, economic, educational and political objectives of the government. They are able to perform this function because of the unique positions they occupy in the hierarchy of ministries and the departments. The most well placed amongst them, such as the permanent secretaries, their deputies and the under-secretaries, make claims to wealth of experience just as they have access to information and data necessary for policy proposals. With their vantage positions, they make policy proposals, spell out all possible consequences and even indicate their policy preferences.[55] The top civil servants see themselves as equal partners in policymaking with their politically appointed commissioners (ministers). The latter do initiate policies, but much is contingent on their education, professional training and knowledge of the complex activities of the government.

In case of a policy disagreement between a federal permanent

64

secretary (the most senior civil servant in a ministry) and his political boss—the Commissioner, the permanent secretary may well put up a fight in order to make his policy preference prevail. As the recently retired Secretary of the Federal Government put it:

> It would be sheer irresponsibility on the part of the civil servant ... to proceed to implement a decision he believes to be wrong. It is part of the function of the civil servant to utilize all legitimate means to persuade the minister (Commissioner) to accept the policy proposals he submits and in which he believes ... moral persuasion rather than force of logic becomes the armoury of the civil servant. There are times even when humor and judicious use of innocent blackmail could bring an otherwise recalcitrant minister Commissioner) to reason.[56]

The implication of Lawson's statement is that top federal civil servants can resort to 'blackmail' to have their policy preferences accepted by their political bosses. It also implies that the civil servants can hardly implement policy proposals which do not enjoy their favor. The role of civil servants is much more appreciated by the military rulers than those appointed commissioners who are their political bosses. Their effectiveness in policymaking is further enhanced by their attendance at cabinet meetings. Although they do not exercise voting power during cabinet meetings, they like every other member of the cabinet, take active part in its discusions and deliberations. Besides, they provide all the data, that inform all Cabinet decisions.[57] There seem to be symbiotic relationships between the military rulers and the top civil servants. Both are career oriented, and are interested in ranks, statuses and promotions. While the civil servants feed the military rulers with ideas, policy proposals, provide them with factual and value premises for fundamental decisions, the military, in turn, shield the civil servants, and allow them to increase their scope of power in decision-making and in administration. It is therefore not surprising that considering the close-knit relationships between the military and the top civil servants, some civilian appointed commissioners are assigned to peripheral roles.

One effect of the dominance of the top civil servants in goal setting and decision making is that most decisions of government tend to be remote from the basic needs of the Nigerians the majority of whom live in rural areas. In a social environment devoid of political parties or other agencies of mass mobilization and participation, it is often difficult for orderly minded top civil servants in air-conditioned offices in Lagos, Ibadan, Kaduna or Enugu to articulate effectively the primary needs of a majority of Nigerians who live in the rural communities. During our discussions with some young planning officers in a federal ministry in Lagos, we asked them how they reflect the needs of most rural Nigerians in their planning efforts. Their immediate answer was: "Who does not know the needs of Nigerians"? The assumption here is that the needs of all the communities in Nigeria including the rural ones are obvious. Besides, there is a further assumption that the degree of needs are the same from one such rural community to another. The assumptions are not always correct. The intensity of needs of basic necessities of life vary from one area to another. The policy outputs of the civil servants are relevant to the extent that they reflect the varying needs of the various publics, especially the rural ones. One implication of this observation is that there is a pressing need to articulate the needs of the rural Nigerians more effectively. This is a job which the civil service and the military as presently structured are ill-equipped to perform, as this requires a form of regional and local participation.

As the federal government retains more national resources, and as the expectations of the Nigerian public on provision of economic goods and services have risen, the federal civil service is increasingly being looked upon in the new federalism to bring about speedy realization of government economic and social programs. However, both the federal and state civil services are faced, to a varying degree with the problem of how to utilize the available societal and financial resources to execute the planned activities.

For a development theorist who is merely interested in economic growth as reflected in statistical aggregates, the Nigerian economy can be said to have performed well. For instance, using the figure 100 as a base, the index of industrial production rose from 100 in 1965 to 374 in 1973. The value of domestic production of textiles as a proportion of total consumption rose from about 5 per cent in 1961 to about 71 per cent in 1971; the index of beer production rose from 100 in 1960 to 260.9 in 1972. Importation of aviation spirit fell about 43 per cent, that of motor spirit by about 76 per cent. Between 1966 and 1972 the index of domestic production of cement rose from 100 to 114; the importation of passenger cars between 1951 and 1971 increased from a little over 3,000 cars in 1951 to 18,000 in 1971. Commercial vehicles increased within the same period from less than 1,000 to 21,000.[58] One can add to these impressive figures by mentioning other achievements in the economic sectors such as the "indigenization process", whereby certain classified industries had been turned into Nigerian Management, and two vehicle assemblies which were opened in 1975. Besides, there is a proliferation of new economic institutions to manage aspects of the economy, such as the Nigerian National Oil Corporation, the Industrial Training Fund, Nigerian Standard Organization, National Supply Company, Sokoto Rima Basin Development Authority, Lake Chad Basin Development Authority, Nigerian Mining Corporation, Nigerian Enterprises Promotion Board,

Capital Issues Commission, Nigerian Bank for Commerce and Industry.[59]

Despite the growth, the economic activities of the government are in the areas of import substitution; development in heavy industries such as iron and steel, petrol chemicals, as well as agricultural modernization is yet to take off.

Mere statistical aggregates tell only part of the story about the performance of an economy. It is also necessary to look into other factors such as the distribution patterns, the main beneficiaries of economic growth and development and the nature of relationships between the urban and the rural areas. When considered in these factors, the elites from all the sectors of the society have benefited most at the expense of the greater majority of Nigerians. Besides the gaps between the urban and rural areas, the poor and the rich, have widened.[60] It is therefore possible for a developing economy such as that of Nigeria to experience considerable growth without necessarily experiencing development. Availablity of enough foreign reserves and well articulated objectives do not portend that development is automatic. Sometimes substantial resources are deployed into activities such as the World Black Festival of Arts and Culture which tend to be symbolic, rather than helpful in relieving the deprivations of rural Nigerians. Such diversion of funds attracted the criticism of several Nigerians. For instance, 17 Anglican Bishops after their Synod meeting at Onitsha called on the government to readjust its priorities; and ensure that the Citizens be provided with good sanitation, water, roads, before it embarked on expensive projects such as proposed colored TV. The Bishops further stated:

> We feel that in a nation where we are living below subsistence level, we can see no justification for the scale of expenditure we understand is proposed for the Arts and Culture taking place in Nigeria this year (1975). In a country where the gap between the 'haves' and 'have nots' has continued to widen, we wonder how fair it is that large sums of money should be expatriated from this country to banks in foreign countries of the world.[61]

Other factors such as lack of executive capacity can forestall the attainment of stated objectives in spite of available means. Economic development can only be meaningful to the average Nigerian in the rural areas when he can with relative ease provide his basic needs such as food, clothing and housing and when he can be mobile without the constraints of bad roads and unreliable transport system. The average rural Nigerian will also like to see the gap between the rural and urban areas narrowed and to have all the social amenities which are available to his counterpart in the cities. The Anglican Bishops also added:

We should like to associate ourselves with all those people who have advocated health, water and electrification as well as for free education to secondary school level. We believe that it is not the will of God that in any country a few should enrich themselves at the expense of the many.[62]

In an effort to carry through the economic and social programs of the federal and state governments the senior civil servants at both the center and its peripheries have extended their involvement in the economic sector, within the past five years. At both federal and state levels, permanent secretaries and their immediate subordinates are appointed chairmen, general managers, secretaries, chief accountants, board members of statutory corporations and agencies such as the National Oil Corporation, the Nigerian Airways, the Vehicle Assembly plants, hotels, banks and housing organizations.

Civil servants justify their increased roles as both civil heads of their complex ministries and managers of statutory corporations by persuasively arguing that they never asked for chairmanship or headship of these corporations. That the military rulers—because of the "efficient" ways civil servants managed the affairs of their ministries —thrust the responsibilities of statutory corporations on them. That before the emergence of military rule, nepotism, tribalism and general inefficiency characterized the management of these agencies and hence most of them ran great losses for the federal government.[63]

The civil servants further pointed out the following advantages since they undertook the management of some of the statutory corporations. That as they do not belong to any political party with partisan interests, they bring the same "objectivity" that characterizes the management of their ministries to bear on the administration of the statutory corporations.[64] That a permanent secretary as a general manager of a statutory corporation is likely to be more knowledgeable than a political appointee, in organizing and management of these agencies. That most of these agencies under their control are no longer liabilities to the government but have started to run along profit lines. Besides, they claim that they do not receive extra benefits for their services in the corporations and the industries. When the issue that they are being overworked was raised, and that there is a limit to what one superior officer can efficiently manage and control, most of the senior officers interviewed both on federal and state levels claimed that the permanent secretaries are combining effectively their headships of ministries and departments with the management of the statutory agencies. They argued that while some permanent secretaries act as part-time chairmen of these bodies, some delegate their board membership to their able subordinates. They also maintained that in some instances permanent secretaries are seconded to the statutory agencies to work full time, and thereby are freed from the responsibilities of the ministries and departments. The fact, however, remains that there are many permanent secretaries who are not only full time heads of their ministries, but are full time chairmen of statutory corporations. They hardly delegate substantial functions and authority to their subordinates. This detracts from the general efficiency of both ministerial and statutory organizations.

This latter group of permanent secretaries who wield effective authority both in the ministries and several statutory corporations had attracted a lot of press criticisms. For instance, one of the *Daily Times* editorial opinions states:

> One of the criticisms leveled against public corporation managements is the injection of civil servants, particularly permanent secretaries, as chairmen of their boards. For one thing, these permanent secretaries are known to hold too many offices, dissipating their energy without being able to concentrate fully on any particular corporation ... Specially civil servants are found to be, by training, service oriented, rather than profit oriented. Hence, they are cautious and averse to taking the kind of risks necessary for the success of commercial enterprise. There is also a tendency on the part of the civil servants to act as watchdogs rather than planners; they also tend to apply to corporations civil service forms and procedures which have the effect of stifling initiative.[65]

One way out, from overloading talented permanent secretaries who have shown some skills in management of men and materials to achieve the desired goals, is to second them full-time to large and complex government corporations such as the Ports of Authority. Others who are equally talented should be concerned only with the affairs of their ministries which have become increasingly complex.

Implications of the "New Federalism"

The "New Federalism" has two major implications which Nigerians must fully address themselves to and resolve in order to take full advantage of their increased oil wealth. First, there is the increased dependency of the state governments and civil services on the federal government as units of unitary administration; rather than as units of government with recognizable spheres of independent activity. Secondly, there are increases in magnitude of problems that detract from the efficiency of the federal and state civil services.

I **Dependency Problem.** We have already discussed how factors such as the centralized political authority, increased structural differentiation and increases in federal largesse have increased the power and authority of the federal government and civil service at the expense of those of the states. The point we need to emphasize here is how the nature of the military command has made the constituent states and their agencies to be more dependent on the central government.

Unlike the pre-1966 federation, the basis of the federal-state relationships in the 'New federalism' derives more on the unity of military
command than on a constitutional provision. In effect, the state governments and civil services do not derive their powers and legitimacy
from the inherent powers of the constitution. Rather, they are
appointed and dismissed at the pleasure of the head of the federal
military government. Although some aspects of pre-1966 Constitution provides some guide for the center-periphery relations in Nigeria,
there are hardly any limits to activities and functions the present
federal government can engage in, besides there are no guarantees of
spheres of activities in which the states as of right have independent
action. Between 1966 and 1976, the federal military government has,
through a number of decrees suspended and modified the pre-1966
federal constitution and thereby increased its powers and functions at
the expense of the states. For instance, the following independent
actions of the federal government illustrate to what extent the basis
of federal-state relations has been altered in favor of the federal
government and its administrative machinery:

(a) On May 27, 1967 the federal military government abolished the
    former four regions and imposed a twelve state structure without
    the consent of the states. This was altered further on February 3,
    1976 with the creation of seven additional states, bringing the
    number to 19.[66]
(b) State governors have been appointed and dismissed at the pleasure
    of the federal government.
(c) National institutions have been created or abolished without the
    consent of the states. The most recent creation is the National
    Council of State.[67]
(d) The basis of revenue sharing between the federal and the states
    has been adjusted from time to time by the federal government
    without seeking the consent of the states.
(e) A decision was reached recently (February 3, 1976) on the
    movement of federal headquarters to a new area without the par-
    ticipation of the states.
(f) The federal government has taken over the control of all Nigerian
    universities including those of Ife and Ahmadu Bello which the
    states were reluctant to surrender.
(g) The federal government has fixed limits for the maximum income
    tax, any state can collect; it also fixes the prices of specified com-
    modities such as cement for all the states in the federation.

Perhaps in a country where in the last decade the national state
was a victim of forces emanating from the regional environment, it is
necessary to strengthen the central political authority. However, there
is a limit centralization of political authority could attain in Nigeria
and it still remains a federation. Given the present balance of power

between the federal and states in Nigeria, which is in favor of the former, some authorities can argue that the Nigerian government is premised more on unitary than a federal principle. This raises the question of what distinguishes a federal government from a unitary one. Without going into the controversy of the two principles of government, it is generally argued that the underlying principle of federalism is that the general or federal and state governments are "each within a sphere coordinate and independent".[68] In a 'true' federation it is presumed that the federal government cannot without express constitutional amendment, encroach upon functions and the powers of the states. This coordinate division of power is stressed by Freeman who argues that

> Two prerequisites seem necessary to constitute a federal government in its perfect form. On one hand, each of the members of the union must be wholly independent on those matters which concern each member only. On the other hand, all must be subject to a common power in those matters which concern the whole body of members collectively. Each member is perfectly independent within its own sphere but there is a sphere in which its independence or rather separate existence vanishes.[69]

Invariably in many federal systems, the constitution occupies a special position of importance, and it is usually a written constitution, while in a unitary system, there may or may not be a written constitution, but it is by no means as 'sacred' as a federal constitution. In a federal system the laws of the constitution are supposed to be the supreme laws of the land. On the other hand, nothing inhibits a unitary government with a parliamentary majority such as exists in Britain from exercising sovereign power. An effective unitary government recognizes no other superior authority. Such powers that other agencies exercise, are delegated to them by the central government. The powers can be withdrawn without causing any constitutional upheaval.

We must emphasize that there are no perfect unitary or federal systems of government. Each federal or unitary system is determined and shaped by peculiar circumstances that it has to contend with. In reality, federations vary from that of the United States where there are in practice coordinate divisions of power between the federal and state governments to that of the USSR where there is an ideal written federal constitution, but the actual practice of government is based on the unitary principle.

In the 'new Nigerian federal system', it is too early to make a categorical statement about the patterns of federal-state relations. Situations are still fluid and in the making. While there are strong unitary trends in the present federal system, one should not conclude that Nigerians have opted for a unitary system, and that regional and centrifugal forces have been finally contained. The present situation is made possible by the presence of a military regime. It is difficult to predict the future pattern of federal-state relations. Though a new federal constitution is in the making, sometimes constitutions do not provide enough understanding about the actual behavior of politicians. After all, the 1960 Nigerian constitution was one of the best ever written federal constitutions based on coordinate divisions of powers, but in practice the locus of effective power lay with the Regional rather than in the federal government.

Although the present patterns of the federal-state relations are still being shaped and will not be normalized until Nigeria adopts a new federal constitution, and the military withdraws from the political process, yet linkages between the two levels of governments are maintained through a number of organs which include: the national council of state, conference of federal and state commissioners, federal and state Public Service Commissions, conference of federal and state officials and through a central planning office in Lagos. We shall briefly highlight the importance of these organs with the exception of the Central Planning Office, which will be discussed in Chapter Four.

(i) National Council of State: This is the newest political organ established by the military regime in 1975. The Council is comprised of the members of the supreme Military Council and the state governors. The Council discusses all matters that are of common interest to the states. As a newly established organ it is too early to assess its effectiveness. No detail is yet available about the range of subjects it discusses and how much independence it enjoys in its deliberations. But given the hierarchical nature of federal military government, and considering the fact that all the state governors are the direct appointees of the Nigerian head of state and are dismissed at his pleasure,[70] the governors can hardly be expected to exercise much independence in the deliberations of the Council. Besides, there is a higher political organ above the Council—the supreme Military Council (S.M.C.), in which neither the governors nor regional interests are represented. The state governors ceased to be members of the Supreme Military Council when Gowon's regime was ousted on July 29, 1975. It is the S.M.C a purely central organ that reaches decisions on such important matters as the creation of new states, the movement of federal headquarters that affect the patterns of federal-state relations. It is necessary to add that on withdrawal of the military regime, both the National Council of States and the S.M.C. will cease to exist, and then whatever constitution that Nigerians agreed upon will provide the legal basis for the center-periphery relationship. But it should be noted that the most important instrument that presently determines the nature of center-periphery relations, including the magnitude of the roles of the federal and state civil services is the Supreme Military Council, a central government organ in which state or regional interests are not represented.

(ii) Federal and State commissioners (ministers): Since the end of the civil war in Nigeria in 1970, there have been regular meetings and consultations of federal and state commissioners (ministers) charged with various functions such as education, works, agriculture, information and the trade industry. Though the commissioners' meetings are advisory, nevertheless their outcomes had strengthened the federal-state linkages. During such meetings the federal and state commissioners map out policy objectives for the consideration and adoption by both federal and state governments. Vital information which influences government decisions is exchanged. The meetings also provide forums for identifying common problems which face various federal and state ministries and departments. Having identified problems, the commissioners usually suggest strategies for their solution.

For instance, the meetings of the federal and state commissioners of education provide a good illustration of the patterns of linkages and cooperation that exist between the federal and state commissioners. Since the federal government announcement in January 1974 of its desire to introduce free and universal primary education throughout Nigeria in September 1976, there have been several meetings of the Federal and state commissioners responsible for education. Through these meetings, the need for the federal-state cooperation to make a success of the program has been realized. The commissioners had also identified problems that will face the execution of the program. These include: shortage of teaching staff; the imbalances in the educational system of the country; lopsided distribution of educational facilities, shortages of classrooms and teaching equipment; handicapped children.[71]

As a result of the concern of both the federal and state governments to make a success of the free primary education scheme, they have already evolved common policy guidelines which provide a basis for action.[72]

(iii) Federal and State Public Service Commissions: Apart from the ministerial linkages, the federal and state public service commissions meet regularly to tackle common problems of selection and recruitment. In order to effectively utilize the available manpower in Nigeria, the Federal Public Service Commission has introduced on behalf of the states a "supernumerary service" whereby graduates are offered employment in the federal public service and seconded to the states in which their services are required. The scheme was first proposed in 1968 and approved in 1971.[73] It was aimed at free movement of high-level manpower such as doctors, technologists, engineers, education officers, scientific and administrative officers. At the request of the state, recruitment action for the supernumerary service is initiated by the federal public service commission. The federal government bore incidental expenses such as transport costs, while the states pay salaries and allowances of supernumerary service officers while in their employment.[74] Though many states, especially the Northern states, showed keen interest when the scheme was introduced. The scheme has not been successful as was originally envisaged. The Federal Public Service Commission, in evaluating the scheme recently stated:

> This scheme has however not been as successful as one would wish because of the reluctance of graduates to work in states other than those of their origin. For instance, out of 300 graduates offered appointments under the scheme, only 131 accepted the offers and in fact most of these are already agitating to be de-seconded to the Federal Service at the expiration of the period of their secondment.[75]

Besides supernumerary service, the Federal and State public service commissions are linked by annual conferences in which they discuss problems relating to recruitment and placement of graduates. The conference held at Port Harcourt in 1971 discussed in depth the problem of finding a sufficient number of teachers for the expanding network of educational institutions in the country. The conference further considered the desirability of coordinating the overseas recruitment efforts of the commission in general and agreed on the ways of streamlining and simplifying the procedures for recruiting teachers from the United Kingdom with the aid of the British Government.[76]

In another annual conference held in February 1975, the conference of Federal and State public service commissioners discussed the problem of placement of University graduates in Nigeria. The chairman of the conference, who is also the chairman of the Federal public service commission, pointed out that most Nigerian graduates including professionals are reluctant to take appointment with the state public services and national corporations such as the Railways and the National Electric Power Authority. Rather they prefer the Federal civil service which is already over-established in some areas.[77] The common problem that confronts the public service commissions, including other recruitment agencies in the private sector is lack of proper coordination amongst the various arms of the government and the private sector responsible for planning manpower needs, and placement of graduates. It is usual for one graduate to receive appointments in three or four places at the same time, thereby making it possible for him to reject an appointment in an area where his services may be most needed.

After examining various aspects of the problem of graduate placement in Nigeria the conference agreed as follows:

(a) that the government (federal and state) should undertake post pupilage training of engineering and para-medical staff, by employing them as pupils and attaching them to projects and reputable companies for the period of their pupilage to enable them to acquire the necessary experience and skills.

(b) that in order to create an equitable balance between demand and supply of skilled manpower, there should be a coordination of the individual efforts in manpower development by the ministries of Education, Establishments, Labor and the Manpower Board . . .

(c) that recruitment tours of all Nigerian universities by all employment agencies in the republic should be organized simultaneously.

(d) that a Working Party be set up consisting of representatives of the civil services, the public and private sectors, the universities and student body, to examine the proposals made at the meeting.[78]

The working party has already been established. With the existing cooperation among the Federal and State public service commissions as well as with the representatives of the private sector, it is left to be seen how well the available high-level manpower can be effectively matched with the available vacancies in both public and private sectors. (iv) Federal and State Officials: There are equally formal and informal linkages between the federal and state civil service officials. Just as the Commissioners charged with the various ministerial responsibilities meet regularly to discuss common problems, top federal and state government officials such as permanent secretaries and directors of professional departments meet often not only to discuss problems and devise solutions but to exchange information and ideas. There are such meetings as those of permanent secretaries charged with finance, information, works, establishment, trade, agriculture and other responsibilities.

An example of an official linkage between a federal and a state ministry is the National Council on Establishments. This body like others such as the Joint Planning Committee of the federal and state ministries of Economic Development and Reconstruction, and the Agricultural Development Committee is an inter-governmental organization. It plays an important role in determining the conditions of service, salaries and wages throughout the public service of the federation. The National Council on Establishment is made up of representatives of the federal and state governments. Its secretariat is at the Federal Ministry of Establishments. Some of its other functions include:

(a) providing consultative machinery on matters such as salaries and material conditions of service affecting the civil services, teachers and government labor.

(b) provides forum for information exchange and discussion of common problems.

(c) provides common services to Federal and State governments in the interest of uniformity and economy of effort.[79]

The Council operates on two levels: the Commissioners' (or full council) meeting. At this level the federal commissioner for Establishments presides. Other state commissioners for Establishment attend with their permanent secretaries as advisers. It was in such full council meetings that details of the implication of Udoji's Public Service Review Commission and the Government White Paper on it was discussed and decisions reached.

The other level is the meetings of the officials. This consists of the Federal and State permanent secretaries of the ministries of Establishment. The officials sort out matters and prepare the ground for the commissioners' meetings. They also consult among themselves and dispose of matters of minor importance.[80]

In other respects officials of the state governments act as the intermediaries of the federal government. For instance, the officials of the state ministries of Works execute or supervise federal projects such as road construction or housing located in their states. Furthermore, the Federal Ministry of Agriculture acquires land, executes its accelerated food program and tree crop rehabilitation through the agency of state government officials. In Chapter Five we shall examine in more detail the housing and agricultural projects of the federal government being implemented through the intermediacy of the Midwestern and East Central state governments.

II. **Problems:** The second implication of the "new federalism" in Nigeria is the magnitude of problems that now face both the federal and state civil services in the performance of their functions. These problems, which include the communications systems, internal conflicts within the services, ethnicity and discipline, corruption, physical infrastructure and organization combine in varous ways to impair the efficiency of the civil services. We shall briefly highlight all the problems with the exception of the last two which will be developed in Chapter Five.

(i) Communication System: To some observers the telecommunication network in the country is not improving, in spite of several millions of naira invested in it.[81] Though from 1970 to 1974 the total number of telephones in the country increased from 70,000 to 109,000, yet the corresponding per capita available telephones show that there are as of now about 1.5 telephones for every 1,000 of the population which is much lower than the estimated average of one telephone per 100 people for developing countries of Africa, Asia and Latin America.[82] Nevertheless, there is often a wide gap between planned targets and actual performance in the communication sector. For instance, of

N125 million planned for the communication sector in the second national development plan, the realized investment after the first three years of the plan was only about N44 million.[83]

What are the consequences of a poor telecommunication network on the work of the civil service? Many officers cannot be reached easily by telephone. The telephone system breaks down so often that points which can be cleared easily by telephone are delayed. Besides, an inefficient telephone system aggravates the communication problem for ministries and departments, especially those with branch offices in other parts of the country.[84] This situation creates a communication gap between the headquarters and the field offices, with the resultant effects of "leakage of authority", delays and inaction by some field officers. Public communication in the country is so undependable that many transnational corporations in Nigeria such as the Shell-BP have their independent communication network. If mere proposals and huge allocations were to restore efficiency in the telecommunication network in Nigeria, much hope would be placed on the proposals and allocations of the Nigerian third National Development Plan 1975-1980. This plan envisaged a total expenditure of N1,107.5 million in the communication sector.[85] The following table demonstrates yearly allocations.

Given the past experiences, which indicated wide gaps between plan targets and performance, one should not be very optimistic in expecting major improvements in the public telecommunication network, just because of a huge allocation of money.

Other constraints, such as executive capacity may be decisive in widening the gap between aspirations and performance.

(ii) Internal conflicts in the services: Apart from the constraints imposed on the efficiency of the service by a poor communication system, the effectiveness of the service is further affected by the hiatus that exists between the superior and subordinate officers, which are known in Nigerian parlance as senior and junior civil servants. As a group the junior civil servants dub their superiors as the "indigenous expatriates" who had inherited and converted all the rights and privileges which the former colonial expatriate officials reserved to themselves. They see them as remote and arrogant officers, insensitive to their needs and unamenable to criticisms.

On the other hand the senior civil servants think that most junior civil servants are lazy and cannot work without maximum supervision. Most of the time, they spend the official time in discussing their promotional prospects, and have little or no commitments to the service.

Viewing each other from a stereotype, harms rather than improves the efficiency of the service. It leads to miscarriage of instructions and information. Directives sometimes flow down to the subordinates

TABLE 12. COMMUNICATION SECTOR INVESTMENT 1975-80 (N)

	Total	1975-76	1976-77	1977-78	1978-79	1979-80
Federal Telecom- munications	1,107.485	153.633	234.094	278.469	271.827	169.462
Postal Services	158,749	15.122	37.963	38.200	37.320	30.144
Nigerian External Telecom- munications	72.100	9,080	16.060	20,940	14.420	12.210
	1,338.944	177.835	288.117	337.609	323.567	211.816

Source: Federal Republic of Nigeria, *Third National Development Plan 1975-80*, Vol. 1, p. 234.

in such clumsy manners that misunderstanding of their meaning and intention is therefore inevitable.[86] Unless the elitist character of the service is modified, "leakage of authority", misapprehension or even fear, will remain a feature of the Nigerian civil service for a long time.

The efficiency of the federal and state civil services is further impaired by the acrimony that exists between the generalist administrative officers and their professional colleagues. Instead of the relationship of these officers to be characterized by "cooperative rational action", it is marked by distrust. The distrust has reached such a level that the Udoji's review report states:

> This spirit of animosity exists between superiors and subordinates, between professionals and administrators, between administrators and academicians. One sometimes gets the impression in observing human relations in the public service that Nigerians do not like each other.[87]

The poor relationships between the administrators and the professionals were highlighted in the aftermath of the Government White paper on Udoji's review recommendations. The professional officers accused the generalist adminstrators of denying them access to the four volumes on grading and pay in which Udoji's new salary gradings were determined. They claimed that, had they been allowed to give the government the benefit of their knowledge of their professions as

78

regards gradings, many of the causes of dissension that followed the publication of the Government White Paper on the report would have been removed, since grading has been the most explosive issue.[88] The professionals argued that the administrators influenced the government decision on the White Paper to their greatest advantage. While it is possible for many permanent secretaries and administrative officers grade 1 to rise to SM7 of Udoji's salary grading, their professional counterparts can only rise to SM5.

The professionals also resent the fact that several permanent secretaries in the service are drawn from the administrative cadre. They see no reason why they should not head ministries which are professional in character, such as the ministries of health and works. In the federal civil service, they noted that only one permanent secretary had been selected and appointed from their class, since independence in 1960.[89] They accused the administrative class of hiding from them useful information necessary for decision making. They further accused the administrative cadre of monopolizing sensitive and powerful positions in the ministries and departments.

Generally, the administrative class deny the accusations of the professional class. They argue that every senior officer in the service has an opportunity of reaching the highest position, provided he has the necessary potential. The administrative class points out that they do not monopolize decision making in the ministries and the departments, and that the senior professional officers have access to the government. Above all, they maintain they neither hide information from the professionals nor prevent them from being promoted or being made permanent secretaries.[90]

The effect of the strained relationship between the professionals and the generalist administrators on the civil service is obvious. It leads to delays, concentration of authority, and reluctance to delegate responsibilities. It also results into inefficient use of available talents in the service. In a country where plan implementation is retarded by lack of executive capacity, it is unnecessary for the available high-level manpower to work at cross purposes, all in the defense of cadre interests.

(iii) Ethnicity and Discipline: Another set of twin problems which are rampant in the service are those of ethnicity and indiscipline. Family, local, ethnic and other primordial ties and loyalties sometimes compete or take precedence over loyalty to the service and the nation. It is not uncommon to find in a typical ministry or department many low skilled staff such as messengers, drivers, cleaners, clerical assistants belonging to the same ethnic groups with the top superior officers of the organization. Considering the nature of the social environment which we examined in Chapter Two, there is nothing alarming about this pattern of patron-client relationship between superior and subordinate officers. Often the expectations in the peripheries of the society is that senior officers should use their privileged positions to deploy as many unskilled labor from their areas as possible within the ambit of what is tolerable, and what will not incense public feelings or ethnic balancing. While patro-client relationships could serve useful empirical functions in the civil service of a developing country such as Nigeria, the problem is, how much of it can be tolerable so as not to seriously impair the effectiveness and efficiency of the service? If patron-client relations are practiced on a wide scale in employment, deployment and promotion of high level manpower the service will gradually cease to be innovative, goal setting and problem solving. The patron-client relation as practiced in the lower cadres of the service has its consequences. It leads to indiscipline. An awareness on the part of subordinates that they have "god-fathers" who will protect them at all times, leads to a disturbing growth of insubordination and disobedience in carrying out lawful instructions or directives of supervisors who are not well placed in the hierarchy of a ministry or department. The patron-client relationship is not the only source of indiscipline. It can also result from lack of training and commitment to goals and objectives of the civil service by newly recruited civil servants. It is observed that the average clerical officer obtains his training on the job:

No training program is arranged for him on the work he is expected to do and on the whole spectrum of clerical functions in the service. He gets his job explained to him for a day or two by his clerical colleague who himself has a poor background knowledge of the general run of clerical work.[91]

Thus, indiscipline, poor work performance are related to lack of training. Yet another cause of indiscipline is lack of adequate office accommodation. Though the federal and state civil services had in the last decade experienced rapid growth in personnel, there has not been a corresponding effort to expand office accommodation. Consequently, there is overcrowding in offices which is not only unhygienic but militates against the ability to concentrate at work. The space provided for registries in some ministries and departments is so inadequate that collection or retrieval of data from registries for officers to carry out their work becomes a difficult exercise. It is not therefore surprising that low output arises as a result of indiscipline, lack of pride in one's work, distractions, dull and drab offices. Remedial measures which have been put forward include spelling out clearly objectives of the civil service and means to achieve them; creation of environments which are favorable to high productivity and pride in one's work. Such environments include decentralization of federal offices, speeding up the building of federal secretariats in the states, provision of adequate office accommodation and structuring relevant training programs for all classes of civil servants.

(iv) Corruption: The most threatening problem that can postpone indefinitely the attainment of economic development in Nigeria and further create hardships and frustrations to millions of Nigerians is corruption. Its incidence has risen with substantial increase of Nigerian oil wealth. The malaise is so widespread that it is practiced in many government institutions and functionaries and at every level of society. Corruption is also practiced in various shapes and forms. At the village level its practice may be less sophisticated but it is equally common. For instance, a village farmer may take a keg of palm wine and some of his farm produce to the local magistrate in order to influence him to decide a case in his favor. The entire community may 'dash' the district officer a goat to influence the location of a government institution in their area. At the state level corruption is much more institutionalized. It pervades the entire network of private and public institutions. It is rampant among government officials, contractors, private international companies and above all the state governors and state officials. It ranges from the wrong use of government property, the abuse of public office for private gains, diversion of huge sums of public funds to private ends, to the exaction of bribes for the award of government contracts.

Recent purges of public institutions in Nigeria, in which 11,000 personnel were involved, including 12 state governors, heads of federal and state ministries and departments, army officers, customs officials, university workers, laborers and cooks, illustrate how widespread corruption is in Nigeria and partly explain the reasons for the ineffectiveness of most public institutions.[92] Ten out of 12 state governors of the ousted Gowon regime, including the administrator of the East Central state were found guilty of appropriating $16 million for their private use.[93] The retired governor of the Northwest state (Sokoto) was found guilty of demanding and receiving bribes and awarding contracts worth several million naira without the knowledge of the state tender board.[94] In the East Central State under Asika's regime, it was said that a total sum of N4.1 million was fraudulently misappropriated in the various state ministries within the 1971-72 financial year.[95] In the North Central state (Kaduna) under the administration of former Brigadier Kyari, vouchers covering a sum of N9.8 million could not be produced for government auditors; besides there were irregularities in the payment vouchers of several ministries.[96] The same story of abuse of public office is true of several retired federal officers. For instance, out of 189 officers purged from the Customs and Excise department, 40 were terminated for misconduct, while 56 were dismissed for gross misconduct.[97]

81

Effects of Corruption: Corruption directly and indirectly affects the execution of public programs. Deployment of huge sums of public money into private use results in the abandonment of projects or their unsatisfactory completion. A case in point is a Federal government road project—Enugu-Nsukka road—(40 miles) which was being executed in behalf of the Federal government, by the East Central State Ministry of Works. The N6.72 million contract was awarded in October 1973.[98] By May 15, 1975, 15 months after the contract was awarded, not more than 15 miles of roads had been paved, and at the cost of N5.35 million.[99] Another case of unsatisfactory completion of a government undertaking due to corruption is that of the construction of the Federal government Labor Office at Maiduguri. Because of poor execution of the project by an indigenous contractor who was apparently under the supervision of building architects, the Federal Commissioner was forced to stop the work. After the Commissioner had inspected the poor quality of the work done, he declared it very unsatisfactory and added that the damage done to the building by the contractor was beyond repair.[100] The Commissioner blamed most of the architects in general who were supervising various Federal government projects for allowing the contractors to 'rape' the nation's largesse unduly.[101]

The important point relevant to efficiency is that a contractor who has made a 'dash' of 10-20 percent to high government officials on winning a government contract cannot be expected to do satisfactory work. He wants to make his gains which often ranges from 20-40 percent of the cost of the contract. In the end, the work is not completed on schedule, nor is it satisfactorily executed. Both the government and the public who are entitled to satisfactory service out of the financial resources invested in projects are ripped off. This breeds frustrations and withdrawal of support, which in turn affects the legitimacy of the government and public institutions. Public institutions lacking in legitimacy can hardly be expected to be efficient. Besides, given the spiral rate of inflation in Nigeria, the time spent by the government officials in negotiating 'kickbacks' increases the cost of projects. Corruption lowers the morale of subordinate officers who work under corrupt superiors. It leads to a 'paintup' behavior which is described in Nigeria as an "eye service". Subordinates engage in an 'eye service' when they pretend to work hard before a superior, but relax to idleness on his departure. Incidence of corruption in government institutions leads to organizational goal displacement. In pursuit of private goals, several officials in public institutions form cliques and informal groups in order to maximize their benefits; all at the expense of the attainment of institutional goals. In effect public institutions which are characterized by a network of patron-client relations and which steadily suffer goal displacement, can hardly be expected to be efficient. It is hoped that the recent purges of public institutions in Nigeria will reduce the incidence of corruption and enhance efficiency. It is however too early to assess its impact.

FOOTNOTES

1. A discussion of public bureaucracy in Nigeria will cover the civil service as well as other statutory corporations such as Nigerian Railways and Ports Authority. We deliberately limit our analysis to the civil service which of course is the central core of public bureaucracy in Nigeria.
2. For details of how Britain acquired Nigeria see James Coleman, *Nigeria Background to Nationalism,* Berkeley and Los Angeles: University of California Press, 1958, pp. 41-50.
3. J. Donald Kingsley, "Bureaucracy and Political Development, with Particular Reference to Nigeria", in Joseph La Palombara, ed., *Bureaucracy and Political Development,* New Jersey: Princeton University Press, 1963, p. 302.
4. H. O. Davies, *Nigeria, the Prospects for Democracy,* London: Weidenfield and Nicolson, 1961, pp. 76-77. See also John H. Kautsky, *The Political Consequences of Modernization,* New York: John Wiley & Sons, Inc., 1972, p. 76. Kautsky states the general goal of all colonial bureaucracies. These include: development of a traditional society as a source of raw material for the advanced country, maintenance of law and order. Establishment of transportations and communication systems are taken as secondary goals, in order to realize the primary goals.
5. E. O. 'Awa, "High Level Administration in the Public Services of Nigeria", *The Nigerian Journal of Economic and Social Sciences,* Vol. 6, No. 1, March 1964, p. 43.
6. H. O. Davies, *Op. Cit.,* p. 76.
7. Ladipo Adamolekun, "High Level Ministerial Organization in Nigeria and the Ivory Coast", in D. J. Murray, (editor) *Studies in Nigerian Administration,* London: Hutchinson Educational Ltd. 1970, p. 13.
8. E. O. Awa, *Op. Cit.,* pp. 43-44.
9. H. O. Davies, *Op. Cit.,* p. 76.
10. Donald Kingsley, *Op. Cit.,* p. 307.
11. H. O. Davies, *Op. Cit.,* p. 77.
12. Ibid.
13. John H. Kautsky, *Op. Cit.,* p. 76.
14. Fred W. Riggs, "Bureaucrats and Political Development: A Paradoxical View", in Joseph La Palombara, ed., *Bureaucracy and Political Development,* New Jersey: Princeton University Press, 1963, p. 123.
15. James S. Coleman, *Op. Cit.,* p. 162.
16. *Ibid.,* p. 154.
17. *Ibid.,* p. 156, quoted from the Report on the Amalgamation of Southern and Northern Nigeria, and Administration 1912-1919, CMD. 468, London: H.M.S.O., 1920, p. 19.
18. Coleman, *Op. Cit.,* p. 163.
19. Lord Hailey, *Native Administration and Political Development in British Tropical Africa,* London; Colonial Office 1942, pp. 171-176.
20. O. I. Odumosu, *Nigerian Constitution,* London: Sweet & Maxwell, 1963, p. 14.
21. John Hatch, *Nigeria: The Seeds of Disaster,* Chicago: Henry Regnery Co., 1970, p. 200.

22. John M. Ostheimer, *Nigerian Politics,* New York: Harper and Row, 1973, p. 23.
23. Dispatch from the Governor of Nigeria to the Secretary of State for the Colonies, December 6, 1944, cited in John D. Chick, "The Structure of Government at the Regional Level", in Frank Blitz, ed., *The Politics and Administration of the Nigerian Government,* London: Sweet and Maxwell, 1965, p. 82.
24. Northern House Assembly Debates, May 1953, p. 42, cited in Odumosu, *Op. Cit.,* p. 91.
25. Adamolekun, *Op Cit.,* p. 14.
26. I. F. Nicolson, "The Structure of Government at the Federal Level", in Frank Blitz, *Op. Cit.,* p. 74.
27. Kalu Ezera, *Constitutional Development in Nigeria:* Cambridge, Cambridge University Press, 1964, pp. 217-218.
28. *Ibid.,* p. 220.
29. A. H. M. Kirk-Greene, "The Higher Public Service", in Blitz, ed., *Op. Cit.,* p. 222.
30. *Ibid.*
31. *Ibid.*
32. Report of the Public Service Commission of Northern Nigeria 1954-1957, paragraph 18, cited in Kirk-Greene, *Ibid.*
33. I. F. Nicolson, *Op. Cit.,* p. 74.
34. Taylor Cole, "Bureaucracy in Transition", in Tilman, ed., *Nigerian Political Scene,* London: Duke University Press, 1962, p. 104. C. F. Federation of Nigerian Staff List Revised to April 1, 1960, Lagos: 1960.
35. *Ibid.,* p. 105.
36. Kingsley, in discussing one of the environmental pressures the civil servants face in Nigeria talked about the "brother-stranger syndrome". One of the outcomes of the syndrome is the pressure on the politicians and civil servants to use their public positions to help their friends and members of their ethnic groups. Kingsley, *Op. Cit.* p. 306.
37. Cole, *Op. Cit.,* p. 102.
38. Udoji Public Service Review Commission: *Main Report,* Lagos: Federal Ministry of Information, 1974, p. 27.
39. *Ibid.*
40. Ezera, *Op. Cit.,* p. 216.
41. *Ibid.*
42. International Bank for Reconstruction and Development, *Economic Development of Nigeria,* Lagos: 1954, pp. 104 & 105.
43. Kenneth Post and Michael Vickers, *Structure and Conflict in Nigeria 1960-1966,* London: Heinemann, 1973, p. 235.
44. John Ostheimer, *Op. Cit.,* p. 62.
45. *Ibid.* p. 64.
46. The account of the series of crises that led to the Nigerian Civil War and the course of the war itself had been given by so many authors. See the following works:
Kenneth Post and Michael Vickers, *Op. Cit.*
S. K. Panter-Brick, *Nigerian Politics and Military Rule,* New York: Oxford University Press,
Rex Niven, The War of Nigerian Unity, London: Evans, 1970,
C. Odumegwu Ojukwu, *Biafra,* New York: Harper & Row, Vol. 1, 1966, Vol. 2, 1969,

Robin Luckham, *The Nigerian Military*, London: Cambridge University Press, 1971,
A. H. M. Kirk-Greene, *Crisis and Conflict in Nigeria A Documentary Source Book 1966-1970*, London: Oxford University Press, 1971.

47. Some of the military decrees that have modified the old Nigerian federal constitution include: Constitution, Suppression and Modification Decree of March 17, 1967, "12 State Decree", May 26, 1966—this decree abolished the former regions.

48. John Ostheimer, *Op. Cit.*, p. 68.

49. *Ibid.*, p. 64. See also John Hatch, *Op. Cit.*, p. 283.

50. Gowon's regime was ousted in a bloodless military coup on July 29, 1975. The leader of the coup, who became the Nigerian Head of State, was General Mohammed. Mohammed was killed in an abortive coup d'etat that was staged by a Colonel on February 13, 1976. Mohammed had within his short tenure in office restructured the 12 Nigerian states into a 19 state system.

51. International Bank for Development & Reconstruction, *Nigeria: Options for Long-Term Development*, Baltimore: The Johns Hopkins University Press, 1974, p. 72.

52. Colin Legum, ed., *Africa Contemporary Record 1974-75*, Annual Survey and Documents, New York: Africana Publishing Company p. B750.

53. Federal Republic of Nigeria, *Recurrent and Capital Estimates of the Federal Republic of Nigeria 1975-76*, Lagos: Federal Ministry of Information, p. XIX.

54. *Africa Confidential*, Vol. 13, No. 20, October 6, 1972, p. 3.

55. C. O. Lawson, *The Role of Civil Servants in a Military Regime*, Lagos: Federal Ministry of Information, 1974, p. 12.

56. *Ibid.*, p. 13.

57. *Ibid.*, p. 14.

58. *Ibid.*, pp. 8-9.

59. Federal Republic of Nigeria, *Third National Development Plan 1975-80*, Vol. 1, Lagos: Federal Government Press, 1975, p. 19.

60. The tentative outcome of the Research on Rural Development on the East Central and South-eastern States of Nigeria by the Department of Political Science, University of Nigeria, Nsukka, reveals staggering needs for basic necessities of life such as food, clothing, housing, water and all season roads in the areas covered.

61. Daily Times, Tuesday, March 4, 1975, p. 1. In the Third National Plan 1975-80, about N122,15 million has been proposed for a color TV program. See Third Plan *Op. Cit.*, p. 274.

62. Daily Times, *Op. Cit.*, p. 1.

63. Lawson, *Op. Cit.*, p. 18.

64. *Ibid.*, p. 19.

65. Daily Times, March 24, 1975, p. 3.

66. Daily Times, Wednesday, February 4, 1976, p. 1.

67. The National Council of State was created by General Mohammed when he ousted General Gowon from office on July 29, 1975.

68. K. C. Wheare, Federal Government, London: Oxford University Press, 1963, p. 5.

69. Freeman, *History of Federal Government in Greece and Italy*, ed., 1893, pp. 2-3, quoted in William Morey, Sources of American Federalism, American Academy of Political and Social Science, Vol. VI, December 1895, p. 281.

70. Captain Akin Adunwo, the Governor of the Western state, was summarily removed from office on September 2, 1975 by the federal Military Government. His place was taken by Col. David Jemibewon.
71. Third National Plan, *Op. Cit.*, p. 244.
72. *Ibid.*, pp. 275-277.
73. Federal Republic of Nigeria, Fifteenth Annual Report on the Federal Public Service Commission for the Period 1st January to 31st December 1971, Lagos: Federal Ministry of Information 1972, p. 14.
74. *Ibid.*
75. Federal Public Service Commission *Memo*, February 1975, p. 3.
76. 15th Annual Report of the Federal Public Service Commission, *Op. Cit.*, p. 15.
77. Federal Public Service Commission *Memo*, *Op. Cit.*, p. 3.
78. *Ibid.*, pp. 12-13.
79. F. S. Williams, *Memo* on Personnel Administration in the Public Service and the Role of National Council on Establishments, Lagos: 1973, p. 3.
80. *Ibid.*, p.4.
81. In the Second National Development Plan, the total planned expenditure for telecommunication is N85.282 million. See Federal Republic of Nigeria, *Op. Cit.*, p. 211. This was later revised to N125 million but only N44 was spent.
82. *Ibid.*, p. 227.
83. *Ibid.*
84. Federal Ministry of Establishment, Paper on *Low Productivity in the Public Services of the Federation*, Lagos: July 1971, p. 26.
85. The Third Plan 1975-80, *Op. Cit.*, p. 230.
86. Federal Ministry of Establishments, *Op. Cit.*, p. 26.
87. Udoji Public Service Review Commission, *Op. Cit.*, p. 12.
88. Daily Times, Saturday, March 8, 1975, p. 7.
89. *Ibid.*
90. During the writer's discussion with a senior administrative officer about the relationship between his class and the professionals, he maintained that in many cases the claims of lack of promotional prospects for the professionals is baseless. He pointed out that the professionals fare worse in those ministries whose permanent secretaries are drawn from the professional class.
91. Federal Ministry of Establishment, *Op. Cit.*, p. 33.
92. The purges of Nigerian public institutions are widely reported in both local and foreign press. See Sunday Times, September 28, 1975, p. 1, New York Times, Sunday, February 15, 1976, p. 1.
93. Daily Star, Wednesday, February 4, 1976, p. 16.
94. Daily Times, Wednesday September 24, 1975, p. 1. See also Daily Times, Friday, November 21, pp. 1 and 32.
95. Daily Times, Wednesday, August 13, 1975, p. 1.
96. Daily Times, Monday, August 25, 1975, p. 1.
97. Sunday Times, September 28, 1975, p. 1.
98. Renaissance, Thursday, May 15, 1975, p. 1.
99. *Ibid.*, p. 16.
100. Daily Times, Tuesday, October 21, 1975, p. 32.
101. *Ibid.*

CHAPTER FOUR

FEDERAL-STATE CIVIL SERVICES: PLANNING ECONOMIC AND SOCIAL ACTIVITIES

The analysis of the civil service planning experience is important to our study, first because it illustrates how environmental factors add to or detract from the scope of activities of federal and state civil servants, especially from 1954 when Nigeria became a federation; secondly the contents of a development plan are policy decisions which embody the main political, social and economic objectives and goals which a government wants to carry out; thirdly the outcome of such policy decisions may have far reaching consequences for the entire society. For instance, it may result in greater or lesser commitment to central political authority; it may bring about greater national integration or disintegration. It could result in the fulfillment of promises or lead into greater frustrations and deprivations. By studying the planning experience of the Nigerian civil service from the colonial period to the present, we hope to shed some light on the changing phases of the federal-state relations in Nigeria and their attendant complexities and problems.

Planning during the Colonial Period—(1946-1960)

Colonial administration did not make planning a primary concern.[1] Planning economic and social activities did not go beyond the encouragement of production of cash crops such as cocoa, groundnuts, and palm produce for export. The limited construction activities such as building of railways, ports and roads were undertaken to give infrastructural support to the colonial regime and to serve the needs of private expatriate firms such as the United African Company (U.A.C.).

The few schools and hospitals that existed were provided mainly through the efforts of Christian Missions.[2] Consequently, the main determinants for the Colonial economic and social activities were not the need of the Nigerians but rather those of the colonial administration and the commercial firms whose expanding commercial activities necessitated the recruitment of more local educated personnel as accountants, clerks and clerical officers. Before the inauguration of the 1946 Colonial Plan, Nigeria remained a predominantly peasant economy, marked by low production, dominance of large private expatriate firms, an absence of manufacture, poor communication systems and an increasing number of educated but unemployed personnel. Describing the conditions in Nigeria at the conclusion of the Second World War, a Nigerian observer stated:

> Most Nigerians remained on their farms, small holdings, village lands, growing their food by the same methods their ancestors had used for centuries past with primitive technology and low productivity. Industrialization was noticeable only by its absence, manufacturers almost being entirely confined to those brought from Britain ... In general, Nigeria slumbered ... The one omen presaging future radical change was the return of a few Nigerians who had sought education abroad.[3]

Given the conditions of Nigeria at the conclusion of the Second World War, and the fact that the Labour Party which was plan-minded became the governing party in Britain, in 1945 the Colonial Administration in Nigeria was directed to prepare a ten-year development plan for the country. This was a sequel to a Parliamentary Enactment in 1945, which established a Colonial Development and Welfare Fund of £120 million, of which Nigeria was allocated £23 million.[4] The plan which was entitled A Ten-Year Plan for Development and Welfare came into effect on April 1, 1946 and was to last up to March 31, 1956.[5] It envisaged an expenditure of £55 million and was partly to be financed by a £23 million colonial grant and through mobilization of local resources—savings and bank loans.[6] However, the plan was interrupted in 1950 as a result of a number of factors which included a shortage of personnel, absence of reliable information and the uncertainties which are attendant on programming cost of projects for such a long period of time as 10 years. In the light of these difficulties the plan was modified in 1950. The new program of activities was to run from 1951-1956. The 1951-56 plan was well under way when it was interrupted by two events. One was the visit to Nigeria by a World Bank Mission in 1953, and the other was a constitutional change in 1954, which made Nigeria a federation of three regions.[7] The constitutional changes granted more financial autonomy and functions to the Nigerian constitutent states. The World Bank Mission recommended the creation of a body whose objective was to provide

> a forum in which the federation and the regions might meet to discuss the many economic problems common to each, not-with-standing their separate constitutional functions and such of their development policies as may have consequences reaching beyond their respective constitutional spheres.[8]

Following the constitutional change and the World Bank recommendations, the 1951-56 Plan was modified and rescheduled to last from 1955 to 1960. This was further extended to 1962. The federal capital program in the 1956-60 plan called for an estimated expenditure of £102 million, while that of the western region called for an expenditure of £102 million, while that of the western region called for an expenditure of £39.8 million; those of the northern and eastern regions were put at £32.5 million and £14.6 million respectively.[9] The Federal program emphasized mainly transport and communication and the planned allocation for this sector alone was 60 per cent of the total planned expenditure.[10]

From the onset, the development plans of this period were constrained by shortfall of funds. The total allocation of Colonial Development funds to Nigeria for the entire period did not exceed £23 million.[11] In the 1955-60 Plan the Federal government expected to raise £57.6 million from internal sources; primarily through excise and import duties, this was not easily mobilized, as the federal government revenue was closely tied to the fluctuations of foreign trade. Considering the depressed condition of the London money market of this period, it was difficult for the Federal Government to raise an anticipated loan of £30 million from the market.[12]

The period was marked by the relative importance of the regional plans which was made possible as a result of their greater financial autonomy. They shared (as of constitutional right) all the receipts which the Federal Government collected from customs and excise duties. The Western Regional Plan was more ambitious, because it received 46 per cent of the statutory allocation, while the Northern and Eastern Regions received only 29 and 25 per cent respectively.[13] The large share that went to the West was due largely to its production of cocoa which was then the largest single item in export tax receipts. The Regional financial autonomy was further aided by the inheritance the three regions had when the Nigerian Produce Marketing Board was federalized in 1954. Moreover, Regional financial autonomy was strengthened further as from April 1955 when the United Kingdom government started paying the Colonial Development Grant directly to them.[14]

Within this period plans were constantly interrupted and plan periods were unduly extended and this inhibited acquisition of discipline which planning and the execution of a sustained program of activities was supposed to impose. Besides, the implementation of plan projects was constrained by the shortage of manpower; especially architects, surveyors and engineers. Given the structure of the National Economic Council (N.E.C.) which was dominated by centrifugal forces, the federal and regional plans were not coordinated. This outstanding weakness was emphasized by Nigeria's 1962-68 plan document which states:

These were not 'plans' in the true sense of the word. More accurately they constituted a series of projects which had not been co-ordinated or related to any overall economic target. Many individual schemes proposed no more than an expansion of existing normal departmental activities, and, in large measure, the schemes aimed at building up the social as much as the economic services.[15]

Apart from some achievements in the transportation and communication sectors, planning during the colonial period did little to induce industrialization or improve agriculture on which the livelihood of the majority of Nigerians depends.

Planning during Independence to 1970—Period of continued Regionalism.

One feature of planning within this period was the dominance of regional forces. As Nigeria was about to attain political independence in 1960 there was need to establish both at federal and regional levels a set of institutions to coordinate planning activities. The most important institutions established in the late 1950s which were used in formulation of 1962-68 First National Development Plan include:

(1) **National Economic Council (N.E.C.).** This body as we pointed out earlier was established in 1955, as a result of the recommendations of the World Bank Mission which visited Nigeria in 1953. After the attainment of independence in 1960, the Council was chaired by the Federal Prime Minister. Its other members were the Regional Premiers, four other ministers from each region and four ministers from the Federal Government.[16]

Although the N.E.C. was the highest planning body in the country its role was advisory. It often met to approve the work done by technical bodies. Officers other than the politicians who were in attendance did not participate in the deliberations of the N.E.C., neither did allow private expert opinions before it. Usually the effectiveness of the N.E.C. as the highest decision making body on matters relating to planning was hampered by the very nature of its composition. The regional delegates saw themselves as regional representatives anxious to share in the national largesse rather than as national officers charged with the overall responsibility for development of Nigeria.[17]

(2) **Joint Planning Committee:** This body was established in September 1958 to act in advisory capacity.[18] The committee was comprised of the officials of the federal and regional governments, and was chaired by the Economic Advisor to the Federal Government. The committee was authorized to coopt experts in various fields, both from within and outside the Public Service, in order to give it the benefit of their specialized knowledge.

Although the committee was supposed to be the highest technical body coordinating federal and regional plans, the committee's role like that of N.E.C. was advisory. Besides it did not meet quite often; as a result, the federal and regional agencies planned separately.

(3) **Economic Planning Unit (E.P.U.).** This was the most important technical planning institution at the federal level. It was located in the Federal Ministry of Economic Development. The E.P.U., for the most of the plan period was headed by a University of Michigan Economics Professor—Wolfgang Stolper. He was assisted by some Nigerian economists and other expatriate economists who were under the sponsorship of the Ford Foundation.[19] The committee was responsible for perspective medium term and annual general equilibrium planning, sectoral and micro-economic planning.[20] It coordinated the planning efforts of the federal Ministries. It was said that dominant analytical features of the 1962-68 Plan were those of the Michigan Professor of Economics.[21]

Apart from these national institutions of planning, there were regional structures in each of the three regions. While the Western region established its ministry of Economic Planning in the early 1950s, the Eastern Region established its own only in 1960. Until 1962, the Northern Region did not have a separate planning ministry; its planning ministry unit was then located in the region's Ministry of Finance.[22]

Formulation of the 1962-68 Plan.

Before the Plan was formulated a number of preliminary studies were undertaken which helped to shape the plan projects:

(i) Economic Survey of Nigeria. This study was undertaken by J. P. C. and portrayed the economic conditions of Nigeria at that time. It provided some planning information with regards to the Gross Domestic Product, the trends in monetary and fiscal policies. It also gave an insight into possible future development of Nigeria.[23]

(ii) Economic Coordination of Transport Development in Nigeria. This report was compiled by a team of economists drawn from the Stanford Research Institute in California. The recommendations on how to achieve linkages of Nigerian road, river, rail and air transport systems were based on their projection of the infrastructural needs of the 1962-68 plan.[24]

(iii) Others were the Ashby Commission on Higher Education, investigations of the hydro-electric possibilities of the Niger and Benue Rivers, a set of national Income Estimates, for the years

1950-57 and a considerable number of feasibility studies on specific industrial projects.[25]

The 1962-68 Development Plan generally aimed at achieving the following objectives: economic annual growth rate of 4 per cent, an increase of per capita consumption by 1 per cent, an increase in the domestic savings ratio from about 9.5 per cent of the G.D.P. in 1960-61 to about 15 per cent in 1975; more equitable distribution of income both among the people and among regions; more jobs and opportunities in the non-agricultural occupations and an increase in the production of export crops.[26]

In order to attain these objectives, the planners placed priority on projects which had immediate 'profitable' returns on the investments. Consequently, there were little investments on education, health and social services, because projects in these sectors were considered to have high recurrent expenditures which reduce funds available for 'profitable' investment.[27] Rather, agriculture, industry and technical education received more attention.[28]

Given the extreme regional features of the Nigerian federation, and dominance of the centrifugal forces within this period, what finally emerged as Nigeria's First National Development Plan 1962-68 in April of 1962, was in fact four different plans—the Federal, Northern, Western and Eastern, all compiled into one plan document. Its lack of nationally directed focus was further emphasized in the five introductory chapters dealing with the objectives, sectoral allocation and financial resources of each of the four governments embodied in the national plan document. The plan provided for public capital expenditure of £676.8 million, while the actual planned expenditure was £663.2 million.[29] Private capital formation was initially estimated to be £389.5 million, and this was later increased to £432 million.[30] As we shall explain later this projected amount was not realized. The two single largest projects in the federal plan were the Kainji Dam which was estimated to cost £68.1 million and the Iron and Steel Mill Complex which was to cost £30 million and which was not executed at the end of that plan period.

It was difficult to have an integrated national plan because the regional centers—Kaduna, Enugu and Ibadan, possessed such a considerable political and material resource base that the federal government was unable to assert its authority over them. As the Regional Premiers struggled to maximize their power at the expense of the federal government, they paid less attention to plan implementation. The N.E.C. which was supposed to coordinate planning efforts in the country, was not effective because of the dominance of the regional interests. The Federal Prime Minister and the regional premiers only resorted to it to reconcile their often contradictory and conflicting

TABLE 13. SOME SELECTED PUBLIC CAPITAL EXPENDITURE IN THE 1962-68 NATIONAL DEVELOPMENT PLAN

Sector	Federal	£ Thousand			Total (National)	% By Sector
		Eastern Region	Northern Region	Western Region		
I. ECONOMIC SECTOR						
1. Primary Production	10,466	30,361	22,494	18,439	81,760	12.3
2. Trade Industry	44,030	12,930	9,864	23,445	90,269	13.6
3. Electricity	94,540	600	1,500	1,500	98,140	14.8
4. Transport	103,957	8,850	24,660	6,350	143,817	21.7
5. Communication	30,000	—	—	—	30,000	4.5
	282,993	52,741	58,518	49,734	443,986	66.9
II. SOCIAL OVERHEAD						
6. Water other than irrigation	1,863	5,100	7,442	9,853	24,258	3.7
7. Education	29,154	8,805	18,949	12,855	69,763	10.5
8. Health	10,304	1,819	3,317	1,636	17,076	2.6
9. Town & Country Planning	23,160	3,306	6,000	9,280	41,746	6.3
10. Cooperatives	—	—	2,439	1,500	3,939	0.6
11. Social Welfare	2,689	534	—	1,500	4,723	0.7
12. Information	2,351	450	88	773	3,662	0.6
TOTAL	69,521	20,014	38,235	37,397	165,167	24.9

Source: Edwin Dean, *Plan Implementation in Nigeria 1962-66*, Ibadan: Oxford University Press, 1972, p. 23.

values. The role of the Federal Prime Minister as its chairman was so nominal that he could not influence the powerful premiers to accept any major decision, which they considered to be against their regional interests. Nigerian political leadership lacked the discipline which is necessary for planning and implementation of projects. The situation was made worse when the conflict among Nigerian leaders resulted in a civil war; plan implementation between 1966-68 was not only suspended in the Eastern part of the country but was seriously impaired in the rest of the country.

Apart from political considerations, perhaps the greatest constraint to planned development was the gap between the plan, aspirations and available resource. Much hope was placed by Nigerian leaders and planners on the external sources of finance, such as contractor finance and loans from the international monetary market. It was assumed that as much as 50 per cent of the money allocated for the public capital expenditure would come from the external sources.[31] The Table 14 below illustrates the gap between the money which was actually available for the federal and state governments' capital expenditures and the amount they expected from external sources.

TABLE 14. FINANCIAL GAP IN PUBLIC CAPITAL EXPENDITURE
(1962-68 Development) £ million

	Federal	Western Region	Eastern Region	Northern Region	Total
Requirement for Capital Expenditure	406.9	90.3	67.7	88.9	653.0*
Available for Capital Expenditure	200.7	25.2	21.8	15.3	263.0
GAP	206.2	65.1	45.9	72.6	389.8
Assumed Foreign Aid	203.5	45.2	33.7	44.5	327.1
Uncovered Gap	—2.7	—19.9	—12.0	—29.1	—63.7

Source: Edwin Dean, *Plan Implementation in Nigeria, 1962-66,* Ibadan: Oxford University Press, 1972, p. 26.
This figure is less than the planned amount of £663.2 million stated above because it excludes the projected underspending of all the governments.

Because of the huge gaps which existed in the federal and regional financial resources, public capital expenditure for the first two years of the plan was only £64 million.[32] By 1966, when the military intervened in the political process, several projects were abandoned and the public sector investment reached only £96 million.[33] There is no doubt that the violence which marked the Nigerian political scene at this time affected the flow of resources from the external sources. For instance, the net private foreign capital inflow into the non-petroleum sector decreased from £60 million in 1965 to £6 million in 1967.[34]

94

The plan's performance was also affected by the shortage of personnel and technically feasible projects. Given the inexperience of the Nigerian planners, most o fthe projects were not adequately studied before they were included in the national plan. As a result of lack of feasible projects, 43 per cent of the planned allocation in the agricultural sector and 33.3 per cent of allocation in the industrial sector remained unspent at the end of the plan period.[35] Other problems which directly and indirectly affected plan implementation included the management problems of the Nigerian Railways, the Lagos and Port Harcourt ports, the national shipping line and the lack of efficiency of the Nigerian telecommunication system.

Planning—1970 onwards: The era of 'New Federalism'

The conclusion of the Nigerian civil war in 1970 saw the establishment of the 'new federalism' marked by increased centralization of political authority which was inherent by the unity of Military command, the weakening of the centrifugal forces which has been made possible by the splitting of the former unbalanced four regions into a 12-state structure (7 new states had been created recently, bringing the total number of states to 19);[36] increased centralization of planning institutions and the greater dependency of the state governments and civil services on their federal counterparts. Before we describe the planning institutions and the planning process which the new political arrangements have made possible, it is in order to shed some light on the state of the Nigerian economy since the conclusion of the civil war.

Changes in the Economy:

The Nigerian civil war seriously affected economic growth and development. The Federal Government had to deploy almost all its resources into prosecuting the war. The estimated total budgetary cost of the war amounted to about £300 million.[37] With the sharp depletion of external reserves the Federal Government resorted to a number of control measures that affected the performance of the economy. These measures include the introduction of capital gains tax of 20 per cent on profits accruing from disposal of assets, a super tax on company profits, specific licensing for a number of exporting areas and for a large number of non-essential consumer goods such as TVs and motor cars.[38] Some of these control measures survived the civil war and have been extended to regulate the prices of designated scarce commodities. The war affected production and manufacturing industries, especially in the Eastern parts of the country. This area also suffered the greatest damages in plant installations and physical infrastructure. However, the increased proceeds from the oil sector have helped to give a face lift to the economy, for instance, the receipts expected from

TABLE 15. CONTRIBUTIONS OF PETROLEUM TO NIGERIA'S GROSS DOMESTIC REPORT (N million)

	1974-75	1975-76	1976-77	1977-78	1978-79	1979-80
1. Gross Proceeds	6,633.1	7,340.3	8,133.0	9,000.1	9,968.8	11,033.2
2. Exports	6,458.1	7,120.3	7,913.0	8,665.1	9,603.8	10,633.2
3. Local sales, changes in stock & other local receipts	175.0	220.0	220.0	335.0	365.0	400.0
4. Immediate Inputs	171.1	191.9	215.8	232.7	271.6	286.9
5. Indirect Taxes	16.8	17.7	18.7	19.7	20.7	21.9
6. Value added	6,445.2	7,130.7	7,898.5	8,747.7	9,676.5	10,724.4

Source: Federal Republic of Nigeria (1975), *Third National Development Plan 1975-80, Vol. 1*, Lagos Federal Ministry of Economic Development, p. 58.

the oil industry in the 1975-76 financial year will exceed 90 per cent of all available sources of foreign exchange earnings.[39]

In the foreseeable future the Nigerian gross domestic product will be tied closely to the proceeds from her oil sector, as the projection in the above table indicates.

The Table 15 illustrates that petroleum will account for the average growth rate of 11 per cent of Nigeria's GDP within the period 1975-80. The present economic trend indicates that Nigeria will for a long time depend on a single commodity—oil—not only to finance her recurrent expenditure but also her capital projects. This dependency will make her vulnerable to the fluctuations of the world demand for petroleum.[40]

Another problem that poses a lot of complexity to the Nigerian economy is inflation. The inflationary pressures have been exacerbated by increases in money supply, shortage of essential commodities, port congestion, 'abnormal' wage and salary increases.[41] Inflation reduces the predictability of the economic performance, as it is difficult to determine cost trends for any given period of time and this poses a lot of problems for planning. Inflation has not only reduced the real monetary values in Nigeria, but has substantially increased the cost of living. The effects of inflation on the majority of Nigerians who still live near poverty level is not made easier by the existing high rate of unemployment.

The New Structure of Planning:

As a result of the increased centralized political authority, and given the additional financial resources available to the national government, the state planning institutions have been integrated into the federal ones not only to reflect the primacy of the federal government and civil service but to ensure the emergence of a more coherent national plan. From 1970 onwards the states could no longer plan independently as they did in the past. Their projects must now receive approval of the federal government before they form part of the national plan.

The principal federal civil service organ, through which the federal government directly controls and coordinates the planning activities of the states is the Federal Ministry of Economic Development and Reconstruction. At the conclusion of the civil war, in 1970, this ministry was revamped and reorganized in order to have it have a development role in both federal and state planning activities. The main functions of the revamped Federal Ministry of Economic Development include the following:

(i) Coordination of economic matters within the federal ministries as well as between the federal and state governments.

(ii) Cooperating with the state Ministries of Economic Development

TABLE 16. FEDERAL MINISTRY OF ECONOMIC DEVELOPMENT AND RECONSTRUCTION

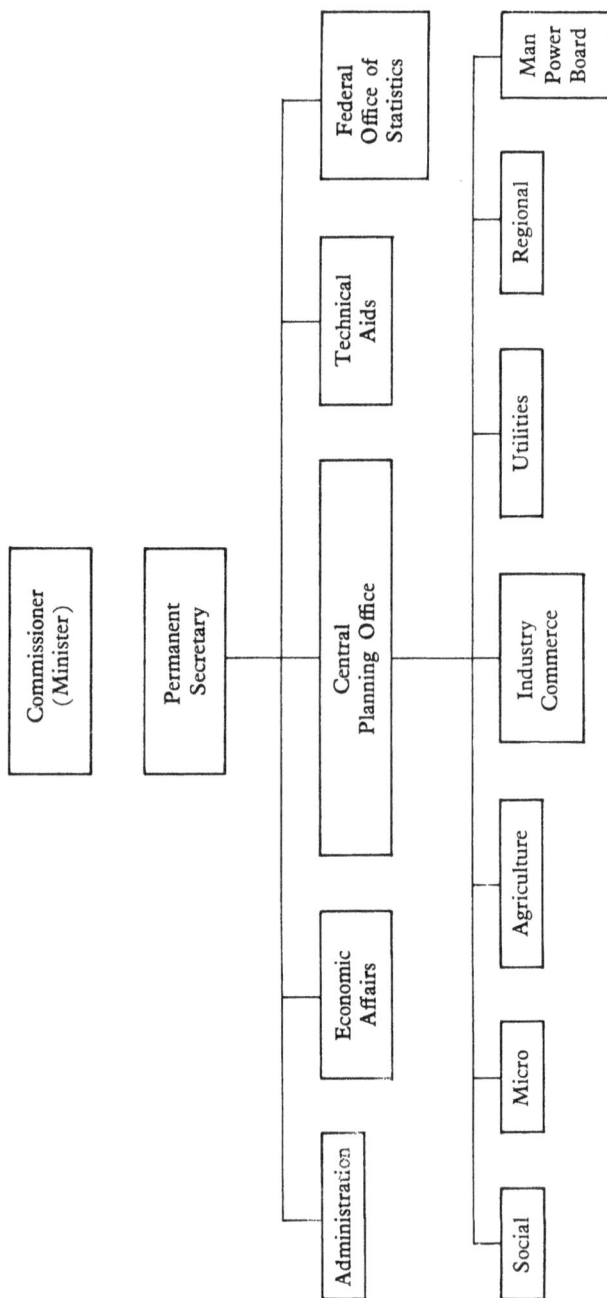

```
                    ┌──────────────┐
                    │ Commissioner │
                    │  (Minister)  │
                    └──────┬───────┘
                    ┌──────┴───────┐
                    │  Permanent   │
                    │  Secretary   │
                    └──────┬───────┘
         ┌─────────────────┼──────────────────────┬──────────────────┐
  ┌──────┴──────┐   ┌──────┴───────┐       ┌───────┴──────┐   ┌───────┴───────┐
  │  Economic   │   │   Central    │       │  Technical   │   │    Federal    │
  │   Affairs   │   │   Planning   │       │     Aids     │   │   Office of   │
  └──┬───────┬──┘   │    Office    │       └──────────────┘   │   Statistics  │
     │       │      └──────┬───────┘                          └───────┬───────┘
┌────┴───┐ ┌─┴──┐  ┌───────┼───────────┬──────────┐           ┌───────┴────────┐
│ Admin- │ │Mic-│  │       │           │          │           │        │       │
│istra-  │ │ ro │  │       │           │          │           │        │       │
│ tion   │ └────┘  │       │           │          │           │        │       │
└────────┘      ┌──┴───┐ ┌─┴────┐ ┌────┴───┐ ┌────┴───┐  ┌────┴───┐ ┌──┴───┐
                │Social│ │Agri- │ │Industry│ │Utilit- │  │Regional│ │ Man  │
                └──────┘ │cul-  │ │Commerce│ │  ies   │  └────────┘ │Power │
                         │ ture │ └────────┘ └────────┘             │Board │
                         └──────┘                                   └──────┘
```

98

Source: Federal Ministry of Economic Development and Reconstruction, Lagos, 1975.

and Reconstruction to formulate national economic policies and draw up national development programmes.

(iii) Coordination of external technical assistance.

(iv) Supervision of intergovernmental cooperation in economc matters both internally and externally.

(v) Collection, analysis and publication of statistical data through the federal office of statistics.[42]

The reorganized Federal Ministry of Economic Development and Reconstruction has five broad divisions consisting of Administration, Central Planning Office (CPO), Economic Affairs, the Technical Aids Division and the Federal Office of Statistics. Each division is responsible to the permanent secretary through its head. The Central Planning Office was created in 1971 to replace the Economic Planning Unit (E.P.U.), following the realization that planning exercise has become increasingly a technical enterprise and could no longer be left to the generalist administrators, who are more concerned with broad matters of policy rather than the technical details of a plan.[43] The C.P.O. has several sections, which include industry, agriculture, transport, research and forecasting, statistics, social, regional development and the national manpower board. It is the most important division within the Ministry and the largest technical planning institution in the country. It has an establishment of over 140 professional planning officers and statisticians of various grades. This represents by far the largest concentration of such professional officers in the federation. As the diagram in table 16 illustrates, the C.P.O. is divided into several sections which are charged with responsibility over a number of draft proposals stemming from either federal or state ministries and agencies. Unlike the E.P.U. the C.P.O. is headed by a Nigerian of a considerable planning experience. It is the C.P.O. that coordinates and harmonizes the development activities of the governments of the Federation.

The State Ministries of Economic Development and Reconstruction have organizational structures which more or less correspond to the federal economic ministry. Some states such as the North Eastern State have simpler organizational structures dominated not by professional planners but by administrative officers. The planning organization in the North East is called the Ministry of Economic Planning and Political Affairs and is attached to the Military Governors office. In other states such as the East Central State, the Ministry of Economic Development and Reconstruction is structured along the line of the Federal Ministry. As in the Federal Organization the Planning Unit is always the largest unit. That of the East Central State contains several professional planners drawn from many disciplines, and unlike in the Federal Organization, the controller of the planning division is also the permaent secretary and the civil head of the Ministry. The planning division of the Ministry is divided into several sections like the C.P.O. These

TABLE 17. EAST CENTRAL STATE STRUCTURE OF THE MINISTRY OF ECONOMIC DEVELOPMENT AND RECONSTRUCTION

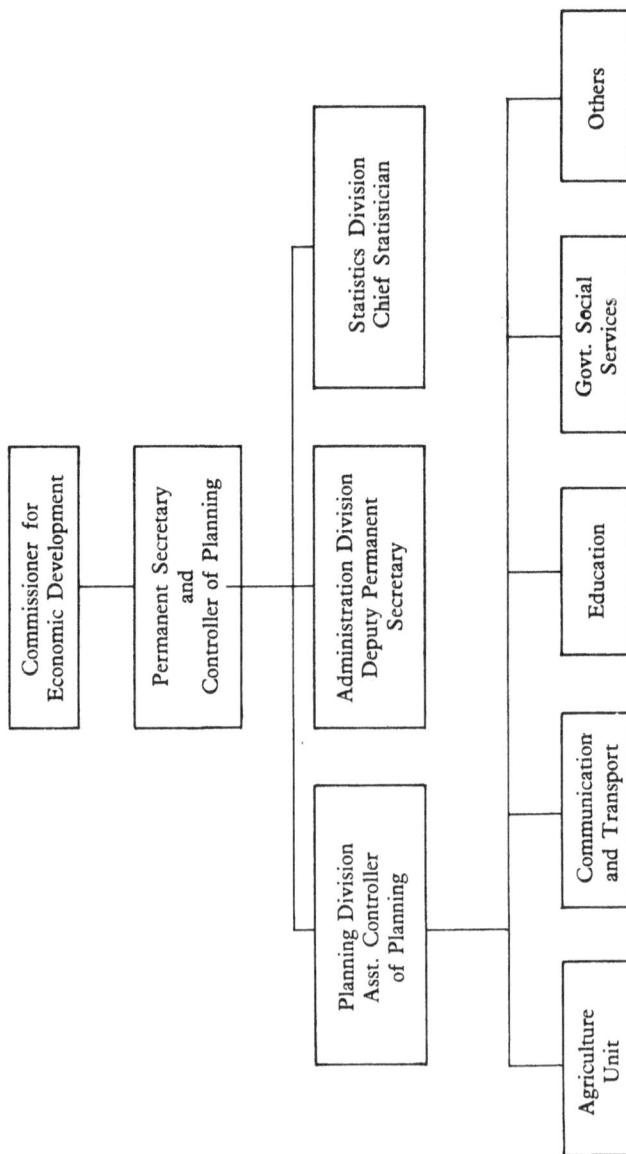

Source: East Central State Ministry of Economic Development and Reconstruction, Enugu, 1975.

sections are charged with responsibility over a number of draft proposals. For instance, all the agricultural projects originating from the State Ministry of Agriculture and the Agricultural Development Agency will go to the Agricultural unit of the Planning division for appraisal. The proposals which receive the approval of the section and the division are transmitted to C.P.O. in Lagos for further appraisal and approval.

In the Midwestern State, the Ministry of Economic Development and Reconstruction is dominated by administrative officers supported by professional planners such as appraisal officers, statistical officers and inspectors of projects.[44] Nevertheless, there is a move to revamp the Ministry with several professional planners and structure it along its federal counterpart.

Planning Process:

Since the end of the Nigerian civil war in 1970, and the establishment of the Central Planning Office in 1971, planning activities of both the federal and the state governments are better coordinated and harmonized. While the First National Development Plan 1962-68 consisted of five separate plans: Federal, Northern, Eastern, Western and Mid-west regions; the Third National Development Plan 1975-80 from which we drew most of our illustrations, is a more integrated plan. The Central Planning Office is the brain and the nerve center for planning activities in Nigeria. It translates the broad objectives of Nigeria's Supreme Military Council into practical guidelines and achievable goals. In collaboration with the Federal Ministry of Finance it determines the main fiscal and monetary policies that should be in operation within a plan period. It also determines the strategy for plan implementation and control. The relationship between the Central Planning Office in Lagos and the State Ministries of Economic Development and other state agencies that initiate plan proposals is in a sense similar to that of a multi-national company with its subsidiary or holding companies. Just as the multi-national companies consult their field offices and subsidiary companies before making decisions which have far reaching consequences for their operations, the C.P.O. in Lagos usually consults the State Ministries of Economic Development as well as other Federal Ministries before reaching decisions on strategies and perspectives of a given plan. Nevertheless, the State permanent secretaries in charge of Economic Ministries and their chief planning officers, like managers of holding companies, are important and powerful men in their own rights. Much initiative and discretion is left to them in appraising the proposals to be included in a national plan. In accepting or rejecting a plan proposal arising from a State Ministry or agency, the Central Planning Office will seek the advice and comments of that State's Ministry of Economic Development.

There is, however, a limit to their power and authority. The power and authority they exercise are determined by the plan objectives and practical guidelines set by the Central Planning Office. The State Ministries and agencies as well as Federal Ministries formulate plan proposals within the context of broad strategy set by C.P.O. and with the knowledge that the C.P.O. can accept or reject plan proposals on the grounds that it acts as the guardian of national interest with regards to planning activities.

The Processes in the Federal, State Ministries and Agencies and the Central Planning Office:

Planning machinery is set into motion when the Supreme Military Council, which is the highest executive and legislative body in Nigeria, directs that a development plan be prepared. The Supreme Military Council determines the broad objectives, priorities and the strategies of the plan. For instance, in the Nigeria's Second National Development Plan (1970-74), some of the objectives included, establishment of Nigeria firmly as a united, strong and self-reliant nation, a great and dynamic economy, a just and egalitarian society; a land of bright and full opportunities for all citizens, and a free and democratic society.[45]

These objectives, although they reflect a broad view of the ultimate aspirations of the society, still remain valid for the Third National Development Plan. Under the Third National Development Plan the specific short-term goals of the Nigerian Supreme Military Council which it hopes will ultimately facilitate the attainment of the board objectives are as follows:

a) increase in per capita income
b) more even distribution of income
c) reduction in the level of unemployment
d) increase in the supply of high level manpower
e) diversification of the economy
f) balanced development
g) indigenisation of economic activity[46]

The main strategy of the Supreme Military Council is to deploy the resources from the oil sector to develop the productive capacity of the economy and thus permanently improve the standard of living of the people.[47] The Supreme Military Council also determines the total amount of money to be spent within a given plan period, although this is often subject to revisions on the basis of actual implementation experiences. For example, the original nominal Investment program of about 2 billion Naira in the Second National Development Plan 1970-74 was revised upwards to 3.3 billion Naira. Some of the reasons given for the upward revision included price inflation, changes in the

TABLE 18. THE FUNCTIONAL RELATIONSHIP BETWEEN THE CENTRAL PLANNING OFFICE AND THE FEDERAL AND STATE MINISTRIES AND AGENCIES

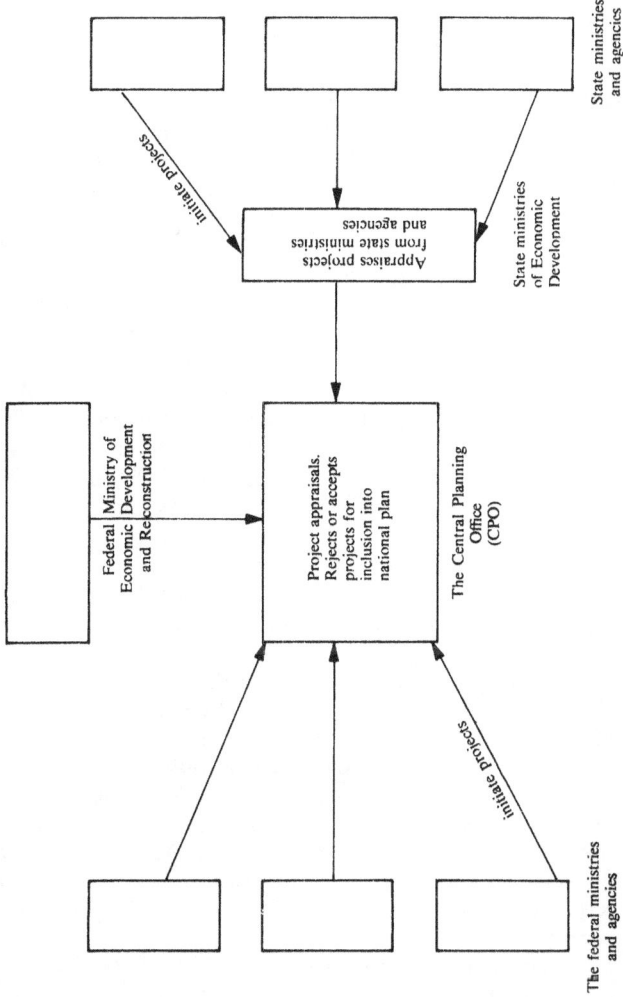

Federal Ministry of Economic Development and Reconstruction

Project appraisals. Rejects or accepts projects for inclusion into national plan

The Central Planning Office (CPO)

Appraises projects from state ministries and agencies

State ministries of Economic Development

State ministries and agencies

initiate projects

initiate projects

The federal ministries and agencies

scope of projects, introduction of new projects and revised costing in the process of project design and implementation.[48]

After the broad intentions of the SMC have been made known, the Federal Ministry of Economic Development and Reconstruction sends out proposal forms to the Federal and State Ministries and other agencies which usually initiate and execute projects. The Ministry also sends out guidelines on how the projects should be prepared. Both the Federal and State Ministries and their agencies initiate projects that they hope to execute within the plan period. They cost the projects after carrying out feasibility studies. The State Ministries and agencies submit their proposals in the appropriate forms through the State Ministry of Economic Development to the Central Planning Office in Lagos. The Federal Ministries and their agencies submit their proposals directly to the C.P.O. In formulating the federal and the state projects the advice of the Federal Ministry which not only mobilizes the financial resources of the Federal Government, but makes the same available to the executing agencies. Its advice as a custodian of Federal Government revenue can up-grade or scale-down the magnitude of the national plan.[49] Before the project proposals are forwarded to the C.P.O. in Lagos, many of the executing Ministries in the states endeavour to ensure that their proposals are technically feasible and that their utility are not in doubt. Evaluation of projects at the state level is made easier, if the state has reliable data and information to draw upon. Evaluation of projects is further facilitated, where the state Ministry of Economic Development has many professional planners. In the Midwest state before projects are forwarded to the C.P.O. a cabinet committee consisting of representatives of Ministries of Economic Development, Finance, Trade and Industry and works vets the state projects.[50]

When the plan proposals from the Federal and State Ministries and agencies are received in the Federal Ministry of Economic Development Central Planning Office, they are sent to the different divisions of C.P.O. Agricultural division for an example assembles all the agricultural proposals from the federal and state Ministries and agencies. The projects are carefully considered along with the recommendations of the division concerned. The state or federal Ministry that proposed the projects under consideration is invited to defend them. In approving or rejecting a project, the C.P.O. takes the following principles into account:

I.   The national interest. A project is likely to be approved if it conforms to the national objective and the stated guidelines of the Federal Ministry of Economic Development. State projects which cut across national interest may be adopted as federal projects. Those that intrude in the domain of the Federal Government may not receive the blessing of the C.P.O. Though, a state which feels strongly about a rejected project may surface it in a higher political organ such as the Conference of Commissioners or in the Supreme Military Council meeting.

II. Comparative cost advantage. The C.P.O. is often cost minded and as much as possible it tries to encourage state Ministries to avoid duplication of projects whose costs are prohibitive. The competitive spirit of the states and desire to enhance state prestige and esteem, induce some states to include in their programs projects which have been well established in other states, and which can easily be expanded to take advantage of economies of scales. It is the task of the C.P.O. to find such projects, trim them or reject them outright.

III. National priorities. Another factor, which the C.P.O. takes into account while appraising federal and state projects is the national priority. It considers each project partly on the basis of how it conforms to the national priority. Left to the states, themselves, each would like to own a beer industry, a textile firm, a university, etc. As the C.P.O. is aware of the National guidelines on each of the above subjects it interprets and applies them while considering the acceptability of any project. For instance, no state can propose building a university without the consent of the Federal Government, even if the state has the resources to do so.

IV. Contribution to the economic growth and development. This is another important yard stick for measuring the acceptance or rejection of projects. As the strategy of the military government is to utilize the resources from the oil sector to finance economic growth and development, it is left to the C.P.O. to ensure that the federal and state projects will promote economic growth and development, as well as create employment opportunities.

One of the major differences between the Third National Development Plan and the other two previous national plans, is the attention paid to the costing of each of the state and federal projects. Most of the projects in the Third National Development Plan 1975-80, were appraised along the principles stated above. The Federal Civil Service relies on the states to identify and articulate in their plans, those peculiar and diverse interests, which otherwise would escape the attention of the federal planners. Moreover, though the federal government enjoys the ultimate sovereign power in Nigeria with its control of the armed forces, as well as the national revenue; it is the states that control most of the farm lands. The federal government acquires land for its agricultural and other developmental projects through the agency of the states, because the state government officials can easily deal with the land-owners than the federal officials. Besides, in Northern Nigeria, most of the land belongs to the state governments. In addition, with almost all the important institutions and organs of the federal government centered in Lagos, the federal government has few well staffed and equipped field offices in the states which it can rely upon to collate and process vital information which is necessary for policy choices.[51] On the other hand, as the states are closer to the people, and can easily reach them not only through mass media and through local government machineries as well as through cultural groups and co-operative unions, they can more easily aggregate the needs of the peripheral people than the Federal Government. Even if the federal governrment desired to deal directly with the people in initiating and processing all the plan proposals, it cannot at present do it, owing to its limited manpower and information resources. It, therefore, has to rely on the states not only to supplement its manpower needs but to abridge its information gap. One of the major criticisms of the last two national development plans was lack of broad participation. As the Federal regime lacks an organ of mass mobilization and participation, one of the effective means of securing a form of participation and involvement in drawing up a national development plan is through the states' agencies and associational infrastructures. Consequently, the Central Planning Office in Lagos works closely with the state civil services and agencies in formulation of national plans.

The Joint Planning Board (J.P.B.)

After the various divisions of the Central Planning Office have appraised projects emanating from the Federal and state governments and their agencies, the approved projects form the basis for a draft plan. The C.P.O. therefore draws up a draft plan and submits the same to J.P.B.—an official body which replaced what used to be the Joint Planning Committee (J.P.C.). The membership is drawn from the federal and state ministries and some agencies of the federal government. The Board consists:

   i. The permanent secretary federal ministry of Economic Development and Reconstruction, as the Chairman.
   ii. The Director Central Planning Office.
  iii. Chief Statistician, federal office of statistics,
   iv. Director Nigerian institute of Social and Economic Research.
   v. Director of Research Central Bank of Nigeria.
   vi. Permanent Secretary Federal Ministry of Finance.
  vii. Permanent secretary ministry of Economic Development and Planning from each of 12 states, each state representative, will have an option of being accompanied by an alternate or adviser.[52]

The J.P.B. serves as a clearinghouse for planning officials all over the country. The members jointly work out the format and criteria for selection of state and the federal government projects as contained in the draft plan. During the Board's review of the draft plan, each state and the federal ministry endeavors to justify its projects. The acceptance of a project depends as noted earlier on a number of factors such as cost/benefit ratio, social and economic utility, compatability with set out national objectives. In effect the J.P.B. harmonizes, coordinates economic policies and planning activities of the federal and state governments and their agencies. It puts forward its recommendations to the next planning organ.

As the J.P.B. has the arduous task of vetoing the state and federal government projects, one may ask, how competent is the Board. Its membership has been criticized because of the predominance of administrative officers who are not professional planning officers. The dominance of administrative officers implies, that some technical questions concerned with planning cannot be handled competently by the Board. Considering the well known conflict between the administrative officers in Nigeria and their professional counterparts, the administrative officers, who exercise relatively superior hierarchical authority can in some circumstances overrule the minority voice of the professional members of the Board. Moreover, the Board is further constrained as a result of conflicts between federal and state officials about projects to be included or left out in the national plan. In order to improve the effectiveness of the Board, it has been suggested that its membership should be enlarged to include more professional and technical experts.[53]

The National Economic Advisory Council (N.E.A.C.)

This is mainly and advisory body drawn from both public and private sectors. The membership includes representatives of chamber of commerce, manufacturers association of Nigeria, agricultural interests and professional associations. Some members especially those from the universities were appointed on their merit.[54] There are altogether thirty-five members, and the Federal Commissioner for Economic Development and Reconstruction is the chairman.[55]

The N.E.A.C. provides a linkage between the private and public sectors. The officials through the N.E.A.C. exchange views with the leading members of the private sector. The main function of the N.E.A.C. is to advise the federal government on planning, economic, and fiscal matters and the harmonization of the activities of the private sectors with the national plan. The C.P.O. provides a secretariat for the Council. The regularity of its meetings is contingent upon, how often the C.P.O. wants its services and thereby summons it. The C.P.O. can request the leading members of the Council, especially the academicians to make studies of particular problems and the projects which the C.P.O. is interested. The C.P.O. is not bound however to accept the outcome of such studies.

Though the Council was established to achieve greater private sector's input in the authoring of a development plan, the Council as

TABLE 19. NIGERIAN PLANNING INSTITUTIONS

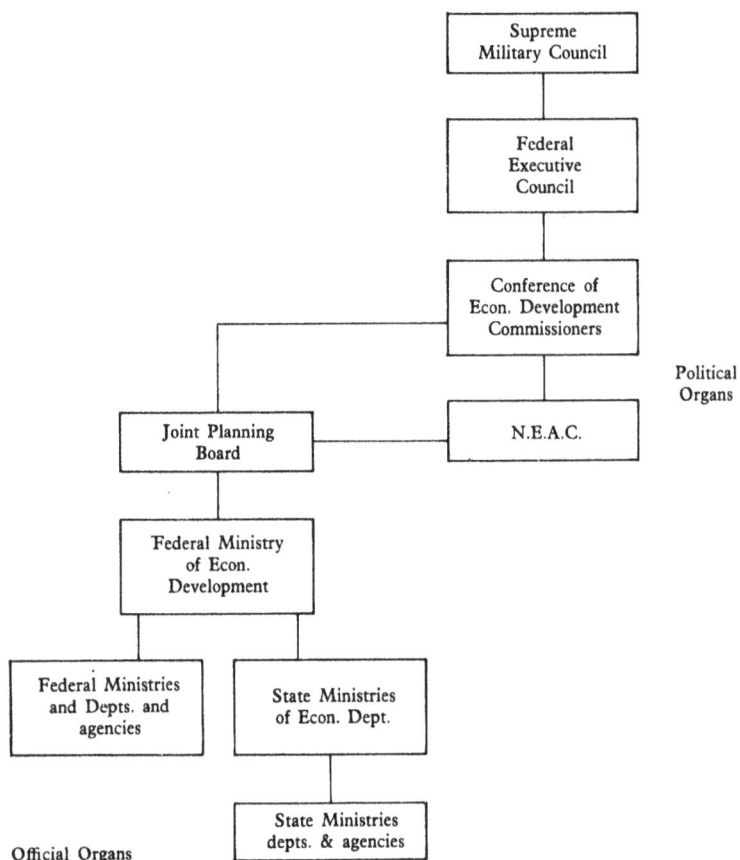

```
                          ┌─────────────────┐
                          │    Supreme       │
                          │ Military Council │
                          └────────┬─────────┘
                                   │
                          ┌────────┴─────────┐
                          │    Federal        │
                          │    Executive      │
                          │    Council        │
                          └────────┬─────────┘
                                   │
                          ┌────────┴─────────┐
                          │  Conference of    │
              ┌───────────┤ Econ. Development │
              │           │  Commissioners    │
              │           └────────┬─────────┘            Political
              │                    │                       Organs
   ┌──────────┴────────┐   ┌───────┴────────┐
   │  Joint Planning    ├───┤    N.E.A.C.    │
   │      Board         │   └────────────────┘
   └──────────┬─────────┘
              │
   ┌──────────┴─────────┐
   │  Federal Ministry   │
   │    of Econ.         │
   │   Development       │
   └────┬──────────┬─────┘
        │          │
┌───────┴────┐  ┌──┴──────────────┐
│  Federal    │  │  State Ministries │
│  Ministries │  │  of Econ. Dept.   │
│ and Depts.  │  └────────┬─────────┘
│ and         │           │
│ agencies    │  ┌────────┴─────────┐
└─────────────┘  │  State Ministries │
                 │  depts. & agencies│
Official Organs  └───────────────────┘
```

108

presently structured and functions does not perform this role effectively. It is argued that most of its members drawn from the private sector are representatives of successful indigenous businesses, who represent their interests, rather than the interests of the entire spectrum of private sector. Their views are always the views of producers, rather than those of consumers. Profit considerations rather than equitable distribution of goods and services guide their thinking. The impact of whatever the consumer interest the Council represents is minimal. Besides, the Council has additional constraint because of its advisory status. As the N.E.A.C. lacks executive power, it can hardly influence the outcome of a development plan in any significant manner. Its lack of power inevitably dampens the interests of otherwise active and informed members.[56]

For the council to narrow the information gap between the public and the private sectors, it needs to change its orientation and structure. The Council should be enlarged and revamped with representatives of the various associational and functional groups in the society such as labor, teachers, traders cooperative societies and farmers. It should be given some executive powers, so that it can participate actively in drafting a national development plan, instead of merely "glancing through" draft plans prepared by C.P.O. The Council should be able to initiate on its own studies whose outcomes will inform the national plan. Furthermore, in the absence of a mobilizing instrument such as a political party or parties, there is greater need in drafting a development plan to secure more input from the private sector, through the participation of the representatives of the various functional and cooperative organizations in the country. Emphasizing the need for increased role for the N.E.A.C. the Udoji Public Service Review Commission states:

> The National Economic Advisory Council needs some reorientation with a view of providing more systematic information on the private sector of the economy. The private sector is an area where the information gap is very wide and the National Economic Advisory Council is supposed to narrow the gap. The performance of the Council has so far fallen below expectation. The performance has been more or less limited to consideration of papers prepared by the Central Planning Office. This is not sufficient. The Council is expected to identify problems independently, to commission its own studies, and make positive recommendations to government on the integration of the private sector in the planning process.[57]

The Council can only perform the type of role which Udoji's review commission envisages, if the structure of its representativeness is broadened and its power increased. At present it only functions at the insistence of the C.P.O., which is not bound to accepting its recommendations.

The Conference of Commissioners Responsible For Economic Development

Another political linkage between the federal and state governments in planning and harmonization of economic policies is the conference of Commissioners charged with economic development and planning. The conference is chaired by the Federal Commissioner for Economic Development and the meetings rotate from one state capital to another. The Commissioners are generally concerned with broad economic and planning policies, rather than technical details of a development plan. They exchange views on common problems, and share each other's planning experiences. Though the Commissioners lack popular electoral base, they are expected to bring the broad spectrum of public interest to bear on the draft plan. The conference also examines the recommendations by the N.E.A.C. and joint planning board. But it does not in any significant manner alter the draft plan presented to it.

The Federal Executive Council

This body functions as the federal cabinet. Its military and civilian members are appointed directly by and owe allegiance to the head of the Nigerian military government. Each of the twelve states is represented in the Federal Executive Council by at least one Federal Commissioner. It is therefore not uncommon for a rejected project of a state to resurface at the Federal Executive Council meeting. The Council examines the draft plan from the joint planning board before it is forwarded to the Supreme Military Council. As the Federal permanent secretaries are in attendance during the Federal Executive Council meetings they are often called upon to clear any doubts which the draft plan may embody. The Federal Executive Council can effect changes in the draft plan. It also endeavours to ensure that the plan proposals conform to the stipulated objectives of the federal government.

The Supreme Military Council

This is the highest political organ and has the last word in approving a development plan. It consists of top military personnel and the state military governors. In the reconstituted supreme military which followed the overthrow of Gowon's regime in July 29, 1975, the state governors ceased to be members of the body. The Nigerian head of state is the chairman. The Council, when compared with its civilian counterpart, National Economic Council (N.E.C.), which it replaced is a much more powerful and coherent organ. The membership of the N.E.C. then consisted of the Federal Prime Minister who was the chairman, regional premiers, four ministers from each region and four other ministers from the federal government.[58] The N.E.C. played an advisory role, and its regional representatives did not see themselves as national actors, but as representatives of partisan interests. In contrast, the Supreme Military Council is not only the most powerful political organ in the country but is more nationally oriented. As the Council functions as the highest legislative and executive body in the country, it has the last word with regards to modification or approval of a development plan. For example, it determined the financial limits of the current Third National Development Plan 1975-80. Moreover, it resolved all the outstanding differences arising out of the federal and state projects. The current development plan became an official document only when the Supreme Military Council gave its approval.

FOOTNOTES

1. John Hatch, *Nigeria The Seeds of Disaster,* Chicago, Henry Regnery Company, 1970, pp. 203-204.
2. For the activities of Christian missionary schools in Nigeria see James S. Coleman, *Nigeria Background to Nationalism,* Berkeley and Los Angeles, University of California Press 1958, pp. 91-140.
3. John Hatch, *Op. Cit.,* p. 214.
4. U.S. Department of Commerce, *Investment in Nigeria,* Washington: Government Printing Office 1957, p. 115.
5. *Ibid.*
6. *Ibid.*
7. International Bank for Reconstruction and Development, *Nigeria: Options for Long Term Development,* Baltimore: The John Hopkins University Press, 1974, p. 23.
8. Cited in U.S. Department of Commerce, *Op. Cit.,* p. 115.
9. Edwin Dean, *Plan Implementation in Nigeria, 1962-66,* Ibadan: Oxford University Press, 1972, p. 12.
10. U.S. Department of Commerce, *Op. Cit.,* p. 116.
11. *Ibid.* p. 112.
12. *Ibid.* p. 116.
13. *Ibid.* p. 114.
14. *Ibid.* p. 112.
15. Federal Ministry of Economic Development, *National Development Plan 1962-68,* Lagos: 1962, p. 6.
16. Wolfang F. Stolper, *Planning Without Facts,* Cambridge: Harvard University Press, 1966, pp. 38-40.
17. Adebayo Adedeji, *Federalism and Development Planning in Nigeria,* Ibadan: Institute of Public Administration, University of Ife, 1969, pp. 25-32.
18. Federal Ministry of Commerce and Industry, *Handbook of Commerce and Industry in Nigeria,* Lagos: Federal Ministry of Information, 1962, p. 24.
19. Dean, *Op. Cit.,* p. 16.
20. Adedeji, *Op. Cit.,* p. 30.
21. Dean, *Op. Cit.,* p. 17.
22. *Ibid.,* p. 18.
23. *Handbook on Commerce, Op. Cit.,* p. 24.
24. *Ibid.*
25. Dean, *Op. Cit.,* p. 16.

26. First National Plan 1962-68, *Op. Cit.*, p. 23.
27. Stolper, *Op. Cit.*, pp. 144-146.
28. Dean, *Op. Cit.*, p. 22.
29. *Ibid.*
30. First National Plan 1962-68, *Op. Cit.*, p. 23.
31. Dean, *Op. Cit.*, p. 25.
32. World Bank, *Op. Cit.*, p. 23.
33. *Ibid.*
34. *Ibid.*, p. 24.
35. *Ibid.*, p. 23.
36. The Mohammed regime which ousted Gowon's administration on July 29, 1975, created 7 additional states on February 3, 1976. This brings the total number of states in Nigeria to 19.
37. World Bank, *Op. Cit.*, p. 24.
38. *Ibid.*
39. Federal Republic of Nigeria, Recurrent and Capital Estimates (1975-76), Lagos: Federal Ministry of Information 1975, p. XXXI.
40. Recently, Iran had a budget deficit of $2.4 billion. This is a result of a shortfall of $8 billion in the gross proceeds from her petroleum export. See Time Magazine, March 1, 1976, p. 44.
41. For the Public service review report which resulted into substantial salary increases in both Nigerian public and private sectors see Federal Republic of Nigeria, *Public Service Commission Main Report,* Lagos: Federal Ministry of Information 1974.
42. Most of the information used in compiling this section is derived from interviews and panel discussions held with the senior officials of the Federal and State Ministers of Economic Development and Reconstruction at Lagos, Enugu and Benin.
43. *Ibid.*
44. Ministry of Economic Development and Reconstruction Benin, interview with Assistant Chief Appraisal Officer, May 8, 1975.
45. Federal Republic of Nigeria, *Third National Development Plan,* 1975-80, Lagos, Central Planning Office, Federal Ministry of Economic Development and Reconstruction, March 1975, p. 29.
46. *Ibid.*
47. *Ibid.*, p. 30.
48. *Ibid.*, p. 13.
49. Federal Ministry of Finance, Lagos. Interview with the Director of Research. The Director says in initiating a national plan, there is a close cooperation and consultation between the Federal and State Ministries of Economic Development with the Federal Ministry of Finance.
50. Ministry of Economic Development Benin, *Op. Cit.*, interview with the Chief Appraisal Officer, May 2, 1975.
51. A survey conducted in parts of rural Mid-west to test the knowledge of the people about the achievement of the federal government, showed that most of the people interviewed attributed the achievements of the federal government, such as road development to the state government. So far as these people were concerned the federal government is far away to be immediately relevant to their needs.
52. Udoji, *Public Service Review Commission, Op. Cit.*, p. 63.
53. *Ibid.*, p. 64.
54. *Ibid.*
55. *Ibid.*

56. During our discussions with senior officials of the Federal Ministries of Economic Development and Finance in Lagos about the planning role of the N.E.A.C., they were of the opinion that it hardly does much. Its lack of power, makes the C.P.O. the chief planning organ. The C.P.O. makes use of it when it desires. It presents a finished draft for the consideration of N.E.A.C.
57. Public Service Review Commission Main Report, *Op. Cit.*, p. 64.
58. Wolfang Stolper, *Op. Cit.*, pp. 38-40.

CHAPTER FIVE

FEDERAL-STATE CIVIL SERVICES AND PLAN IMPLEMENTATION

As we pointed out in the last chapter, Nigeria has since 1946 adopted development planning as a strategy of not only accelerating economic and social development, but as a means by which successive regimes endeavored to secure compliance with and support for their policy choices. It has therefore drawn up relatively 'excellent' plans sometimes, with expert assistance from the international bodies, and yet she had not realized the magnitude of industrial and social development which her plans in theory were to make possible. For, while the planning process involves exercises in imagination and theories and concern only political decision makers and their technical experts, plan implementation poses more problems and complexities and requires several inputs of various kinds of resources which are often in short supply in countries as underdeveloped as Nigeria. Plan implementation also generally involves the cooperation of the entire society as well as the effective deployment of the societal physical and social infrastructures. Moreover, as plan documents are in a sense a system of payoffs, and positive inducements to the various groups and sectors in the society, the level of implementation ultimately helps to determine the degree of legitimacy grant the wider society makes to the incumbents of central and regional authority roles.

This chapter is divided into two sections. The first section analyzes the main problems which constrain plan implementation in Nigeria and thereby help to frustrate the attainment of planned societal objectives. The second section is a case study of three federal projects which were implemented through the agency of state governments and civil services. These case studies shed further light on the problems and complexities of plan implementation, and the lags that exist between paper plans and actual achievements accomplished during plan implementation.

PROBLEMS OF PLAN IMPLEMENTATION

In Chapter Three we discussed a number of problems such as poor communication, ethnicity and corruption which detract from the effectiveness of the federal and state civil services. Here we shall analyze three more problems which pose great constraints to plan implementation in Nigeria. These problems are related to physical infrastructure, organizational resource and management and outmoded agricultural technology. Considering the extent these problems constrained the implementation of Nigeria's 1962-68 and 1970-74 development plans, there are hardly doubts that they constitute the most challenging threats to the successful implementation of the 1975-80 development plan which is more ambitious in financial allocation and magnitude of projects than the two previous plans.[1]

1. **Infrastructure:** The overall importance of infrastructural support to Nigeria's economic development cannot be overemphasized, because a successful plan implementation largely depends on the effectiveness of the services rendered by the country's public physical infrastructures such as the roads, railways, ports and shipping line and airways. The Nigerian federal government recognizes the significance of an effective transport system when it states that:

> an effective transport system has to support the growth and development of agriculture, commerce and industry with efficient movement of people and goods throughout the country.[2].

In general the Nigerian transport system is characterized by poor coordination, misinvestments, operational deficits, lack of maintenance, inadequate utilization of human and natural resources and poor management and operational control.[3]

As a result of lack of effectiveness in coordination, the use of some branches of the transport system is on the increase while others are steadily declining. For example, the road transport between 1965-70 rose by about 18 per cent and the water transport dropped to 10 per cent of its pre-war level.[4] An analysis of each of the branches of the transport sector, will highlight the problems it poses for plan implementation.

Roads: The greatest demands on the Nigerian Transport system are made on the roads. Given the vastness of Nigeria and the spread of its population, the country is not adequately served with road networks. For instance, out of the total length of 55,000 miles of roads that existed in Nigeria in 1970 only about 10,000 miles were properly paved and covered with bituminous.[5] Several of the roads are narrow and poorly constructed and they lack adequate drainage systems and regular maintenance.

Road construction and maintenance are not properly coordinated The existing practice whereby the federal roads are maintained through the agency of state ministries of works had proved to be unsatisfactory.[6] Often the roads are left to deteriorate to the extent that they constitute death traps during the rainy seasons. Besides, the roads carry more heavy traffic and trucks than they originally were designed to carry.

Consequently, severe damage is inflicted on them. In 1969, it was estimated that the number of vehicles that ply the Nigerian roads was between 67,000 and 79,000, including 28,000 to 30,000 trucks and buses and 31,000-38,000 motorcycles[7]. Most of the passenger vehicles are concentrated around Lagos which has not yet evolved an adequate ring road system around its immediate vicinity and this causes one of the world's worst traffic jams and 'go slows' in the city. Many of the Nigerian roads and bridges were seriously damaged during the civil war, and some of them especially in the East Central state are still in deplorable condition.

Road development and construction in Nigeria are made difficult by the shortage of foreign and indigenous construction firms with considerable wealth of experience and expertise in road construction. Increasingly, both the federal and state governments find it difficult to attract private international construction firms to help in the construction of networks of roads in Nigeria.

Implication of Poor Road Networks to Plan Implementation

The Nigerian road system cannot cope with the increased demands made on it by increased traffic in men and materials which the growing economy and the implementation of the third national development plan require. Consequently, there are increases in cost of transportation and this is being reflected in the cost of projects, far above what had been shown in the plan documents. It is also difficult to move construction materials in time to places where they are needed, and this results in increases in cost implementation as well as an extension of periods for project completion. Increased heavy traffic inflicts more damage on the roads and thereby constrains the economy as a whole. Considering the inadequate maintenance of the roads and bridges and the poor highway control system there are likely to be more accidents on the roads within the present plan period and this will imply more cost to human lives, vehicles and construction equipment.

Although the federal government has made proposals to establish maintenance organizations in order to make the Nigerian roads safer and more reliable, the plan has not yet taken off. Given the constraint of manpower and equipment it is doubtful that the road maintenance organizations will make impressionable impact within the current development plan period.

Furthermore, given the shortage of both foreign and indigenous construction firms with experience and expertise in road building, it is not likely that the total planned expenditure of N5.34 billion covering 50,000 kilometres of roads can be successfully executed within the 1975-80 plan period.[8] Several projects are likely to remain incomplete at the end of the plan period and will spill over to the next plan period.

116

Railways: The Nigerian Railway was established as a government department in 1898 and was made a statutory corporation in 1955.[9] As statutory public corporation it was expected to operate as a commercial concern, although the federal government retained powers over broad policies.[10] The corporation has so far not justified the early hopes placed in it. In spite of the fact that it operates under conditions of heavy traffic demands, long haul, easy train and spare track capacity and despite regular subsidies it receives from the federal government, the corporation has operated in deficit in every year but one during the past 15 years.[11] Its freight liftings have substantially declined from 850,000 tons in 1958-59 to 350,000 tons in 1970-71.[12] Its operations deteriorated further between 1971 and 1974 and its deficits increased substantially.

TABLE 20. NIGERIAN RAILWAYS DEFICITS 1969-74

Year	Deficit (N million)
1969-70	10.3
1970-71	15.8
1971-72	22.2
1972-73	21.8
1973-74	23.1
TOTAL N	93.2

Source: Federal Republic of Nigeria, Third National Development Plan 1975-80, Vol. 1, Lagos: Federal Ministry of Economic Development 1975, p. 214.

As Table 20 illustrates, the Nigerian Railway Corporation has within 1970 and 1974 sustained a loss of N93.2 million. A number of reasons are responsible for the declining fortune of the corporation. First there is the problem of management. The management of the corporation has had long history of internal conflict and struggle for power and influence, and this led to impaired operational efficiency. When the management is not engaged in polemics over operational policies it is constantly harassed by labor disputes and 'wild cat' strikes. Poor management is partially responsible for under utilization of human and material resources. Empty wagons are not always moved in time to the points where they are needed. Nor could the corporation guarantee regular and scheduled service to its customers. Unreliable and unpredictable service has diverted several railway customers to road transport which is more expensive. Hence, the inefficiency of the railways impose extra consts to the economy as a whole.

The second reason for NRC's operational loss is the aftermath of the Nigerian civil war. The corporation was hard hit by the civil war; it lost about 6,000 employees of various skills and its Eastern branch was closed down during the war.[13] Besides its rolling stock was extensively depleted as the result of the war and the remaining ones are generally inadequate for the needs of the corporation and partly obsolete for the increased functions it has to perform.[14]

The third reason for the increased problems of the corporation is the obsolete track system. The present route was built between 1898-1965 and spans over 2,178 miles, with less than a standard 3ft 6in gauge. The rail route is characterized by extensive track curvature, light weight rails, weak bridges, steep grades and obsolete signalling systems and this limits train speeds at times to as low as five miles per hour.[15]

Other problems that help reduce the efficiency of the railways include the high defects in its diesel engines, heavy backlog of repairs and maintenance work, extensive detention time at stations, poor facilities for passengers and an unreliable communication system. Implications. The inefficiency of the Nigerian railway poses severe consequences to both Nigerian economy and to succesful plan implementation. It constitutes a major drain on the public largesse. The corporation does not meet its economic share of total transport demand in the country. Given the unreliability and unpredictability of its operation, goods and construction materials cannot be taken to places at the time they are needed. The delays not only increase transport costs but results in noncompletion of projects according to the programmed schedules. The delays ultimately raise the cost of implementing projects. Besides, several heavy equipments that could be cheaply moved by rail are diverted to the road transport which is more expensive. Despite the federal governments planned expenditure of N885 million[16] to improve the service of the NRC, within the next five years it is doubtful considering the past records of the corporation and its poor management that it can cope with the increased movements of men and materials which the current development plan calls for. Besides it will take several years before the planned investment can yield significant results.

The Ports Authority and National Shipping Line. Another branch of the Nigerian transport system whose services have fallen far below heavy traffic demands is the Nigerian Ports Authority (NPA). The Authority was established as a statutory corporation in 1955 to operate and manage the country's ports along commercial lines. The Authority owns and manages six sea ports—Lagos, Port Harcourt, Calabar, Warri, Burutu and Koko. Lagos and Port Harcourt are the largest ports, with 18[17] and 8[18] berths respectively. On the whole the authority has 29 berths. The Authority is also responsible for the maintenance of its facilities including the dockyard and the dredging of the ports and their approaches.

The management of the Ports Authority has in recent years demonstrated its inability to cope with the heavy traffic demands at the Lagos and Port Harcourt ports. The congestion at the ports reached a crisis situation throughout 1975, when in the month of October alone there were over 400 ships awaiting off loading at the Lagos port.[19] The management of the Authority's ports was. adversely affected by the loss during the civil war of some of its most experienced and skillful staff. Operational efficiency is further impaired by what a government statement described as

inadequate system of collection and dissemination of internal information, delays in customs clearance, vehicular traffic congestion in the port areas and shortage of certain types of equipment in operational equipment (and) high incidence of cargo losses from breakage and pilferage in the ports.[20]

The consequences of the inefficiency of the Nigerian ports in the economy and plan implementation are quite obvious. Delays at the port which average five to six weeks for a cargo ship through 1975 had imposed staggering difficulties on all Nigerian importers, exporters and consumers alike. Long waits of ships at the ports are accompanied by increases in shipping charges, which the authority transfers to import costs as part of its social overhead. This implies that the costs of all imported commodities including all the construction materials necessary for plan implementation are unduly expensive because of the congested ports. Besides, as ships are not off loaded in time, materials necessary to complete projects at specified schedules are not delivered at the time and places they are needed. As goods are held up for unpredictable periods of time at the ports, artificial scarcity is created in the local markets and this accelerates the inflationary pressures, which are reflected in the disproportionate increases in prices. This poses a lost of complexities and uncertainties to plan implementation, as cost of goods and services cannot be effectively monitored at any given period of time.

The operational problems of the Nigerian Ports Authority are not helped by the 'lame' services of the Nigerian National Shipping line (NNSL) which was established in 1958.[21] The NNSL has a fleet of 13 ships, four of which are described as "over-aged". Despite government subvention the shipping line operates at financial loss.[22] This is partly due to mismanagement and rapid turnover of personnel. Other reasons that help to account for its ineffectiveness include excessive maintenance cost in time and money, unreliable cargo ships and undependability of its services due to constant ship withdrawl. Consequently, the Nigerian Shipping Line is only able to carry 7 per cent of the Nigerian sea traffic.[23]

Airways: The Nigerian Airways Corporation was established in 1959 and has a monopoly of all domestic air service. It also operates scheduled international services to several West African countries and Europe. Its American service is limited to flights to New York and this is carried out in collaboration with the Pan American World Airways. The corporation has only 11 aircraft comprising 5 Fokker 27s, 2 Boeing 707s, 2 Boeing 737s, and 2 Fokker 28 jets. Owing to its management problems the corporation has not turned its favorable domestic operational conditions into profit. Its services are not dependable, as flight schedules are altered with little or no notice. Long waits at the airports are the rule rather than the exception. The corporation is equally deficient in such other areas as engineering, maintenance facilities, communication equipment, accommodation and other support facilities. Given the operational and the management problems of the Nigerian airways it does not carry its economic share of the increasing Nigerian traffic demands.

In summary, all the Nigerian physical infrastructures including power and water supplies are plagued by both operational and management problems and are not able to cope with the changing and expanding needs of the Nigerian economy. The demand for road, shipping and air services exceeds the capacity of existing utilities to meet them. The situation is made worse by lack of coordinated transport policy in the country. Although there is a federal ministry of Transport which directs transport policies, it does not have full power in initiating and executing overall policy for transportation in the country. Its planning role is shared with the Transport Division of the Federal Ministry of Economic Development. Besides the budget allocation for improvement in any of the branches of transport sector it determined and controlled by the Federal Ministry of Finance. Despite, the huge planned expenditures directed towards improving the physical infrastructures they are likely to constitute major constraints to plan implementation during the current (1975-80) plan period.

2. **Organizational Constraint.** Perhaps the most intractable constraint achieving the objectives of Nigerian third national development plan is the one posed by inadequate organizational resources. Lack of adequate organizational resources is reflected in shortages of all levels of manpower, poor organizational coordination and in the inability of organization structures to adapt to the changing needs of the economy. Shortage of Manpower: In the Nigeria there is a shortfall in the supply of manpower at management, professional and intermediate levels. The shortage of management staff at a time, both the federal and state governments are expanding their economic activities poses the greatest setback to implementation. As the economic and planning functions of the federal and state governments have substantially increased, the federal and state civil services have increasingly become forms of "Economic Bureaucracies". Increased economic functions

of the federal and state civil services require therefore the availability of more administrative entrepreneurs who are experts in combining development inputs in innovative ways, in order to translate the objectives contained in paper plans into concrete achievements. But there is a dearth of such innovative administrative entrepreneurs in the Nigerian federal and state civil services. The catalogue of failures as we pointed out above in the operations of the Nigerian ports Authority, Railways and the Airways indicates that the other branches of the public service equally lack experienced and innovative entrepreneurs. The permanent secretaries at both the feredal and state levels who constitute the "bulk of administrative entrepreneurs", by their training and experience, lack the expertise and the orientation which the implementation and management of such technical projects as vehicle assemblying plant, petrol chemical industries, and liquefied natural gas call for. The management problem is further compounded by such environmental contraints as the pressures on the permanent secretaries by friends, ethnic affiliations, townspeople, to side track the civil service rules in order to extend to them favors such as employment and government contracts.[24] Yielding to such pressures reduces the efficiency of the service.

The problem of manpower is not confined to management there is equally a shortage of all kinds of professional officers and intermediate level manpower. The shortfall is most acute for all kinds of construction engineers, irrigation and agricultural engineers, architects, surveyors, doctors, dentists, pharmacists, farm managers, foremen, technologists, technicians and skilled artisans of all grades. The shortage of professional manpower is made worse by Nigeria's 'preference' for mere academic qualifications, and the dissolution in the 1960s of the Nigerian colleges of Arts, Science and Technology which were then the main sources for the provision of intermediate level manpower. These institutions were enmeshed into Ahmadu, Ife and Nsukka Universities. Consequently, most of the executing ministries in Nigeria lack an adequate number of professional staff and technologists who can design and execute increasingly highly technical projects.

The implementation of projects is further constrained by the 'fragmentation' which exists in the internal structure of both federal and state civil services. As we pointed out in Chapter Three the civil services are divided into various conflicting groups such as administrative, professional, intermediate and lower groups. There is further polarization into senior and junior civil servants. These internal divisions and conflicts inhibit coordination. It does not facilitate the role of the civil services as a coherent organization engaged in a "cooperative rational action" in order to achieve societal objectives.

Although the federal government recognizes the constraint posed by the shortage of manpower to plan implementation, it does not seem that its solution will obviate it in any significant manner. The federal government estimates that it would require an additional 49,210 high level manpower in order to successfully execute the projects embodied in the 1975-80 plan. Its manpower budget for the same periods provides for 43,350 high level manpower, leaving a gap of 5,660.[25]

TABLE 21. ANTICIPATED SOURCES OF HIGH LEVEL MANPOWER SUPPLY 1975-80

Source	Anticipated Number
1. 1975-80 graduates turned out by local universities	28,000
2. Supply from local non-University institutions	4,000
3. Supply of graduates from overseas institutions	1,600
4. Other external supplies of qualified Nigerians	3,000
5. Supply through upgrading from intermediate category	6,150
TOTAL	43,550

Source: Federal Republic of Nigeria, Third National Development Plan 1975-80, Vol. I, Lagos: Federal Ministry of Economic Development, 1975, p. 378.

There are so many problems surrounding the government's manpower estimates. There is no evidence that the required manpower will be available or produced when they are needed. While the production of 28,000 local graduates can be a future possibility, the manpower needs of the current development plan are immediate and pressing. In fact, there were several spillovers of projects from a more modest 1970-74 plan into the 1975-80 plan because of the shortage of manpower.[26]

Besides, the main productive sectors of the economy can hardly benefit from new university graduates who lack practical experience. Equally important to organizational strength is the stock of practical experience the graduates possess. As there are very few large industrial establishments in Nigeria, many Nigerian students in engineering and allied fields do not have adequate opportunity to gain practical experience during their training; as a result most of them have to learn their jobs for periods ranging from one to several years before they can be productive in any real sense. Experience has shown that industries and construction firms are reluctant to employ professional graduates lacking in practical knowledge.[27] Even if the government succeeds in getting its 28,000 high level manpower from local institutions of high learning within the plan period, those of them who would be deployed to the construction industry and who are lacking in practical experience would constitute more of a liability than an asset to the needs of plan implementation.

122

While the government proposal to attach students and fresh graduates to industrial establishments, in order to make them acquire practical experience, may be beneficial in the long run, its utility for the current development plan is doubtful.

Besides the government estimates for external manpower supply is not based on verifiable statistical data, rather it is premised mainly on a statistical bulletin of the number of Nigerians going and returning from overseas. Apart from the occasional recruitment tours undertaken by the federal and some state services abroad, there has never been any sustained effort to find out the number of Nigerians who are qualified and working abroad. There is no doubt that there are several qualified and experienced Nigerians teaching and working in several institutions in Europe and America who require some incentive to be attracted home. Given the comparatively favourable conditions under which many Nigerians serve abroad it is not likely, as the federal government optimistically hopes, that the most qualified, experienced and better paid among them can return to Nigeria to assist in the implementation of the 1975-80 development plan without any incentive packages.

In summary, the implications of shortfall of skilled manpower at all levels are quite obvious. First the skills, expertise, technical information and degree of management which the present national development plan requires are more than the federal and state civil services, in fact the entire public bureaucracy can cope with. The successful execution and profitable management of such technical and complex projects as the petro-chemical industry require a highly centralized, penetrative and well coordinated administrative machinery which the present federal and state civil services have not yet evolved. For instance, outside Lagos and the few scattered urban centers in Nigeria, the presence and the activities of the Federal Civil Service are hardly noticed or felt by the majority of Nigerians who live in the peripheries of society. Sometimes, the ineffectiveness of the federal and state civil services does not stem from any deliberate unwillingness on the part of the senior civil servants to assume administrative leadership, rather part of their problem is that they are overwhelmed by the sheer complexity of the tasks before them. Given their lack of knowledge of modern administrative techniques and considering the poor communication network that characterizes the entire services, as well as the absence of reliable body of technical information, the federal and state civil services tend to be inflexible to the changing needs of the growing economy and the peculiar demands of plan implementation. Consequently, successful plan implementation is easily attainable on those small scale projects which call for less development inputs of organization, management, technology, communication and information.

123

3. **Outmoded Agricultural Technology.** In 1975, out of the estimated labor force in Nigeria of about 19.22 million, 17.90 million representing 64 per cent of the entire labor force are engaged in one form of peasant farming or another. Only 2.18 million representing 7.8 per cent of the labor force are engaged in wage employment, while 7.90 million representing 30.7 per cent of the labor force serve as unpaid household workers and unpaid apprentices.[28]

The important fact that emerges out of this statistical analysis is that Nigeria remains essentially an agricultural country despite the increased contributions of the petroleum industry into its Gross Domestic Product.[29] Agriculture will continue for a long time in the future to provide means of livelihood to millions of Nigerians in spite of Nigeria's effort to accelerate the pace of industrial development.[30]

Despite the important position agriculture occupies in the economy, Nigerian agriculture as we pointed out in Chapter Two is characterized by a sharp decline in production of both export and food crops, shortage of skilled manpower, underutilization of labor and above all an outmoded production technology. The bulk of agricultural production is done by peasant farmers whose average land holdings are between 3-7 acres. The machinery used for production consists mainly of hoes, cutlasses and other primitive hand tools.[31] Given the outmoded farming technology the area under cultivation represents only 11 to 16 per cent ·of the land potentially suitable for agriculture.[32] Several constraints inhibit agricultural modernization in Nigeria. The most significant constraint is the one which is related to the problem of "technology transfer". As we pointed out earlier, the majority of the farmers are peasants who are ignorant of modern farming techniques. They are often unwilling to experiment with new methods of farming or improved variety of crops, as their existence depends on their meager farm products. The greatest challenge the Nigerian authorities face in increasing the productivity of agriculture, both quantitatively and qualitatively is how to transfer modern techniques of farming to millions of people who live in rural areas. The problem of "technology transfer" is exacerbated by lack of sufficient number of agricultural extension staff who could practically transmit the available knowledge and distribute the improved crop varieties to farmers. Shortage of qualified agricultural personnel is so acute, that several millions of farmers cannot be reached in the foreseeable future. It is estimated that throughout the Nigerian agricultural sector there are only 3,000 senior personnel, 12,000 intermediate level staff and 9,000 other skilled workers.[33] Apart from the shortage of personnel, technological transfer is also constrained by the limited information on variety of crops, soil texture, suitable agricultural equipment, methods of preservation, which is currently available for the farmers' use. Until recently the federal government was peripherally involved in agricultural production. Its role up to 1965 was confined to fundamental research on cash crops such as cocoa, palm oil, groundnuts, and cotton, rather than on food crops such as cassava, yams, rice which form the staple food for all Nigerians.[34] Concentration on a sustained and coordinated research program on all kinds of Nigerian crops, and the transmission of the outcome of such research to farms is still at the pilot stage.

The backwardness of Nigerian agriculture is also related to the land tenure system in the country. While generally most of the land in the northern states of Nigeria are owned by the state governments, there are several fragmented land holdings in the south, especially in the East Central state, where shortage of farming land and high density of population have contributed immensely to the protracted land disputes over utilization of land. While 'communal' and government ownership of land in Northern Nigeria does not hold sufficient incentives for individual farmers to invest much effort and resources in land development, fragmented land tenure system in parts of Southern Nigeria militates large scale mechanization of agriculture.

Agricultural modernization in Nigeria is also inhibited by inadequate supply of credit institutions. Though commercial banks extend credits to some medium and large scale private farmers, they are often unwilling to do the same to small farmers. Agricultural cooperatives are increasingly becoming popular in several parts of Nigeria, yet their activities do not extend to more than 5 per cent of the farming population.[36] Furthermore, the efforts of the federal government in establishing a National Agricultural Credit Bank is yet to benefit millions of farms who have no knowledge about the existence of such credit facilities. Agricultural development is further constrained by lack of an adequate supply of such other support inputs as fertilizers, insecticides, price incentives, reliable transport and distribution system and irrigation facilities. Land under irrigation is considerably limited. Only about 36,000 acres are irrigated and mainly in Northern states which in some areas have only 20 inches of annual rainfall. The major constraint against expansion of irrigation facilities includes lack of essential data on water resources, topography, crop soil acceptances and crop husbandry procedures.[37]

In summary, outmoded technology, problems of technology transfer and inadequate coordination of the federal and state governments efforts constitute a major impediment to agricultural development in Nigeria. Insufficient manpower and lack of modern management techniques result not only in underutilization of land and labor resources, but in poor project design and execution.

Modest success in implementation are more likely to be attained in those projects which require less agricultural inputs of technology manpower, and management, as well as in those small scale projects which hold immediate and direct incentives to millions of peasant farmers. Besides, plan implementation is also likely to be assured in those other projects in which the federal and state governments pool their resources through such mechanisms as task forces and project teams. As long as the problems and constraints confronting Nigerian agriculture persist there will continue to be gaps between paper plans and actual plan accomplishments.

Bearing in mind the various constraints that inhibit implementation we shall now discuss the execution of three federal projects in which two states acted as the intermediaries of the federal government. The projects are: the first phase of the federal national housing scheme in the Mid-west and East Central state; the tree crop rehabilitation scheme in the East Central state; and the accelerated food program in the Mid-west.

THE IMPLEMENTATION OF THREE PROJECTS

The first project—the federal housing scheme—is an ongoing project in all the states of the federation which slipped over from the second national development plan 1970-74 to the Third Plan 1975-80. The federal government has already committed several millions of naira on the project. It is hoped according to the revised schedule that the fourth phase of the project would be completed in 1979/80 and this would then lay a solid foundation for other 'gigantic' housing programs of the federal government. This project involves much more input of organization, management, technology and material resources than the states can readily afford to mobilize and therefore the possibilities of successful implementation are limited.

The last two projects were agricultural programs whose ultimate objective was to increase food and cash crop production as well as improve living standards of the rural population. We can hardly overemphasize the need for increased production of *food* and housing *units* as important goals of state building, for any regime which neglects these goals in Nigeria can easily fall into trouble. The two agricultural projects are small-scale projects requiring less input of management, organization or technology. Besides, they hold more direct incentives to the farmers who were involved.

Background of the Federal National Housing Scheme.

Until recently, the federal government was not involved in any large scale housing scheme for low income workers in Nigeria.

The conclusion of the Nigerian Civil War in 1970 and the increased economic activities and opportunities in the urban areas had resulted in large scale movements of people from rural to urban centers all over the country. This rural-urban migration has created acute accommodation problems in such townships as Lagos, Ibadan, Enugu, Aba, Jos,

126

Kaduna, Kano, Ilorin, and Calabar. The problem has been exacerbated by hundreds of thousands of soldiers in these cities who share the available accommodation with their civilian counterparts. The accommodation problem in cities like Lagos has reached a crisis point requiring a "task force" action. It was therefore welcome news to most low-income group Nigerians when the Nigerian head of state in his 12th Independence Day Anniversary Broadcast on the 1st October 1972 announced a National Housing Program for low-income group workers. In the broadcast he stated that the first project, in the program would involve construction of 54,000 housing units, 10,000 of which would be in Lagos, 4,000 in each of the remaining eleven state capitals. ' These figures have since been revised upwards to 60,000 housing units, of which 15,000 would be constructed in Lagos, 5,000 in Kaduna, and 4,000 each in the remaining state capitals.[38]

The construction of 60,000 housing units all over the federation between 1973 and 1980 is regarded by the federal government as the first phase in a long-term National Housing Program. The preliminary estimates for the first project was estimated to cost the federal government N1,500 million, and the sum of N180 million was provided in the 1974/75 capital estimates for the construction of the first 22,250 housing units.[39]

Our study of the implementation of the first phase of the federal housing project in the Mid-west and the East Central State will be aided by recapitulating briefly events that took place between October 1, 1972, when General Gowon made his pronouncement and December 1974 when the project took off in most of the state capitals.

Unlike other Nigerian big projects, such as the Iron and Steel industry which are non-starters, immediate steps were taken towards the implementation of the first phase of the national housing program, in January 1973, three months after General Gowon's announcement. Two Romanian consultants, Messrs. Ion Comino and Victor Sebestyen, were employed by the federal government to carry out within six weeks feasibility studies on the national housing scheme. Terms of reference for the technical study included the following:

1. To make the services of experts available to assist in appraising the existing designs of state governments and make recommendations to the federal government for the execution of up to 40 percent of the Housing program, approved in each state in the first phase of the federal government housing scheme.
2. To assist the federal Housing Authority as required in the selection of contractors and in negotiations on contract prices for the execution of the programs in the states.
3. To undertake with immediate effect the study and selection of the standard housing designs to be constructed in each of the states.
4. To initiate the study and selection of the construction system to be

adopted with a view to reducing costs and improving completion time.

5. To make detailed recommendations to the Federal Housing Authority on the physical planning studies leading to the production of master plans for the main urban areas or satellite towns in which subsequent housing is to be executed. In working on this, the consultants should take into consideration the work done by the Greek firm of Doxiados in respect to 20 urban centers in the country.

6. To advise on the structure which the federal housing Authority should take and assist the government in establishing the authority.

7. To prepare training programs for carefully selected Nigerians in various disciplines connected with the construction industry based on forecasts in the Report on the large number of professional indigenous personnel required in the next 10-15 years. The program should be in two main categories:
    (a) middle-grade technicians and artisans
    (b) professionally qualified personnel.

8. To assist the Federal Housing Authority in establishing a Research and Design unit.

9. To advise on the setting up of industries which will produce building materials.

10. To submit to the Federal Housing Authority by January 1975 a carefully drawn-up Ten-year Housing Program to follow this project.[40]

The Romanian consultants worked hard and kept to time stipulated for the study. In company with four senior officials of the federal government, the Romanian consultants visited all the states in the federation and held discussions with state functionaries on the Housing problems in each state. They were shown the possible sites for the projects in most of the states.

The report of the feasibility study was compiled and presented to the federal government about the middle of June 1973, 8 months after the housing program was announced. The highlights of the main body of the report are as follows:

(i) The first part of the report dealt with the housing problem generally. It stressed the need for adequate housing which it claimed came next to food in importance. It touched upon the quantitative aspects of housing which it said depended very much on how many funds are available, and the level of priority accorded to housing in the scheme of things in any country. It recommended a long drawn-out master plan for housing which is expected to gather momentum as more funds and more technical expertise become available. The report recommended, in view of the rapid growth of population in Nigeria, the need for embarking upon a bold housing scheme to cater not only for urban areas but also for the rural communities. On the assumption that the report would be accepted the consultants estimated that it would be possible by 1981 to construct 30,000 housing units per year, thus building about 800,000 dwellings between 1981 and 1985.[41]

The second part of the report dealt with the problems of housing in the various states of Nigeria and unearthed the following information about the states.

(i) All the state governments are experiencing a drift of population from rural to urban areas, resulting in serious human, social and economic problems.

(ii) As all the states aim at achieving even development, the need for adequate housing in the divisional headquarters has become rather pressing.

(iii) Ten of the twelve states could have liked to share all its 4,000 housing units among its divisional headquarters.

(iv) All the states agreed to make land available for the project. In two of the states (North East and Lagos), they would like the federal government to pay compensation for the land to be acquired for the project. The other states would be prepared to offer land free to the federal government provided all the states would be treated alike.

(v) Most of the states have Housing Corporations or some other similar agencies; and those which have not yet established such bodies have plans to do so. The state governments would want the federal government to merely make funds available to them, while leaving them free to construct the building in accordance to their own plans and designs.

In this section of the report, the consultants recommended that a standard medium size dwelling should be comprised of one sitting-dining room, and two bedrooms with necessary facilities. It also noted that building materials, designs and executive capacity throughout Nigeria were in short supply and stressed the need for importing building materials and expertise to supplement local resources.

The report dealt with the lack of well-kept statistical evidence with regard to the population, dwellings, fixed capital labor force, industries and lack of physical planning activity throughout the country. It recommended that Nigerian specialists and professionals in various fields relating to the building construction industry should be associated with a foreign Institute to be commissioned to conduct studies in three main areas:

(a) physical planning

(b) the study and selection of the types of apartments to be constructed, and,

(c) the study and selection of the construction systems to be adopted. The studies, the consultants hope will make it possible to embark on large-scale building construction without occurrence of grave errors; it

129

also recommended that the Nigerians who would be associated with a foreign institute in the studies should not be its employees, rather they should be joint partners.

The report also concentrated on the machinery for executing the Federal Housing program. It recommended that, while fullest use should be made of private enterprises in the execution, a central body at the Federal level with branches in the 12 states should be established. In order to combat the acute shortage of building materials the report also recommended that the construction industry should be fully industrialized, with the state governments, the federal government and private indigenous enterprises participating to the fullest extent, and where necessary in partnership with foreign investors. This recommendation involves expansion of the existing factories producing building materials such as cement, asbestos, roofing sheets, window and door frames, tiles, sanitary equipment and paints. The feasibility report did not end here, it went into detail on the location of the industries which should produce these materials and the necessary road network to be provided to make transportation easy and relatively cheap. The report equally recommended keeping proper and detailed records of expenditure of the schemes in each state, what has been achieved in concrete terms as this will facilitate control.

The report stressed the need for efficient management of finished houses. It recommended that whatever buildings are put up until 1979 should be allocated entirely on the rental basis. In the consultants' view this would ensure that houses would be occupied by people who need them most and that structures would be kept in good repair all the time, thus preventing premature deterioration.

Finally, the report recommended that the states should have the following obligations:

(a) land for the execution of the programs should be made available to the federal government free of charge by each state.

(b) state governments should ensure that building programs are executed from the funds made available to them in accordance with the designs worked out and strictly in' keeping with the established work schedules.

(c) states should provide the necessary execution needs, guidance, and control of the works in accordance with the regulations to be established by the federal government.

(d) allocation of the dwellings to be provided must be carried out strictly in accordance with the principles laid out by the federal government.

(e) each state should ensure that adequate administrative and maintenance machineries for the buildings are well established and fully equipped to discharge their functions effectively.

130

(f) the states must prepare, beginning from January 1, 1974, and, in accordance with the schedules established by the federal government the next building stage. This stage should be guided by the urban planning drawings approved for each town.[42]

In making its recommendations the Romanian Consultants took into account the general shortage of building materials and executive capacity in Nigeria. It also realized the necessity for the federal government which provides the funds to establish the principles that should govern the execution of the housing project. Given the manpower constraints in the country the report also recognized the need for the federal government to seek the cooperation of states in ensuring the speedy execution of the project. In August 1973, two months after the report was submitted to the federal government, it was approved; and the government initiated the following steps for the implementation of the scheme.

Firstly, an *ad hoc* committee of officials, made up of permanent secretaries of federal ministries of mines and power, works and housing, establishments, finance and another permanent secretary from the cabinet office was constituted to arrange the execution of the National Housing Scheme. The duties of the committee which was chaired by the permanent secretary of the ministry of mines and power included design approval, invitation to tenders, award of contracts, preparation of drafting instruction for a decree to establish the Housing Authority.[43]

However, the *ad hoc* committee was short lived, following the establishment of the Federal Housing Authority. The Authority became a "department" under the Federal Cabinet Office in Lagos, with a permanent secretary as head of the department. The Housing Authority inherited the responsibility of the *ad hoc* committee of the officials, in addition to its other powers.[44]

Secondly, in August 1973, the Nigerian head of state wrote to all the state military governors, informing them of the decisions of the federal government on the national housing schemes. This was followed by a meeting in Lagos in September 1973, in which the states sent representatives. The representatives were further briefed in detail about the housing project.

Thirdly, the federal government employed the Romanian Consulting Institute, "ROMCONSULT" as consultants for the implementation of the scheme. Under the terms of the agreement which was signed on May 4, 1974, the institute would provide a team of experts for three years in the first instance, who would form the designing and consulting arm of the Federal Housing Authority. In addition, the institute would carry out some other studies connected with the program.

With all these steps taken, it was possible for the Nigerian head of state to lay the foundation of the first phase of the scheme in Lagos

131

and North Central States on the 25th and 28th of September 1973 respectively.[45]

The first phase of the project had started in one form or the other in the 10 remaining states of the federation. However, this study concentrated on the execution of the project in the two states—Mid-west and East Central.

Implementation in the Mid West and East Central States.

As in the other states of the federation the first phase of the federal government housing scheme in the Mid West and East Central states involved construction of 250 housing units. There is nothing special about the figure 250, as it represented a small proportion of 4,000 housing units to be constructed in each of the 11 states. It was hoped that by the time the first batch of 250 was completed, some measures would have been taken to ensure an adequate supply of the building materials required for the construction of others.

Before the two states started acting as the agents of the federal government in the implementation of the first phase of the national housing scheme within their areas of authority, they signed a contract with the federal government. As agents of the federal government, the states through their housing authorities would invite tenders for contracts, negotiate with contractors, select the winners, award contracts and enter into agreements with contractors on behalf of the federal government. The state governments were also responsible for supervising construction, issuing work certificates and accounting to the federal government before money was released to them.

It was further stipulated in the agreement that the states would provide land free of charge, topographical measurements, soil reports, and general layout drawings, according to the urban planning designs of the town, the designs and bills of quantities and execution of the work for roads and drainage, water supply, sewage, electrical network etc.

It was also agreed that out of the 250 housing units to be constructed in the first phase, 12 per cent should be one bedroom type housing units, 75 per cent two bedroom type and 13 per cent three bedroom housing units.

Construction in the Mid West.

The Mid West government acquired land for the first phase of the project in Benin city. The site is situated one mile off Benin, along Benin-Auchi Road.[46] Considering the urgency attached to the project the state government established a "task force" for its implementation. The task force consisted of a representative of the military governor's office, police, air force, permanent secretaries of ministries of works, finance, land and housing and also a representative of Bendel Construction Company. The chairman of the task force was permanent secre-

132

tary of the ministry of land and housing. The main term of reference of the task force is to ensure that the first phase of the federal housing scheme in the Mid West was satisfactorily executed. The task force set out immediately to work. The Ministry of Works prepared the site which took cognizance of appropriate areas for nurseries, primary schools, dispensaries, shopping centers, community centers, parks, etc. The layout was prepared in such a way that it complied not only to the stipulation of the Benin town planning Authority but also to the directive of the Federal government housing authority. There were also provisions in the plan for football fields and tennis courts. The task force worked so hard that it was possible for General Gowon to lay the foundation of the project during his official visit to Mid West state in December 1973.

To facilitate speedy completion of the project, five construction contractors were employed. The main contractor was the Bendel Construction Company which was responsible for the construction of 186 housing units. The remaining 64 houses were constructed by four indigenous contractors. The four indigenous contractors completed their buildings according to schedule because of the limited number of houses each of the contractors had to erect.

On the other hand, the Bendel Construction Company, the government construction agency, spread out all its resources at once. It started construction of its 186 housing units at the same time. Considering the shortage of building materials which was country-wide, and the manpower constraint the company could not complete the houses within the scheduled time. The company has, however, roofed all the houses and is at present giving them finishing touches.

Though all the 250 housing units in Benin are almost completed, the infrastructures—roads, drainage, electricity etc. are yet to be completed. The Nigerian Energy and Power Authority which contracted installation of electricity has not kept to schedule. The Ministry of Work is yet to complete the construction of the access roads, while the state water board is still expected to connect the site with water. We were however, informed that money has been made available to these bodies for the installation of all the utilities so as to make the place habitable.

The construction of the project in the Mid West faced a number of problems which impeded its earlier completion.

Firstly, there was the problem of communication with Lagos; according to the procedure of releasing funds, the Romanian Consultants who liaised between Lagos and Benin had to give their approval to each stage of the work completed before money was made available. It was said that the consultants did not pay regular visits to the site to certify completed work, and this delayed the release of funds. Constant visits were made to Lagos in order to get things done.

Secondly, other government agencies such as the National Energy and Power Authority and the State Water Board, whose services were needed, were not represented in the task force committee charged with implementation of the project and hence did not appreciate the necessity of supplying their services according to schedule. The secretary of the task force committee had to write to these agencies several times to execute their own portion of the project.

The indigenous contractors would have completed their buildings earlier than they did, if all the designs were ready when the foundation for the project was laid in December 1973. Furthermore, the Bendel Construction Company which won most of the contract, took more than it could conveniently "bite" By over extending itself, it lacked the executive capacity which would have ensured completion of its contract according to schedule.

Besides, the state government was in such a hurry to achieve results that the task force in charge of the project approved the use of septic tanks for each housing unit, instead of a central sewage system which is preferable.[47]

Execution in the East Central State

The contract for the construction of the first phase of the National Housing Scheme at Enugu, capital of East Central State, was given to the Housing Development Authority (HDA) of the state.[48] According to the edict that established the Housing Authority in 1970, it was charged with the responsibility for development, construction and management of houses for acquisition and rentals by the public. Although the Housing Development Authority is a government agency, it is authorized to enter into agreement with public and private bodies for construction work. It was not surprising that the East Central State government being the agent of the federal government for the purposes of the national housing scheme in the state gave the contract to its Housing Development Authority.

As in the Mid West, phase 1 of the federal government scheme in East Central consisted of construction of 250 housing units, including roads, drains construction and sewers. The project is located in the Trans-Ekulu area of Enugu.

Unlike the Mid West where the construction of buildings, roads, sewers and other facilities were contracted out to several contractors, all the construction work at Enugu is being carried out by the Housing Development Authority. There are differences in the construction "strategies" of the two states. While the Mid West established a special committee of officials as a task force to ensure speedy completion of the project, the housing Development Authority regarded the federal housing scheme in the state as merely one of its several contracts.[49] There was no special urgency attached to the project as in the Mid

134

West. Despite the fact that the Housing Authority stretched out its executive capacity unduly it has made some progress with the construction of the buildings and roads at the building site. When we visited the site (in April 1975) over 32 houses had been completed with roofs, ceilings and primed with paint; 23 other houses had been completed with roofs but had no ceilings, while 16 others had roof trusses and purline and gable ends built up. 30 buildings had been completed to wall plate level and 12 others had reached lintel level and part wall plate. Substantial progress had also been made on storied terrace blocks while block one had been completed up to roof level, block two had reached wall-plate level, block 3 lintel level, while block 4 had its deck cast.

Much progress has been made by HDA in the provision of infrastructure at the layout. The most difficult part of the surface water sewer had been laid. The estate roads had been laid out and the scraping of existing ground level, extraction of roots and disposal of surplus material completed. The roads had also been graded to formation level including the compaction of sub-base.

In spite of the progress made by the HDA, the completion of the project is behind schedule. On investigation, the Housing Development Authority attributed this to a number of pressing problems.

Firstly, there is a problem of shortage of building materials, particularly bricks, concrete blocks, and asbestos roofing sheets. The authority has in fact resorted to imported steel panels in building walls of some of the bungalows.

Secondly, the Udoji new salary awards had adversely escalated prices of both building materials and labor. The Housing Development Authority pointed out that since its commencement of the federal contract, there has been an increase in the prices at which it purchased building materials, but there has been no increase in the contract prices. The situation has been worsened since the Udoji salary awards. The Authority claimed that most of its construction workers received 200 per cent salary increases. The general effect on the contract is that labor and material costs combined have risen approximately 200 and 250 per cent.[50] The Authority is finding it difficult to complete the contract at the original price and is pressing hard for a review of the original contract sum.[51]

Though the first phase of the federal housing scheme in the Mid West has almost been completed, while some progress has been made in the construction of the scheme in the East Central State, the completion of the scheme in the two states as well as in several other states of the federation has lagged behind schedule determined originally by the federal government. According to that schedule the first phase of the project in the two states as in all the states including Lagos would have been completed on March 31, 1974, the second phase on March

135

31, 1975, while the third and last phases would be completed on March 31, 1976 and September 30, 1976. A new schedule for completion of the last phase of the project has been fixed for 1980.

It is doubtful whether the first phase of the project would be completed by March 31, 1976. The causes of the delay as we noted in the study of the execution of the project in the Mid West and East Central states obviously include inflation, shortage of building materials, executive capacity and organizational problems.

Though there are external inputs to inflation in Nigeria, this has been accelerated by internal sources. The general shortage of building and other essential materials in Nigeria as we pointed out above is partly caused by the congestion of Lagos' port and the faulty distribution system. At any one moment within the past 9 months there was an average of 200 ships waiting at Lagos port to be offloaded.[52] Some of the ships wait as long as 3 months. Such unusual delay results in scarcity of essential commodities including building materials. They also add to inflationary pressures. Inflationary pressures had in addition been supported by the faulty distribution system which makes transportation of construction materials very expensive. It is common to find some essential materials in parts of the country while they are lacking in other parts. This is partly caused by the inadequate transportation system as well as fuel shortage which hit Nigeria since December 1974. It is ironic that a country which is a major exporter of crude petroleum suffers an acute fuel shortage. Besides shortage of building materials is also caused by the massive construction programs which Nigerian Third National Development Plan 1975-80 involves. Here and there, there is public and private construction work going on. This includes roads, bridges, army barracks and offices. Construction work as well as release of money into the economy contributed here to spiral inflation which in turn gave rise to substantial increases in prices of building materials and other essential commodities.

Unless the Nigerian federal government finds solution to the congestion at Lagos and Port Harcourt, the faulty distribution system, fuel shortage, as well as increased importation of building materials, the prices of these commodities will continually be on the increase. This will effect adversely the completion date for all the four phases of the project which has been put for 1980. Besides the cost of the project originally estimated at N500 million and revised upward to the sum of N1.5 billion naira in the third national development plan 1975-80 would have been doubled by the end of the plan period.[53]

The problem of shortage of building materials can be combated partly by expansion of the local industries which produce materials such as cement, asbestos and rods. This is however a long term measure which can scarcely have beneficial effects on the implementation problems of the current development plan.

Another problem which impedes speedy execution of the federal housing scheme as noted earlier is inadequate supply of executive capacity. The two main contractors—the Bendel Construction Company and the Housing Development Authority—engaged in the construction work in both Mid West and East Central states had their manpower stretched to the utmost.

There is no evidence of better executive capacity in the other states of the federation; the problem is even worse in the new Northern states. The federal and state governments could expedite the solution to the problem by speeding up the training of manpower, both locally and abroad, but this can hardly produce immediate significant results in order to aid the implementation of current plan projects. Besides, it is not easy for both the federal and state governments to attract international private construction companies with experience and expertise in building construction.

Another problem which inhibits progress in the construction of the buildings is organization. The Federal Housing Authority as presently constituted is too remote from the construction scene to be very helpful. Though the federal government has recently (June 1975) announced the creation of the Ministry of Urban Development, Housing and Environment, which would inherit the duties of the present housing authority and more, the ministry has yet to ramify its organizational structure as to direct effectively the construction of houses in the states. It has not yet established field offices in the states and cannot therefore coordinate the construction of the federal housing schemes effectively. Besides, its management role is likely to be constrained by the shortage of high level manpower.

In summary, the success of the implementation of a national housing scheme of the magnitude described above calls for inputs of such organizational, management, information, technological and material resources which neither Mid West, East Central nor any other state in Nigeria possess in ample quantity and quality. The inadequate supply of these necessary resources will in the foreseeable future constrain the speedy implementation of all phases of the Federal Government housing projects in all the states of Nigeria, especially in the Northern States.

The Implementation of the Tree Crop Reclamation Program in the East Central State

Background of the Project

This project was a cooperative venture between the federal and East Central State governments.[54] The latter acted as an agent to the former. The palm and rubber plantations established in the East Central state during the 1962-68 development period had suffered neglect as a result of the Nigerian Civil War. The farmers were not able, even three years after the Civil War, to resume regular maintenance and harvesting of the palm and rubber trees.

The aim of the cooperative venture which lasted from August 1973 to March 1974 was to assist farmers to reclaim 22,220 hectares (55,000 acres) of palm trees and 3,232 hectares (8,000 acres) of rubber trees.[55] The implementation of the project involved extensive movement in distribution of seedlings, fertilizers, insecticides, and above all intensive supervision of both field and headquarters staff. This required the provision of an adequate number of both heavy and light vehicles, such as lorries, touring vans, motor cycles and bicycles. Three Honda 90 motorcycles and 7 Raleigh bicycles were purchased for the newly created administrative division of the State, while 2 Mazda station wagons[56] were purchased for movement of project officers and committee members who often went to the field for spot checks. The federal government provided the money for the purchases.

A task force committee made up of federal and state government officials was established to implement the project. The state chief agricultural officer was the chairman, while the federal principal agricultural officer resident in East Central state was the secretary of the committee. The committee compares favorably in its composition with the one which supervised the implementation of the first phase of the federal government housing scheme in the Mid West. The Federal Ministry of Agriculture at Enugu provided a secretariat for the task force. The committee handled the day-to-day running of the program.

Implementation:

The implementation of the project entailed distribution of palm and rubber nurseries to farmers to replace dead ones, application of fertilizers around palm and rubber trees after the weeds were removed. Successful reclamation of a rubber as well as a palm tree meant that the farmer had underbrushed the weed-ridden plantation and cleared the palms by removing ferns and dead fronds. Some 4,666 farmers benefited from the palm tree rehabilitation program; reclamation grants amount to N116,478.23 were paid to them, while 1,820.30 tonnes (1,784.60 tons) of nitrate of potash fertilizer was also distributed to them.[57] This program after implementation achieved about 93 per cent of the target. The Table 22 shows the details of achievement in the main agricultural zones into which East Central State is divided.

The difference of 2,063.23 hectares between the target and achieved figures is accounted for mainly by the fact that some of the plots did not qualify for the reclamation exercise because they were excessively damaged through war destruction. Farmers also, in some areas, notably Abakaliki and Orlu, preferred food crop farming to the reclamation programs.

Rubber Trees: The implementation of the rubber program achieved 94

TABLE 22.
1973/74 TREE CROPS RECLAMATION PROGRAMME
OIL PALM FIELD ATTAINMENT (HECTARES)

Location IN ZONES	Original figures (Hectares)	Reclaimed figures (Hectares)	Percentage performance	No. of bene- ficiaries
Aba	2,974.65	2,462.18	82.8	482
Abakaliki	1,915.36	1,494.48	78.0	313
Awka	2,519.34	2,355.12	93.2	490
Enugu	1,358.05	1,092.21	81.6	226
Nsukka	633.27	1,021.31	161.3	156
Okigwi	1,964.25	1,625.09	82.7	379
Orlu	1,069.39	569.24	53.2	184
Owerri	1,527.93	1,486.52	97.3	359
Onitsha	1,104.13	1,385.11	125.4	250
Umuahia	3,299.47	3,284.52	99.5	576
Erei farm settlements	869.41	673.59	77.5	197
Igbariam (farm settlement)	923.75	880.32	95.3	427
Ulonna North farm settlement	556.11	556.11	100	240
Ulonna South	325.62	325.62	100	164
Ohafia farm settlement	1,039.50	734.88	70.7	223
Totals	22,060.23	19,946.30	93.3	4,666

Source: Final progress report on 1973/74 Tree Crops reclamation programme. Federal Ministry of Agriculture. Enugu. pp. 2-3

per cent of its target of reclaiming about 3,232 hectares or pre-war established plots. Some 475 farmers benefited from the program; this number of farmers was also trained in the technique of rubber tapping. Reclamation grants totaling N12,845.00 were paid to the farmer-participants, while the following rubber tapping equipment was also distributed to them: 390,000 latex cups, 260,000 cups hanger wires, 390,000 latex equipment, 1,400 collecting buckets and 1,400 tapping knives.[58] The rubber program took place in the 8 rubber zones of East Central State, as well as at Ohaji and Ulonna (North) state farms. Table 23 shows details of the accomplishments made in the 8 rubber zones of the state.

No rubber trees were reclaimed at Ulonna State farm because its rubber trees were disqualified, as they lacked adequate tappable trunks. The tree crop reclamation is a good illustration of a federal project in a state, which was successfully executed by joint cooperation of the federal and state governments. The task force committee which consisted of the federal and state government officials operated smoothly, which facilitated decision making and execution. Once the program was approved and money provided it was relatively easy for the task force to execute the project. The only major constraint that affected it was lack of personal vehicles by state and government inspection officers. This militated against regular field inspection. We understand that a special arrangement has been made for provision for transportation for these officers so that future programs will be well supervised. There has been the need to strengthen the staff strength of the federal ministry of agriculture in the state, as interest of the federal government in joint participation in agricultural development has increased.

In conclusion, apart from the constraints mentioned, the federal government funded the project adequately: N41,804.30 remained as a balance out of N500,000 which the federal government allocated to

TABLE 23.
1973/74 TREE CROPS RECLAMATION PROGRAMME
RUBBER FIELD ACCOMPLISHMENT (IN HECTARES)

Location	Original Areas (Hectares)	Area Reclaimed (Hectares)	Percentage Performance	No. of bene- ficiaries
Aba Zone	494.50	454.50	91.9	54
Abakaliki Zone	157.96	62.22	40.3	9
Awka Zone	54.34	95.55	175.8	19
Okigwi Zone	445.61	161.20	36.2	28
Orlu Zone	118.90	116.35	98	23
Onitsha Zone	69,90	82.42	117.9	19
Owerri Zone	752.05	631.65	85	79
Umuahia Zone	534.90	560.75	104.6	107
Ulonna state Farm	208.06	–	–	–
Phaji state Farm	432.08	430.87	99.7	137
Total	3,268.30	2,595.51	94.4	475

Source: Final Report on 1973/74 Tree Crops Reclamation Programme Federal Ministry of Agriculture Enugu, p. 5.

the execution of the project.[59] It is important to stress that the rehabilitation of the tree crop project in the East Central State succeeded primarily because it made less demand on inputs of organization, management, technology and information. Besides it held immediate direct incentives to farmers who participated in the program. There was also better coordination of federal and state civil services' efforts.

140

The Accelerated Food Program in the Mid West
Background of the Project:

Following the national seminar on agricultural development held at Ibadan in July 1971, in which serious note was taken about the rising prices of food, low cereal yield and low farm incomes, the federal government decided as a matter of policy to accelerate food production in the 12 Nigerian states. The government decided to induce farmers through extension staff to use improved seed varieties so as to increase their productivity.[60]

The objective of the federal government is to make Nigeria self-sufficient in cereal by 1980. In order to make this goal feasible, the federal government sponsored a team of Nigerian agriculturists drawn from the state and federal ministries of agriculture to visit Tunisia, Kenya, the Philippines, Mexico and India to study the organization of their accelerated food production programs. The Nigerian delegation was convinced after its study trip, that a form of "green revolution" was possible in Nigeria. Following the report of the delegation, a survey team of Nigerian and International experts was formed to investigate the agricultural situation and make recommendations to the federal military government on how such a program could be initiated in Nigeria. The report of the team generally referred to as the "Spragne Report", was accepted by the federal military government and the national Accelerated Food Production Program was based on the recommendations of the team. The most salient features of the recommendations include:

i.   accelerated food programs in Nigeria should concentrate on maize, rice, wheat, sorghum, millet and cassava;

ii. research and extension efforts should be commodity rather than discipline oriented;

iii. massive efforts at training both research and extension staff involved in the project, in all available institutions in the country and abroad;

iv. the project should test new crop varieties on farmers' fields for yield and acceptability in order to speed up the transfer of research results to farmers;

v.   the project should ensure the availability of all necessary inputs— seeds, fertilizers, insecticides, storage and marketing facilities to farmers;

v.   the program should encourage the transfer to the private sector, the supply and distribution of the inputs with the production of seed by government continued only to the small scale production of high quality yield;

vii. the program should promote the processing of cereals.[61]

141

Machinery for Implementation:

The execution of the project was carried out by a special committee known as 'state steering sub-committee'. The state chief agricultural officer was the chairman, while the federal principal agricultural officer resident in Mid West was the secretary. Other members included: representatives of planning and community farms sections of state agriculture; chief research Officer of the Ministry, and the farmer's union.

The field office of the federal ministry of agriculture in Benin provided secretarial facilities.

The state steering sub-committee supervised the execution of the project. The federal government provided N37,000,[62] with which all the necessary inputs such as fertilizer, mini-kit boxes of maize were purchased. It was out of the funds that all claims for transport allowances for field officers were paid.

Three hundred farmers participated in the experiment. They were provided with mini-kit boxes of maize seed, which had been tested at the sub zonal centers of the Mid West.

The mini-kit boxes contained a variety of improved maize. The farmers were also provided with fertilizer. They planted the improved varieties of maize along with their own local maize. Their work was supervised by state agricultural extension staff.

As a result of the experiment, most of the farmers involved in the projects realized the advantages of the improved varieties of maize. However they are still reluctant in doing away with their local varieties, until they are further assured that the improved varieties when planted on a large scale will attain success. The steering sub-committee has proceeded cautiously knowing that old habits die hard. For this reason many more experiements involving several farmers have been planned for the future. In 1975, the experiment would involve 500 farmers from the various sections of the state. The federal government had already provided N50,000 for the 1975 experiment.

It is planned that, after further tests had been carried out, the improved varieties which had been accepted by the farmers would be multiplied, and parcelled out into minikits and sold to farmers. The seeds would be tied with all necessary inputs as to ensure that the farmers would achieve the full potentials of the seeds.

Though the pilot project which involved only 300 farmers could be described as moderately successful, its importance should not be over stressed because there are still several constraints to be surmounted before the improved varieties of maize and other crops can be widely accepted by the farmers. Even though the improved varieties of maize have a higher yield and contain more protein, their major defect is hardness, as a result many prefer the poor proteinous and low yielding variety. There is, therefore the need to improve the quality of the new variety of maize further in order to soften its hardness. Secondly, the experiment was carried out with very few farmers, there is the greater problem of communicating the outcome of the experiment to the millions of farmers not only in the Mid West but in other states of the Federation.

Deployment of several hundreds of extension staff into the scheme will be imperative, of which there is a shortage in both the federal and state governments. If the crucial function of transmitting information to the thousands of farmers both in Mid West and other parts of Nigeria would be successfully carried out, there is need for the services of thousands of agricultural extension staff to assist the farmers because increased production of food and export crops can be achieved in Nigeria to the extent that millions of farmers acquire modern techniques of farming as well as accept improved varieties of crops. Consequently, lack of adequate agricultural staff will be a constraint for a long time on the implementation of both federal and state government agricultural projects.

Another constraint to the acceleration of technological transfer is that of harmonization of the federal and state priorities in agriculture. The federal grants and other allocations to the states for agricultural purposes will achieve the desired national objectives if the state agricultural priorities synchronize with those of the federal government. While the immediate goals of the federal government are directed towards provision of infrastructure for agricultural modernization, as well as the transmission of benefits of research to farmers, that of the Mid West state aims at achieving agricultural modernization through large commercial farms. Hence, while through the accelerated food program in the Mid West, the federal government target was the individual farmer, the immediate target of the Mid West Government was the successful establishment of large commercial farms at Warranke and Igbanke.

Differing priorities create problems of control and coordination. The federal government provided all the money and other agricultural inputs necessary for the execution of the project, while the state provided the labor. The state government wanted however to control the funds and capital equipment allocated to the project. At present the federal office of agriculture in the state is understaffed and has little authority for decisionmaking. Hence, the senior officials not only aspire to direct the actions of the federal officials, but also they wish to deal directly with the headquarters of the Federal Ministry of Agriculture, rather than its field office.

As we noted at the beginning of the chapter, the modernization of agriculture in Nigeria is constrained by several factors which include outmoded technology, poor coordination and management, and lack of adequate support inputs. These problems are likely to constrain the implementation of several agricultural projects in the current 1975-80 development plan. Successes in plan implementation are more likely to be attained in those small scale projects which make fewer demands on organization, management and technology and which hold direct incentives.

On the whole the 1975-80 development plan contains projects and programmes of greater magnitude and complexity than either the federal or state governments have resources to cope with. The gaps between the government's anticipated and available organizational and management resources help to create lag between the objectives of the plan document and the actual plan accomplishments.

FOOTNOTES

1. For the problems that constrained the implementation of Nigeria's 1962-68 Development Plan, see Edwin Dean, *Plan Implementation in Nigeria 1962-66,* Ibadan: Oxford University Press, 1972. The evaluation of the performance of Nigeria's 1970-74 Plan is contained in the introductory chapter of the current 1975-80 Plan. See Federal Republic of Nigeria, *Third National Development Plan* 1975-80, Vol. 1, Lagos: Federal Ministry of Economic Development, 1975, pp. 11-27.
2. *Ibid.,* p. 199.
3. *Ibid.*
4. International Bank of Reconstruction and Development, *Nigeria: Options for Long-term Development,* Baltimore: The John Hopkins University Press, 1974, p. 88.
5. *Ibid.*
6. Third National Development Plan 1975-80, *Op. Cit.,* p. 205.
7. I.B.R.D., *Op. Cit.,* p. 88.
8. Third National Development Plan 1975-80, *Op. Cit.,* p. 205.
9. *Ibid.,* p. 214.
10. I.B.R.D., *Op. Cit.,* p. 88.
11. Third National Development Plan 1975-80, Vol. 1, *Op. Cit.,* p. 213.
12. *Ibid.*
13. I.B.R.D., *Op. Cit.,* p. 88.
14. Third National Plan 1975-80, Vol. 1, *Op. Cit.,* p. 216.
15. *Ibid.*
16. *Ibid.*
17. *Ibid.,* p. 220.
18. I.B.R.D., *Op. Cit.,* p. 89.
19. Time described in detail the impact on the Nigerian economy of having 400 ships wait for several weeks in Nigerian ports. See Time for Monday, October 27, 1975. Also see Daily Times, August 27, 1975, p. 1.
20. The Third National Plan 1975-80. Vol. 1, *Op. Cit.,* p. 221.
21. *Ibid.* p. 224.
22. I.B.R.D., *Op. Cit.,* p. 89.
23. The Third National Plan 1975-80, Vol. 1, *Op. Cit.,* p. 225.
24. Edwin Dean, *Op. Cit.,* p. 152.
25. The Third National Plan 1975-80, Vol. 1, *Op. Cit.,* p. 376.

26. The projects that spilled over from the 1970-74 Plan to the 1975-80 Plan, partly as a result of manpower problems, include: the federal housing scheme, iron and steel industry, several road and bridge projects, such as the nine mile Oturkpo Road, Shagamu-Benin Road, Imo River Bridge.
27. Third National Plan 1975-80, Vol. 1, *Op. Cit.*, p. 384.
28. *Ibid.*
29. In 1974-75, the Petroleum and other mining industries accounted for 45.5 per cent of Nigeria's Gross Domestic Product, while Agriculture accounted for 23.4 per cent. By 1980 Agriculture is estimated to account for 18.4 per cent of the G.D.P., while petroleum and mining will be responsible for 37.1 per cent. See *Ibid.*, p. 50.
30. Assuming that most of the projects in the current 1975-80 Development Plan are successfully executed, only 580,000 new jobs are expected to be created in the wage employment sector. *Ibid.*, p. 374.
31. I.B.R.D., *Op. Cit.*, p. 78.
32. *Ibid.*
33. The Third National Development Plan, Vol. 1, *Op. Cit.*, p. 380.
34. I.B.R.D., *Op. Cit.*, p. 81.
35. The National Accelerated Food Program, which is still in the pilot stage, is one technique which the federal government seeks to use, in order to transfer modern techniques of farming and a variety of improved crops to thousands of farmers.
36. I.B.R.D., *Op. Cit.*, p. 81.
37. *Ibid.*, p. 79.
38. Federal Housing Authority *Memo* (1974) 1 June 1974, Annex V.
39. *Ibid.*, p. 4.
40. *Ibid.*, Annex 1, pp. 1-3.
41. *Ibid.*, Annex III, p. 2.
42. *Ibid.* pp. 9-10.
43. *Ibid.*, Annex of the *Memo.*
44. During the 1975-76 budget speech General Gowon announced the intention of the federal government to create six additional ministries of which the Ministry of Housing and Urban Development will be one. In June 1975 the creation of the Ministry of Housing as well as the appointment of a permanent secretary was announced. The permanent secretary who was in charge of the Housing Authority became the permanent secretary of the New Federal Ministry of Housing.
45. Federal Housing Authority *Memo, Op. Cit.*, p.3.
46. The information and data used in writing this section of the chapter were derived from interviews and discussions held with key officials of Bendel Construction Company—a government agency—and the Ministry of Works.
47. According to progress reports which the Federal Housing Authority receives from the state, Mid West is among the states which have performed well in the execution of the first phase of the National Housing scheme.
48. The East Central State Housing Development Authority was established by Edict in 1970. See the East Central State Gazette No. 32, Vol. 1 of September 10, 1970.
49. The ECS housing authority, while working on the Federal housing scheme, had several other works at hand. These included construction of Army barracks at Ohafia, staff quarters for Advanced Teachers Training College, Owerri.

50. See Housing Development Authority: *Progress Report on Projects HDA/BM/75/1* of 1975, p. 5.
51. *Ibid.*
52. Several piecemeal attempts had been made to decongest the port, but none had succeeded. The Federal government has announced plans to improve the port facilities. This may take several years to yield results.
53. Federal Republic of Nigeria, *Third National Development Plan 1975-80,* Vol. II, project summary, p. 379.
54. The discussion in this section of the chapter was compiled from the discussion and interviews held with officials of both Federal and State Ministries of Agriculture and Natural Resources.
55. *Final Report on 1973/74 Tree Crop Rehabilitation,* Federal Ministry of Agriculture, Enugu, p. 1.
56. *Ibid.,* p. 6.
57. *Ibid.,* p. 1.
58. *Ibid.*
59. *Ibid.,* p. 7.
60. This section of the chapter was compiled from discussions with the principal agricultural officer in charge of the Federal Department of Agriculture, Mid West Field Office, Benin City.
61. O. F. H. Oyaide, "The Philosophy and the Concept of the National Accelerated Food Production Program", unpublished.*Memo,* 1974, p. 2.
62. The principal agricultural officer in charge of federal field office in Benin gave the statistics of what has been spent in the project in 1974.

CHAPTER SIX

CONCLUSION

We have argued that in Nigeria as in several other African states, the crux of development problems, whether viewed in terms of integration of the state with the society or slow pace of economic development is lack of legitimated national authority. To a varying degree each African regime is primarily concerned with the problems of building and maintaining a legitimated and consolidated national authority out of congeries of interests and groups that constitute the wider society.

In our study we identified and discussed the various powerful groups and legitimated authorities in the wider environment which not only challenge the national authority but constrain the effectiveness of the federal government and civil service to induce development through national planning. In our view, the attainment of other goals of development can only be facilitated when those who occupy authority roles at national level are able to earn the legitimacy of the population. In conclusion, we will therefore re-examine the various techniques and mechanisms through which successive regimes in Nigeria have sought to create legitimated national and regional authorities and institutions.

When Britain effectively established its rule in Nigeria, in 1900, it lacked adequate material resources to secure compliance with its policies either by the use of coercion or elaborate system of positive induce-ments. Consequently, it coopted[1] local rulers and adopted a system of colonial administration which has come to be known as "Indirect rule",[2] in order to legitimize its rule. The system of indirect rule, as we pointed out in our study involves power and authority sharing between the colonial officials and the traditional authorities at the local, district and provincial levels. Under the system, the visible authorities that the majority of the people interacted with in their daily activities were the local rulers rather than the colonial officers. The granting of legitimacy to the colonial administration was 'indirect'. The local authorities earned the legitimacy of their subjects and in turn granted part of it to the colonial authorities. "Power sharing" and the incorporation of traditional rulers into the colonial administrative structure were more complete in those areas of Nigeria as Northern Nigeria which had earlier evolved elaborate administrative infrastructures such as tax, police, court and civil service structures. Through these structures the colonial officials achieved their basic objective of maintenance of law and order and consolidation of their rule. In return the colonial officials allowed the traditional rulers to exercise some administrative and judicial authority over their people with minimal supervision. On the

147

other hand, the incorporation of local authorities into colonial administration was least successful in those areas of Nigeria such as parts of Eastern and Western Nigeria where the traditional political structures were highly segmented and atomized. Undoubtedly it was from these areas that the legitimacy of the colonial administration was most successfully challenged and depleted.

Although the system of indirect rule helped for a while to legitimize the colonial authority, in the long run it did not serve as a dependable source of legitimizing the central political authority in Nigeria. First, its utility was successfully challenged by the educated Nigerian elites who could not be assimilated in the administrative structure. Second, wherever the "system of indirect rule" has been successful as in Northern Nigeria and Uganda, it granted more legitimacy to the local authorities and denied the same to the national authorities and institutions. For instance, it was the highly legitimated *emirates* in Northern Nigeria and the historic kingdoms in Uganda that resisted most, the emergence of strong and legitimated central authority in Nigeria and Uganda respectively. Consequently, creation and development of legitimated central political authority are greatly constrained in those fragmented and less integrated societies where traditional rulers effectively share in the power and authority of the central regimes.[3]

Even where 'cooptation' of a traditional ruler into a central political structure in order to legitimize authority does not involve power and authority sharing as in the case of such older polities as Britain and Japan, it is difficult to achieve a similar situation in Nigeria because none of the Nigerian traditional rulers could generate the same amount of legitimacy to the entire political system as the Queen of England or the Emperor of Japan does. Rather, Nigeria is an amalgam of diverse peoples and hundreds of historic groups and traditional authorities which have varied cultural norms and heritages. They also lack common and stable expectations about behaviors appropriate for various incumbents of authority roles at the national level. Under the circumstances it is difficult if not impossible, in order to legitimize the national political authority to incorporate the differing traditional authorities into Nigeria's central political and administrative structures.

As the process of cooptation of traditional authorities to legitimize the central authority has been less useful, the Nigerian leaders, since the attainment of political independence, have made less use of it than the colonial officers did. Rather, they have coopted the new educated elites from various sections and groups in the society into the central leadership structure to form what is generally referred to in Nigeria as a "broad based" national government. It is generally hoped that the national political authority and national institutions would be legitimated, if, the elites that constitute the central leadership structure are drawn from the various historic groups and the centrifugal forces which

148

constitute the society. Thus, a typical leadership structure in Nigeria as well as in several African states often comprises a coalition of interests, groups, and subnational groups, often with varying orientation which ranges from communalism to nationalism.[4] In an effort to legitimate the exercise of authority, the various elites coalesce to create political units actually capable of regulating behaviour and stabilizing expectations.[5] Besides the resultant leadership structure often pays considerable attention to distributing the available government positions and senior positions in the public bureaucracy according to the strength of various groups.[6] However, the fragmentation that exists between the various groups that comprises the leadership structure has not so far permitted the emergence of a strong legitimated national authority, which is able to command the loyalty and affection of the wider society.

Under the circumstances, each group in the wider society sees representation in the central leadership structure as a zero sum game. Those who consider themselves unrepresented in the structure generally may withdraw their support from the state or at least remain indifferent to its activities. The violence and military coups that have characterized several regimes in Nigeria, as well as in several African states in the past 10 years indicate that so far, forming leadership coalitions and "broad based" governments have not led to building up a reservoir of good will and affection for the exercise of national authority.

Another technique which successive regimes in Nigeria and in several African states have adopted in building legitimacy for national authority and institutions is that of constitution making and the creation of new political structures. To be sure, constitutions and political structures which have successfully survived and adapted to the changes and vicissitudes of time may serve to build up a reservoir of legitimacy for a given political system. In such a situation leaders can secure compliance with their policy choices because they can reckon and sometimes take for granted the stocks of legitimacy which various groups and individuals have invested in the institutions and the structures over a long period of time.

Nigeria has spared no efforts in making, inaugurating and discarding constitutions and political structures. Yet these constitutions and structures do not engender much legitimacy. For instance, between 1922 and 1966, Nigeria had over six different constitutions with accompanying structures and institutions. First, there was the Clifford's Constitution of 1922 which was in operation between 1923 and 1946. This constitution did not engender any legitimacy for the activities of the central government, primarily because it did not grow out of the needs of the wider society. Besides it did not provide institutional framework through which the diverse people who constitute the Nigerian society could interact, discuss their common problems, reconcile their differences or perhaps develop some ties and affection for one another and to the nation. The Clifford's Constitution was followed by those of 1946, 1951, 1954, 1959 and the Republican one of 1963.[7] The 1946 constitution provided an institutional framework for the centrifugal forces and thus weakened the legitimacy of the central legislature, because its members were elected through the regional electoral colleges. The 1954 constitution turned Nigeria into an "unbalanced" federal system of government, in which one of the constituent parts was able to "capture" the federal authority. It was further hoped that the 1954 federal constitution which made formal and elaborate provisions for federal and regional power and legislative lists, human rights, as well as structures and institutions such as parliament, supreme court, would "grow" and serve as a means not only of unifying the diverse peoples of Nigeria, but of generating strong affections for incumbents of authority roles both at regional and national levels. As later events were to prove, the hopes were misplaced and frustrated, because the federal constitution did not originate as a result of the needs of the population, but was merely an expedient instrument which was arrived at after a series of 'trade offs' and compromises first among Nigerian politicians and second, between them and British colonial officials in London. What ever legitimacy the constitution and its institutions might have embodied was completely eroded because the politicians between 1959-66 while serving their private interests, did not show any restraints in undermining the spirit of the constitution. For instance, the 1962-63 national censuses were manipulated and inflated.[8] Besides the federal election of 1964, the West regional elections of 1965 were all manipulated and rigged. In order to win the regional election in the West, Akintola violated all the rules that govern parliamentary elections—nominations were refused, electoral officers kidnapped or dismissed, so that many opposition candidates could not place their nominations, ballots were made available to government party members before polling began, election returns were falsified and candidates with a minority of votes were declared elected.[9]

Under the circumstances, the various groups in the wider society who helplessly watched the 'raping' of the constitution and its institutions did not develop any strong ties and affections for them, because they did not view them as valuable and beneficial organic mechanisms that should regulate their behaviour or stabilize their shared expectations. Besides, the frequent rate and easiness under which new constitutions were drafted, revised, modified, ridiculed, manipulated, suspended indicate vividly how little they serve as dependable sources of legitimating the activities of the occupants of authority roles. Most African constitutions and structures have had insufficient time to prove themselves and become rooted in the wider environment. As 'new'

150

constitutions and political structures do not acquire values and special sanctity over night, Nigeria may have to wait for a long period of time before whatever constitution she finally decides upon can gain root in its cultural environment and thereby generate legitimacy for the incumbents of authority roles.

Political parties have also been commonly used by Nigerians as well as several African states as means of legitimating their political authority. Between 1950 and 1966, Nigeria had three dominant political parties: the Northern People's Congress (NPC), National Council of Nigerian Citizens (NCNC) and Action Group (AG). Given the multi-faceted nature of the Nigerian social environment, which was marked by three powerful ethnic groups, none of the three parties was able to gain widespread support all over Nigeria. Rather, each of them was dominant in a particular region and was primarily supported by a major ethnic group. Although the NCNC and later AG endeavoured to expand their base of support in other parts of Nigeria, the NPC remained in name and structure essentially a communal party deriving most of its support from "native" authorities. Throughout their period of existence the Nigerian political parties were by no means mass parties with precinct support.[10] Neither were they coherent organizations bound together by common interests, purposes or close affection. Rather, they were mainly a coalition of various interests, functional and cultural associations, and traditional authorities which were originally brought together as independent movements.[11]

Besides, none of the parties had an 'independent' funding. But as a result of their control of regional governments, they were 'integrated' as semi-official organs of government and held together by patrimonial relations. The control of a regional government conferred each party a resource base to dispense patronage offices, contracts to the various groups, and individuals who constitute the party coalition. In return, the various groups granted specific legitimacy to the parties and acted as the clients of the party leaders in the provincial, district and local areas.

In Northern Nigeria the integration of the party within the structure of native authorities was more complete than either in the West or the East. In that region the traditional rulers rallied support for the party; in return the party rewarded them with appointments to boards, corporations and commissions.[12] While the Nigerian dominant and regional oriented parties were not instruments of mass mobilization, they provided means of control. In addition, they served as a means of recruiting people into the role of leadership or incorporation of real and potential enemies of regional regimes. The important fact to note is that, while the parties legitimated the regional governments, they did not serve as reservoirs of legitimacy grant to the federal government. Consequently, none of the Nigerian political parties earned enough legitimacy as to grant the same to the federal authorities.

Another technique which Nigerian leaders as well as African regimes have adopted in building legitimacy is the espousal of one form of ideology, or another. However, the plural nature of the African states had inhibited the emergence of a type of ideology, that can have a common appeal to all the diverse groups that constitute the wider society. Some of the ideologies are so diffuse that they have little utility in earning legitimacy to the central regime. For instance, Senghor's "Negritude" which is a form of cultural nationalism is so intellectually oriented that is has no grassroot support. The espousal of various forms of "African socialism" such as Obote's "Common Man's Charter", Kaunda's "Humanism" and Mobutu's "Authenticity" should be viewed as a means by which African leaders sought to create legitimacy for their regimes and thereby consolidate national authority.

In Nigeria, particularly between 1954 and 1966, there was no single ideology that "captured" the imagination of the population. Rather, there were congeries of diffuse ideologies which ranged from 'communalism' through a form of populist democracy, to "democratic socialism". However, between 1962 and 1966 the various ideologies in Nigeria crystalized into two major principles—the 'communal" principle which espoused greater autonomy for regional communal groups in a loosely bound federal system and a "centralist" principle which espoused greater national integration and consolidation of the central authority. The amount of coercion and manipulations which the advocates of each principle used in "selling" their 'political religion' and winning 'reluctant' converts not only threatened the existence of Nigeria as a political community but eroded whatever stock of legitimacy that the federal government had accumulated and in the process led to the intervention of the military into the political system.

Closely allied to ideology is the "ethnic appeal", or what is usually referred to in the literature as "tribalism". Ethnicity which is a 'modern phenomenon in several African states performed both positive and negative roles in Nigeria. First, the ethnic associations and cultural unions served as a useful mechanism for mediating discontinuities and traumas that inevitably accompany any process of modernization. Second, they helped migrants from rural to urban areas not only to adjust to their new urban settings, but to 'survive' the vicissitudes of market economy. Besides, the ethnic associations and cultural unions performed useful welfare functions, such as award of scholorships and the establishment of markets and schools.[13] More importantly the ethnic groups provided the most dependable and the cheapest means with which the regional governments in Nigeria were legitimated between 1954 and 1966. The support which each of the three Nigerian regional governments derived from a particular ethnic group helped to account for the effectiveness of the regional governments and their civil services within the period. However, while the three major ethnic groups: Hausa/Fulani, Yoruba and Igbo, granted legitimacy to the Northern, Western and Eastern regional governments respectively, they invariably denied the same to the federal government and the civil service. Furthermore, each of the major ethnic groups viewed representation in the federal government and civil service as an objective to be achieved at all costs. Consequently, the struggle between the three ethnic groups for dominant positions at the federal level not only alienated the small ethnic groups but as we remarked in Chapter Three reduced the effectiveness of the federal service. Deference and close affections to the ethnic group contributed to the emergence of "exclusive" and regional policies such as the "Northernization policy" which characterized Nigerian political process between 1960 and 1966. These policies were dysfunctional not only because so many Nigerians were denied their rights as a result of their ethnic identity, but because they helped to erode the legitimacy of civilian leaders. Besides ethnic politics exacerbated the differences and jealousies among the various peoples of Nigeria. It attenuated the associational sentiments and the desire to work together for the accomplishment of common purposes.

Finally, Nigeria and several developing states in Africa have relied essentially upon "payoffs" or positive inducements as a means of securing compliance with and support of their policy choices. "Positive inducements" elicit "Willing" compliance of individuals and groups by responding to their instrumental values which are usually specific. In all cases of 'payoffs' there is a form of bargaining or negotiation between a regime and different groups, sectors, and institutional interest groups in the society, such as the bureaucracy, police, and trade unions which usually constitute the legitimacy 'core' of an emergent African state. Invariably regimes use such inducements as salary increases, promotions, appointments to boards and agencies, acceleration of economic and social changes through national planning to "buy" the support of various groups and sectors in the society. Consequently, all African regimes—both military and civilian, are to varying degrees dependent on their civil services to secure compliance with their policies. In some instances as in the case of Dahomey and Senegal, the regimes' dependence has attained such a degree, that central political authorities in these countries can hardly "survive" for a period of time without active support of their civil servants. In fact, the key 'industry' in some of these countries seems to be "administration". Dumont succinctly remarks:

> The principal industry of these countries at the moment is administration. It is not productive and simply adds to general costs. Such costs should be reduced but in fact are swollen to the point where

personal expenses alone absorb 60 per cent of internal income in Dahomey.[14]

In Dahomey the continuous protests of civil servants had crippled all efforts to institute any form of administrative reforms. They have equally frustrated all government's austerity measures. In Senegal most of the government revenue goes to the maintenance of the civil service at the expense of funds for investments and development.[15] In Ghana, in order to assure itself of the continuous support of the civil servants, the military regime was compelled to restore car and "bush" allowances and other privileges which Busia's regime had earlier cancelled.[16] Consequently the need to earn the support of the civil service compel many African regimes to invest their meager societal resources in the maintenance of over-expanded bureaucracies; even when the other needs of society suggest investment in other objectives and goals.

In Nigeria, the degree of dependence on the federal and regional civil services to mobilize support differed considerably between the civilian and military regimes. During the civilian regime particularly between 1954 and 1966, the politicians depended more on the ethnic groups and the regionally oriented political parties than on the civil services to secure compliance with and support of their policies. Within that period, the federal and regional civil services were more compliant institutions, and the politicians were sometimes able to secure their support, not by positive inducements, but by mere manipulations and playing one group off against another. These manipulations not only affected the performance of the civil servants particularly in Western Nigeria, but compelled them to engage in acts of "Survival". Murray succinctly expressed the problem in western Nigeria at this period (1962-66):

> Governments were preoccupied with surviving and civil servants acted without knowing who their masters were to be from day to day. Working in conditions of such uncertainty, officials did not know what political support would be forthcoming for what policies nor what political conditions they would be dealing with. Nor were officials able to make plans for changes in government and thus foster good relations between themselves and the politicians.[17]

The emergence of the military into the Nigerian political process in 1966 has significantly altered the power and importance of civil services with regard to mobilization of support for the policy choices of both federal and state governments. Given the military's lack of expertise and sophistication, in the complicated process of ruling, and also taken into account the desire of military rulers to legitimize their political authority, which they acquired by coercion, they found the civil servants the most convenient and dependable source of earning legitimacy to their rule. But the legitimacy grant from the civil ser-

154

vants to the military has price tags. For instance, in 1974 the federal and state civil servants in Nigeria won an extremely generous salary increase from the military regime.[18] Despite the substantial increases, which in some instance gave some categories of civil servants 100 per cent raises, several civil servant groups and unions ignored the federal government's ban on strikes and plunged the nation into a series of wildcat strikes that nearly ousted the military government. In order to placate the civil servants and earn their continued support the military regime gave in to their demands and consequently their salaries were further revised upwards. This had not only accelerated the pace of inflation in Nigeria but has subsequently increased the cost of implementing government projects.

The legitimacy grant to the military rulers has further earned the civil servants increases in their power and the scope of their activities. For instance, senior federal civil servants attend cabinet meetings and participate actively in making decision choices.[19] Several of them, in addition to the headship of their ministries and departments, also serve as chairmen of statutory boards, corporations and government commercial companies. The senior civil servants have become so 'visible' in the political process that some of them tend to overshadow the civilian appointed commissioners in influencing the decision choices of the military rulers. This had attracted the criticism of some observers and well placed Nigerians. For instance, an observer remarked:

Of late some of these 'supercrats'. (Higher servants) have recently dropped the traditional faceless image of civil servants and have taken to making public speeches and have lauded the current position of government officials saying they are equals of commissioners and are initiators of policies and not mere executors of them.[20]

In the same vein, an experienced politician, Alhaji Isa Kaita commented on the increased "autonomous" power of the civil servants:

So many civil servants found themselves in positions of power, so much so that one has to virtually 'worship' them in order to obtain favours or have service rendered. They are no longer the obedient servants they profess to be ... They are now more or less above that.[12]

The greater involvement of senior civil servants in policy choices, and the running of government corporations and commercial companies undoubtedly reduce their capacity to superintend the implementation of projects assigned to their ministries. In general, civil servants tend to exercise less "autonomous" power in those African countries such as Kenya, Ivory Coast and Tanzania where the central political authority derives part of its legitimacy from the accumulated prestige of the rulers. Nevertheless, the civil service as an institution remains a force in all the emergent states of Africa because of its sensitive position and its near monopoly of technical information and expertise. Most of them are to varying degrees expanded beyond what is functionally relevant; because they are utilized to incorporate the growing large number of secondary school graduates.[22] Substantial civil service reforms can only be undertaken by a regime which has a dependable base of legitimacy and which have alternative sources of technical information and expertise.

Apart from seeking the support of the civil services through specific inducements, successive regimes in Nigeria, as well as in several African states, have sought to widen their sources of legitimacy by promising "attractive payoffs and inducements to more groups and sectors in the wider society. Generally, they endeavour to achieve this through one form of national development plan or the other. Consequently, most of the regimes had often drawn up "excellent" development plans which hold out such promises and inducements as acceleration of economic and social changes, "full" employment, increased social services. However, experience has shown that it is much easier to draw up a development plan which contain ambitious payoffs to the various sectors than it is to implement them. Implementation is constrained by a combination of such factors as lack of material resources, poor physical and social infrastructures, corruption, organizational malintegration, poor management and out moded technology. By far, the greatest constraint that helps to create gaps between the societal aspirations and actual plan accomplishment is inadequate monetary supply. Lack of monetary resources imposes more constraints in such countries as Dahomey, Mali, Upper Volta, Togo, Niger, Senegal than it does to such other countries as Gabon, Zambia and Nigeria which have mineral resources. The extent of planning activities by the civil service and the magnitude of 'payoffs' that are "promised" to the various sectors in the society are largely dependent on available and anticipated resources of a particular regime.

For instance during Nigeria's first national plan period (1962-68) much hope was placed on foreign monetary resources for funding key projects in the plan. Then, it was hoped that 50 per cent of £663.7 million[23] planned expenditure for the public sector would come from the foreign sources.[24] There was a shortfall in the net cash inflow from foreign sources and consequently most of the promises and 'payoffs' to the sectors and groups such as the construction of the iron and steel industry were not redeemed. In fact, the diversion of the available resources within the remainder of that plan period to secure compliance through coercion, eroded the legitimacy of the federal government.

Since the conclusion of the Nigerian civil war in 1970 and the increases in the price of crude oil in 1973, the financial outlook of Nigeria had improved drastically. For instance, Nigeria's estimated revenue for the 1975-76 financial year is N5,25 million.[25] This figure represents an increase of N2,124 million or 68 per cent over the approved estimates for 1974-75, or an increase of 142 per cent over the actual revenue collected in the 1973-74 financial year.[26] In 1975-76, it was planned that after the current expenditure had been deducted the federal government would have a net surplus of N2.23 billion and this would be transferred to development funds. The implication of Nigeria's improved financial outlook is that the federal government has now more capacity to use financial leverage to make more positive inducements to the various groups and sectors in the society and in the long run increase its stock of legitimacy. In fact, the pattern of financial allocation in Nigeria's third national development plan reflects her monetary buoyancy and increased payoffs to the various sectors and groups. For example, the allocation to the transportation and the communication sectors in the third national plan (1975-80) is twice the total amount of money spent by both the federal and state governments in the public sector during the second plan period (1970-74). Other sectoral allocations in the third plan are five or six times more than the equivalent allocations in the previous plan.

It is important to remark that availability of money alone does not make for successful implementation. Much depends on how money is effectively combined with other resources to accomplish the desired objectives. In our view too much more money than an emergent state has capacity to handle may lead to an unprecedented waste of resources and high incidence of corruption as it was evident in Nigeria, especially between 1970 and 1975. Such malaise as corruption erodes rather than enhances legitimacy of a regime and undoutedly this contributed to the fall of Gowon's regime in 1975.

TABLE 24. SOME SECTORAL "PAYOFFS" IN THE
1970-74 AND 1975-80 DEVELOPMENT PLANS (N MILLION)

SECTOR	1970-74	1975-80
Agriculture	173.195	1,300
Mining	88.523	1,400
Transport and Communication	54.523	5,500
Education	254.579	1,500
Health	112.029	400
Administration	476.396	3,000
TOTAL	1,158.900	13,000

Source: Federal Republic of Nigeria: Third Plan 1975-80, pp. 25 and 53.

To sum up, the danger in Nigeria seems less that the federal government a.:d civil service possess more power and authority to overawe the society; than the fear that they do not have enough legitimated authority to carry out their increasing economic and social functions and thereby earn the support of the powerful interests and other legitimated authorities in the wider environment. The regime in Nigeria, like others in Africa, is still confronted with the problems of institution building, which among other things include the integration of the state and society, creation of new political and social structures and infusing them with goals and values. Furthermore, Nigeria's powerful ethnic groups still have to learn how to accommodate each other and transfer their primary loyalty and affection to the national state. Individuals and groups still have to develop "associational sentiments" and 'trust' which are necessary in organizing and working together for the attainment of common purposes.[27] The problem is that political integration cannot be achieved over night nor once for all. It is a difficult process requiring skillful statesmanship and leadership. Besides institutions and structures that are able to serve as a reservoir of legitimacy to national political authority take longer periods to mature through successful survival and adaptation to the changes and vicissitudes of time.

By winning a civil war, and safeguarding the territorial integrity of Nigeria, the military regime has made a moderate start in the long and difficult process of institution building. Though military men everywhere hardly make good statesmen, Nigerian military rulers have, nevertheless accomplished a major restructuring of Nigeria's federal system by abolishing the previous four regions, dividing that unbalanced structure into a 19-state system. This has strengthened the center-periphery relationship and assured effective representation for the interests of minorities. In addition, the military regime has recently carried out minor purges and administrative reforms which are directed towards improving the efficiency of the civil service. Undoubtedly these actions earn more legitimacy and allegiance for the federal government. To be sure, Nigeria is not yet out of danger or 'crisis' situation, for new constitution and political structures are yet to be created and legitimated. Nigerian rulers equally have to devise popular means of assuring orderly and peaceful successions of leadership and government.

In the absence of legitimating ideology and political institutions and structures, all claims by Nigerian national and regional leaders to the people's legitimacy and primary identification must ultimately be won, justified or lost through performance and 'payoffs'.[28]

In the final analysis, it is by demonstrating effectiveness, particularly in the economic sector, and by granting extensive positive inducements to the various interests, individuals, legitimated traditional authorities and other groups in the wider society that occupants of national authority roles can induce them to act as "intermediate organizations"[29] not only in legitimating the national authority, but securing compliance with, and support for, their decision choices. Given her increased "windfall" resources, Nigeria stands a better chance than most other poor African states to demonstrate effectiveness by achieving economic development.

FOOTNOTES

1. A regime or an organization may resort to the process of "cooptation" to legitimize its activities when it is constantly challenged by powerful interests in the environment, and its 'survival' is at stake. A classic illustration of an organization which adopted "cooptation" strategy to legitimize its activities and thereby ensured its survival is the Tennessee Valley Authority (TVA). 'Cooptation', particularly an informal one, involves modification of goals and power sharing. See Philip Selznick, *TVA and the Grass Roots*, Berkeley and Los Angeles: University Press, 1949.

2. For the elaboration of the concept of "Indirect Rule", see the following works: Sir Frederick Lugard, *The Dual Mandate in British Tropical Africa*, 4th Edition, London: Colonial Office, 1940; Lord Hailey, *Native Administration and Political Development in British Tropical Africa*, London: Colonial Office, 1942. Margery F. Perham, *Lord Lugard, Vol. II: The Years of Authority 1898-1945*, London: Collins, 1960; *Native Administration in Nigeria*, London: Oxford University Press, 1937.

3. In Uganda, the Kabaka of Buganda, a traditional ruler who shared power with Obote, constituted Buganda as a "state" within the State of Uganda. Obote forcefully eliminated the Kabaka and appropriated the power enjoyed by Uganda's historic kingdoms.

4. "Communalists" is used here to refer to leaders who espouse principles which are directed towards greater consolidation of ethnic communities at the expense of the emergence of strong and legitimated national political center. Melson and Wolpe use the concept in the same sense. See Melson and Wolpe, *Nigeria: Modernization and Politics of Communalism*, East Lansing: Michigan State University Press, 1971, pp. 1-35.

5. Gerald A. Heeger, *The Politics of Development*, New York: St. Martins Press, 1974, p. 50.

6. Charles Anderson *et al.* refer as "ethnic arithmetic" the process of sharing leadership positions according to ethnic strength. "An effort is made to distribute the visible leadership functions within the state in some rough proportion to the strength and selfconsciousness of primary groups within the polity. In this way the primary groups have a psychic assurance that their communal interests are being defended and that there is no risk of the state being converted into an engine of hegemony of one cultural group over another". See Charles Anderson, Fred Mehden *et al., Issues of Political Development*, Englewood Cliffs, N.J.: Prentice Hall, Inc., 1976, p. 77.

7. For the strands of thoughts and ideas behind the Richards Constitution of 1946, see Lord Hailey, *Native Administration and Political Development in British Tropical Africa*, London: Colonial Office, 1940-42, pp. 168-175.
   For the provisions of the Constitutions of 1951, 1954, 1959 and 1963 see the following works: Kalu Ezera, *Constitutional Development in Nigeria*, Cambridge: Cambridge University Press, 1964; O. I. Odumuosu, *Nigerian Constitution*, London: Sweet & Maxwell, 1963. See also James Coleman, *Nigeria Background to Nationalism*, Berkeley and Los Angeles: University of California Press, 1958.

159

8. For what seems to be a fairly accurate population figures of the Nigerian census of 1962-63 which was never made public, see James O'Connell, "Political Integration: the Nigerian Case", in Arthur Hazelwood (ed.), *African Integration and Disintegration,* London: Oxford University Press, 1967, p. 169.

9. John Hatch, Nigeria: *Seeds of Disaster,* Chicago: Henry Regneny Company, 1970, p. 278.

10. Elsewhere in Africa, there have been attempts to build mass parties with varying degrees of success and failure. CCP in Ghana and TANU in Tanzania are typical African "mass" parties.

11. James Coleman and Carl G. Rosberg succinctly described the nature of African one party system, "The single party with few exceptions has been the end product of a succession of amalgamations in which pre-existing pluralism and competition were not necessarily extinguished, but merely subsumed under a more inclusive organizational level. In effect, competing parties within an emergent state often become competing factions within a one party state". See Coleman and Rosberg, Jr., "African One Party States and Modernization", in Claude E. Welch, ed., *Political Modernization,* Belmont: Duxbury Press, 1971.

12. C. S. Whitaker, *The Politics of Tradition,* Princeton: Princeton University Press, 1970, p. 375.

13. For some of the social functions of ethnic and cultural associations in Nigeria, see E. O. Awa, *Federal Government in Nigeria,* Berkeley and Los Angeles: University of California Press, 1964. See also Audrey C. Smock *Ibo Politics,* Cambridge: Harvard University Press, 1971.

14. Rene Dumont, *False Start in Africa,* (2nd Rev. ed.) New York: Praeger, 1969, pp. 78-90.

15. In 1963, the Senegalese government spent 48 per cent of its recurrent revenue to sustain the bureaucracy. See Henry Bretton, *Power and Politics in Africa,* Chicago: Aldine Publishing Co., 1973, p. 222.

16. *Ibid.,* p. 223.

17. J. D. Murray, "The Western Nigerian Civil Service Through Political Crises and Military Coups", *Journal of Commonwealth Political Studies:* VIII, 2 Nov. 1970, p. 234.

18. For the Reports on which the new salary scales were based, see Federal Republic of Nigeria, *Public Service Review Commission Main Report,* Lagos: Federal Ministry of Information, 1974.

19. For a deeper insight into 'powers' which the civil servants have acquired under a ten-year military rule in Nigeria, see D. O. Lawson, *The Role of Civil Servants in a Military Regime,* Lagos: Federal Ministry of Information, Dec. 1973.

20. Africa Confidential, Vol. 15, No. 15, March 8, 1975, p. 6.

21. Alhaji Isa Kaita, in Mahumud Tukur ed., *Reform of the Nigerian Public Service,* Zaria: The Institute of Administration, Ahmadu Bello University, 1971, p. 28.

22. Kenya is said to have 230,000 registered as unemployed. Each year 150,000 school leavers enter the job market, primarily seeking employment in public bureaucracies. See Colin Legum, ed., *Africa Contemporary Record,* 190/71, London: Rex Collings, 1971, p. B118.

23. Edwin Dean, *Plan Implementation in Nigeria,* 1962-66, Ibadan: Oxford University Press, 1972, p. 24.

24. *Ibid.,* p. 99.

25. Federal Republic of Nigeria, *Recurrent and Capital Estimates of the Federal Republic of Nigeria, 1975-76,* Lagos: Federal Ministry of Information, 1975, p. XXXVI.
26. *Ibid.,* p. XXXVII.
27. Myron Weiner, "Political Integration and Development", *Annals of the Academy of Political and Social Science,* CCCLVIII, March 1965, p. 62.
28. Seymour Lipset argues that the extent of building a legitimated political authority in the new states depends on the capacity of their regime to démonstrate effectiveness in economic developmcnt. See Seymour M. Lipset, *The First New Nation,* New York: Basic Books, Inc., 1963, p. 46.
29. For the elaboration of the concept of intermediate organizations and how they are used as stable subassemblies in building complex organizations, see Martin Landau, "Linkage, Coding and Intermediacy: A Strategy for Institution Building", *Journal of Comparative Administration* 2, 4 (February 1971), pp. 91-109.

BIBLIOGRAPHY

GENERAL

Abernathy, David. "Bureaucracy and Economic Development in Africa" *The African Review*, Vol. No. 1, March, 1971

Ake, Claude. *A Theory of Political Integration*, Home Wood: The Dorsey Press, 1967

Almond, G. and Coleman, J. S. (eds) *The Politics of Developing Areas*, Princeton: Princeton University Press, 1960

Almond, G. and Powell, G. C. *Comparative Politics A Developmental Approach*, Boston: Little Brown and Co., 1966

Almond, G. and Verba, S. *The Civic Culture*, Boston: Little Brown and Co., 1965

Anderson, Charles W. *et al. Issues of Political Development: Domestic Violence in Congo*, Englewood Cliffs, New Jersey, Prentice-Hall Inc., 1967

Apter, David. *The Politics of Modernization*, Chicago: The University of Chicago Press, 1965

Barnard, C. I. *Functions of the Executive*, Cambridge: Harvard University Press, 1938

Bendix, Reinhard. *Nation Building and Citizenship*, New York: John Wiley & Sons, 1964

Benson, George C. S. *et al. Essays in Federalism*, Claremont: Institute for Studies in Federalism, 1961

Binder L. *et al. Crisis and Sequences of Political Development*, Princeton: Princeton University Press, 1971

Black, C. E. *Dynamics of Modernization*, New York: Harper and Row Publishers, 1966

Black, C. E. and Thornton, Thomas, eds. *Communism and Revolution* Princeton: Princeton University Press, 1964

Braybrooke, D. and Lindblom, A. *Strategy of Decision*, New York: Free Press, 1963

Brzezinski, Z. K. *The Soviet Bloc*, Cambridge: Harvard University Press, 1960

Carter, Gwendolen M. ed. *African One Party States*, Ithaca: Cornell University Press, 1962

Chenery, H. B. "The Role of Industrialization in Development Programs" American *Economic Review*, May 1955

Coleman, J. S. "The Resurrection of Political Economy" *Mawaze*, 1967

Coleman, J. S. and Rosberg, C. G. *Political Parties and National Integration in Tropical Africa*, Berkeley and Los Angeles: University of California Press, 1964

Curie, David P. ed. *Federalism and New Nations of Africa*, Chicago and London: University of Chicago Press, 1964

Deutsch, K. W. *The Nerves of Government: Models Political Communication and Control*, New York: Free Press, 1963

Deutsch, K. W. *Nationalism and Social Communication*: Cambridge: M.I.T. Press, 1966

Deutsch, K. W. *et al. Political Community North-Atlantic Area*, Princeton: Princeton University Press, 1957

Deutsch, K. W. and Folz, W. J. eds. *Nation Building*, New York: Atherton Press, 1966

Easton, David. *A Framework of Political Analysis*, New Jersey: Prentice Hall Inc., 1965

Easton, David. *A Systems Analysis of Political*, New York: John Wiley and Sons, 1965

Edwards, L. *The Natural History of Revolution*, Chicago: Chicago University Press, 1970

Eisenstadt, S. N. *Modernization: Protest and Change*, Englewood Cliffs, N.J.: Prentice Hall Inc., 1966

Eisenstadt, S. N. *The Political Systems of Empires*, New York: Free Press, 1963

Eisenstadt, S. N. *Essays on Comparative Institutions*, New York: John Wiley and Sons, 1965

Elazar, Daniel J. *American Federalism A View from the States*, New York: T. Crowell, 1966

Emerson, Rupert. *From Empire to Nation*, Boston: Beacon Press, 1966

Etzioni Amitai. *The Active Society*, New York: Free Press, 1968

Etzioni, Amitai. *Political Unification: A Comparative Study of Leaders and Forces*, New York: Holt, Rinehart and Winston, Inc., 1965

First, R. *Power in Africa*, London: Penguin African Library, 1971

Finkle, J. L. and Gable R. W. *Political Development and Social Change*, New York: John Wiley and Sons Inc., 1971

Friedrich, C. J. *Trends of Federalism in Theory and Practice*, New York: Frederick A. Praeger, 1968

Geertz, Clifford. "The Integrative Revolution: Primordial Loyalties and Live Politics in the New States," in Geertz ed. *Old Societies and New States: The Quest for Modernity in Asia and Africa*, New York: Free Press of Glencoe Inc., 1963

Helleiner, "Development Policies for Africa in the 1970's" *Canadian Journal of African Studies*, Vol. IV; No. 3, 1970

Hirschman, A. O. *Development Projects Observed,* Washington: Brookings Institution, 1967

Hirschman, A. O. *Journey's Towards Progress,* New York: Twenty Fund, 1963

Hirschman, A. O. *Strategy of Economic Development,* New Haven: Yale University Press, 1958

Hodgkin, Thomas. *Nationalism in Colonial Africa,* New York: New York University Press, 1966

Hughes, A. J. *East Africa: The Search for Unity,* Baltimore: Penguin Books, 1963

Huntington, Samuel P. *Political Order in Changing Societies,* New Haven: Yale University Press, 1968

Huntington, S. P. and Moore C. H. eds. *Authoritarian Politics in Modern Society,* New York: Basic Books, Inc., 1970

Ilchman, Warren and Uphoff, N. T. *The Political Economy of Change,* Berkeley and Los Angeles: University of California Press, 1969

Ilchman, Warren and Uphoff, N. T. *The Political Economy of Development,* Berkeley and Los Angeles: University of California Press, 1972

Jacob, Philip E. and Roscans, James, B. *The Integration of Political Communities,* New York, J. B. Lippincott, 1964

Janos, A. C. "The One Party State and Social Mobilization: East Europe Between the Wars" in Samuel P. Huntington and Clement H. Moore eds. *Authoritarian Politics and Modern Society,* New York: Basic Books Inc., 1970

Johnson, Chalmers. *Revolutionary Change,* Boston: Little Brown, 1964

Jowitt, K. *Revolutionary Break Through and National Developments,* Berkeley and Los Angeles: University of California Press, 1971

Kamarck, Andrew M. *The Economics of African Development,* New York: Praeger, 1971

Katz, D. and Kahn R. *The Social Psychology of Organisations,* New York: John Wiley and Sons, 1966

Kautsky. *The Political Consequences of Modernization,* New York: John Wiley, 1972

Kedourie, Elie. *Nationalism,* New York: Praeger, 1960

Kohn, Hans. *The Idea of Nationalism,* New York: Macmillan, 1948

Kuper, Lee and Smith, M. G. *Pluralism in Africa,* Berkeley and Los Angeles: University of California Press, 1969

Lee, J. M. *African Armies and Civil Order,* New York: Praeger, 1969

Lewis, A. *The Theory of Economic Growth,* New York: Harper and Row Publishers, 1970

Lewis, A. *Development Planning,* London: George Allen, 1966

165

Leys, Colin "Politics in Kenya: The Development of Peasant Society" *British Journal of Political Science,* Vol. 1 Part B. July, 1971

Leys, C and Robson, P. *Federation in East Africa: Opportunities and Problems,* London: Oxford University Press, 1965

Learner, Daniel. *The Passing of Traditional Society,* New York: Free Press, 1958

Lipset, Seymour. *The First New Nation: The United States Historical Perspectives,* New York: Anchor Books Doubleday Inc., 1967

Livingston, W. S. *Federalism and Constitutional Change,* Oxford: Clarendon Press, 1966

Lloyd, Peter C. *Africa in Social Change,* London: Penguin Books, 1966

Lofchie, M. (ed). *The State of Nations,* Berkeley and Los Angeles: University of California Press, 1971

Luckham, A. R. "A Comparative Typology of Civil—Military Relations," *Government and Opposition,* Vol. 6 No. 1 Winter, 1971

Lury, D. A. and Robson, P. (eds). *The Economics of Africa,* London: George Allen and Unwin, 1969

Meier, G. M. *Leading Issues in Economic Development,* New York: Oxford University Press, 1970

Meier, Richard. *Development Planning,* New York: McGraw Hill Book Co. 1967

Montgomery, J. S. and Siffin, W. J. (eds). *Approaches to Development Politics, Administration and Change,* New York: McGraw Hill, 1966

Morgenthau, R. S. *Political Parties in French Speaking West Africa,* London: Oxford University Press, 1964

Nelson, Kasfir, "Development Administration in Africa: The Balance of Politics and Administration", *Canadian Journal of African Studies,* 3. 11, Winter, 1969

O'Connell, James. *The Political Class and Economic Growth,* Nigerian Journal of Economic and Social Studies, B, March, 1966

O'Connell, James. "The Inevitability of Instability", *The Journal of Modern African Studies,* 5, 2, 1967

Olerunsola, Victor A. (ed). *The Politics of Cultural Sub-Nationalism in Africa,* New York: Anchor Books, Doubleday & Co., 1972

Perham, M. *Lord Lugord Vol. II: The Years of Authority 1898-1945,* London: Collins, 1960

Perham, M. *The Colonial Reckoning,* New York: Alfred Knopf, 1962

Pant, Y. P. *Planning in Undeveloped Economics,* Allahabad, Incham Press, 1955

Pratt, R. C. *The Administration of Economic Planning in a New Independent State,* The Tanzanian Experience, 1963-66. Journal of Commonwealth Political Studies, Vol. V. No. 1 March, 1967

Pye, Lucien, *Politics Personality and Nation Building—Burma's Search for Identity*, New Haven: Yale University Press, 1962

Pye, L. W. *Aspects of Political Development*, Boston: Little Brown and Company, 1966

Pye, Lucien W. (ed). *Communications and Political Development*, New Jersey: Princeton University Press, 1963

Riggs, Fred G. *Administration in Developing Countries*, The Theory of Prismatic Society, Boston: Houghton Mifflin & Co., 1964

Riker, W. H. *Federalism: Origin, Operation and Significance*, Boston: Little Brown & Co., 1964

Rivkin, Arnold. (ed). *Nations by Design*, New York: Anchor Book, 1968

Rosberg, C. G. and Coleman, J. S. *Political Parties and National Integration in Tropical Africa*, Berkeley and Los Angeles: University of California Press 1964

Rotbert, R. I. *The Rise of Nationalism in Central Africa*, Cambridge, Mass: Harvard University Press, 1965

Rustow, D. A. *A World of Nations: Problems of Political Modernization*, Washington, D.C.: The Brookings Institutions, 1967

Scott, W. R. and Blau, P. M. *Formal Organizations*, San Francisco: Chandler Publishing Company, 1962

Simon, H. A. *Administrative Behavior*—Second Edition, New York: The MacMillan Company, 1957

Simon, H. A. and March J. G. *Organizations*, New York: John Wiley & Sons Inc., 1958

Spiro, Herbert J. (ed). *Patterns of African Development*, New Jersey: Prentice Hall Inc., 1967

Stolper, W. F. *Planning Without Facts*, Cambridge: Harvard University Press, 1966

Thompson, Victor, *Modern Organization*, New York: Alfred Knopf, 1961

Tinbergen, J. *Development Planning*, New York: McGraw Hill Book Co., 1967

Tinbergen, J. *Design for Development*, New York: McGraw Hill Book Co., 1967

Tinbergen, J. *Central Planning*, New Haven: Yale University Press, 1964

Waterson, A. *Development Planning*, Baltimore: John Hopkins Press, 1965

Werber, Max. *The Theory of Social and Economic organizations*, (ed). New York: Free Press of Glencoe, 1964

Welch, Claude ed. *A Revolution and Political Change*, Belmont California: Duxbury Press, 1972

Welch, Claude. *Political Modernization,* Second Edition, Belmont, California: Duxbury Press, 1967

Wheare, K. C. Federal Government 4th Edition, Galaxy Book, New York: Oxford University Press, 1964

Wilensky, H. L. *Organizational Intelligence: Knowledge and Policy in Government and Industry,* New York: Basic Books Inc., 1967

Wildavsky, A. *The Politics of Budgetary Process,* Boston: Little, Brown and Company, 1964

Zolberg, A. R. *Creating Political Order,* Chicago Rand McNally and Co., 1966

Zolberg, A. R. "Patterns of National Integration" *The Journal of Modern African Studies,* Vol. 5 No. 4, December, 1967

Zolberg, A. R. "Military Rule and Political Development in Tropical Africa" in Jacques Van Doorn ed. *Military Profession and Military Regimes,* Moulton: The Hague, 1969

168

NIGERIA: BOOKS & ARTICLES

Abner, Paul, "Modernization and Political Disintegration: Nigeria and Ibos", *The Journal of Modern African Studies*, Vol. 5, 1967

Aboyade, Ojetunji, *Foundations of an African Economy, A Study of Investment and Growth in Nigeria*, New York: Praeger, 1966

—— "A General Critique of the Plan" *Nigeria, Journal of Economic and Social Studies*, July 1962

Adamolekun, Ladipo, "High Level Ministerial Organization in Nigeria and Ivory Coast", in D. J. Murray (ed.), *Studies in Nigeria Administration*, London: Hutchinson, Educational Ltd., 1970

Adedeji, A. *Federalism and Development Planning in Nigeria*, Ife: Institute of Administration, 1969

Anyiam, F. *Men and Matters In Nigerian Politics 1934-58*, Yaba, 1959

Arikpo, Okoi, *The Development of Modern Nigeria*, Baltimore: Penguin Books, 1967

Awa, E. O., *Federal Government in Nigeria*, Berkeley and Los Angeles: University of California Press, 1964

Awolowo, Obafemi, *Awo: The Autobiography of Obafemi Awolowo*, Cambridge: Cambridge University Press, 1961

Azikiwe, Nnamdi, *Political Blueprint for Nigeria*, Lagos: Zik's Press Ltd., 1943

—— *A Selection from the Speeches of Nnamdi Azikiwe*, Cambridge: Cambridge University Press, 1961

Bascom, W. R. "Social Status, Wealth and Individual Differences Among the Yoruba", *American Anthropologist*, Vol. 53 No. 4, October/December, 1951

—— "Urbanization Among the Yoruba" *American Journal of Sociology*, Vol LX No. 5, March 1955

Bello, Sir Ahmadu, *My Life: The Autobiography of Sir Ahmadu Bello the Sultan of Sokoto*, Cambridge: Cambridge University Press, 1963

Biobaku, S. O. *The Egba and their Neighbours 1842-1872*, Oxford: Clarendon Press, 1963

Blitz, Franklin, ed. *The Politics and Administration of Nigerian Government*, London: Sweet and Maxwell, 1965

Bretton, H. L. *Power and Stability in Nigeria*, New York: Praeger, 1962

Burns, Alan, *History of Nigeria*, London: Allen & Unwin, 1955

Cole, Taylor, "Bureaucracy in Transition" in Tilman (ed.), *Nigerian Political Scene*, London: Duke University Press, 1962

Coleman, J. S. *Nigeria: Background to Nationalism*, Berkeley and Los Angeles: University of California Press, 1958

Collins, Robert, *Nigeria in Conflict*, London: Seeker and Warburg, 1970

Crowther, Michael, *The Story of Nigeria*, London: Faber, 1962

Dean, Edwin, "Non-economic Barriers to Effective Planning in Nigeria 1962-66", *Economic Development and Cultural Change*, Vol. 19, No. 4, July 1971

—— "Factors impeding Implementation of Nigeria's Six Year Plan", *The Nigerian Journal of Economic and Social Studies*, March 1966

—— *Plan Implementation in Nigeria 1962-66*, Ibadan: Oxford University Press, 1972

Dudley, B. J. "Federalism and Balance of Political Power in Nigeria" *Journal of Commonwealth Studies*, Vol. IV, March 1966

Eicher, Carl and Lindholm, C. (eds.) *Growth and Development of Nigerian Economy*, Michigan State University Press, 1970

Enahoro, Anthony, *Fugitive Offender*, London: Cassell, 1965

Ezera, Kalu, *Constitutional Development in Nigeria* (2nd edition), Cambridge: Cambridge University Press, 1964

Hodgkin, T. L. *Nigerian Political Parties*, London: Penguin, 1961

Johnson, Samuel, *History of Yorubas*, Lagos: C.M.S. Bookshop, 1956

Kilby, Peter, *Industrialization in an Open Economy: Nigeria 1945-1966*, Cambridge: Cambridge University Press, 1969

Kingsley, D. J., "Bureaucracy and Political Development with Particular Reference to Nigeria", in Joseph Lapalombara ed. *Bureaucracy and Political Development*, New Jersey: Princeton University Press, 1963

Lloyd, P. C., *et al.* eds. *The City of Ibadan*, London: Cambridge University Press, 1967

Mackintosh, J. P. *Nigerian Governments and Politics*, London, Allen and Unwin Ltd., 1966

Melson, R. and Wolpe, H. eds. *Nigerian Modernization and Politics of Communalism*, Islandsing: Michigan State University Press, 1971.

Murray, D. J. ed. *Studies in Nigerian Administration*, London: Hutchinson Educational Ltd., 1970

—— "The Western Nigerian Civil Service Through Political Crises and Military Coups", *Journal of Commonwealth Political Studies*, VIII. 3. November 1970

—— *The Work of Administration in Nigeria*, London, 1969

—— "Interest Groups and Administration", in A. Adedji (ed.) Nigerian Administration and its Political Setting, London, 1968

O'Connell, James, "The inevitability of Instability", *The Journal of Modern African Studies*, Vol. 5 No. 2, 1967

Onyemelukwe, C. C. *Problems of Industrial Planning and Management in Nigeria*, New York: Columbia University Press, 1966

Panter-Brick, S. B. "The Right to Self Determination" The application to Nigeria, *International Affairs*, Vol. 44 No. 2 1968

Perham, Margery, *Native Administration in Nigeria*, London: Oxford University Press, 1937

Post, K. W. J. *The Nigerian Federal Elections of 1959*, Oxford: Oxford University Press, 1963

Post, K. W. and Vickers, M. *The Structure and Conflict in Nigeria 1960-66*, London: Heinemann, 1973

Royal Institute of International Affairs: *Nigeria, the Political and Economic Background*, London: Oxford University Press, 1960

Schwarz, F. A. O., *Nigeria: The Tribe, The Nation or The Race*: The Politics of Independence, Cambridge: M.I.T. Press, 1965

Sklar, Richard, *Nigerian Political Parties: Power in an Emergent African Nation*, New Jersey: Princeton University Press, 1963

Smock, A. C., *Ibo Politics*, Cambridge: Harvard University Press, 1971

Smythe, Hugh and Smythe, M. *The New Nigerian*, Stanford: Stanford University Press, 1960

Stolper, W. F. "How Bad is the Plan", *Nigerian Journal of Economic and Social Studies*, Vol. 6, No. 3, Nov. 1964

—— "Economic Development in Nigeria", Journal of Economic History Vol. XXIII No. 4, December, 1964

—— *Planning Without Facts*, Cambridge: Harvard University Press, 1966

Stokke, Olav, "System Transformation in Nigeria: Cooperation and Conflict", *Nordic Journal of International Politics*, 3, 4, Vol. VI, 1971

Tilman, R. O. and Taylor Cole, eds. *The Nigerian Political Scene*, Durham: Duke University Press, 1962

Tukur, Mahmud (ed.), *Reform of the Nigerian Public Service*, Zaria: Gaskiya Corporation, 1971

Whitaker, C. S., *The Politics of Tradition Continuity and Change in Northern Nigeria 1946-1966*, New Jersey: Princeton University Press, 1970

Williams, Babatunde A. *Political Trends in Nigeria 1960-1964*, Ibadan: African Education Press, 1964

NIGERIA: OFFICIAL PUBLICATIONS

Agricultural Development in Nigeria 1965-1980, FAO Rome 1966

Annual Report of the Federal Department of Agriculture 1973-74, Federal Department of Agriculture Lagos, 1974

Proceedings of the National Agricultural Development Seminar Ibadan, 1971

Recurrent and Capital Estimates of the Government of the Federal Republic of Nigeria 1973-74 Lagos, Federal Ministry of Information 1973

Recurrent and Capital Estimates of the Government of the Federal Republic of Nigeria 1974-75, Lagos, 1974

Recurrent and Capital Estimates of the Government of the Federal Republic of Nigeria 1975-76. Lagos Federal Ministry of Information, 1975

Federation of Nigeria, National Development Plan 1962-68, Lagos, 1962

Federal Republic of Nigeria, Second National Development Plan, 1970-74, Lagos, 1970

Federal Republic of Nigeria, Second National Delevopment Plan 1970-74, First Progress Report, Lagos, 1972 and Second Progress Report 1974

Federal Republic of Nigeria, Guidelines for the Third National Development Plan 1975-80, Lagos

Federal Republic of Nigeria, Third National Development Plan 1975-80, Vol I & II, Lagos, 1975

Federal Republic of Nigeria, Public Service Review Commission Main Report, Lagos, September 1974

Lawson C. O. The Role of Civil Servants in a Military Regime. Lagos, 1973

History of the Federal Government Housing Programme, from October 1972 to date, Lagos, 4th June, 1974

National Housing Programme: Preparation for the Construction of Houses for the 1974/75 Financial Year, Lagos, 1974

East Central State Housing Development Edict, 1970

East Central State Housing Authority, Progress Report on Projects. Enugu, 1975

Paper on Low Productivity in the Public Services in the Federation, Lagos, July 1971

172

Personnel Administration in the Public Service and the Role of the National Council on Establishments' *Memo, Lagos,* 1973

Report of the Special Committee of the Three Whitely Councils on the Review of the General Orders, Lagos, 1973

Guide to Technical Assistance in Nigeria, Lagos, 1965

External Grants and technical assistance, Lagos, 1974

The Philosophy and Concept of the National Accelerated Food Production programme. *Memo,* 1974

Final Report by the Task Force Committee on Oil Palm Reclamation Programme 1972/73

Final Report by the Tree Crops Development Committee, 1973/74

White Paper on Development Administration in Mid Western State of Nigeria

Fifteenth Annual Report on the Federal Public Service Commission for the period 1st January to 31st December, 1971, Lagos, 1972

Minutes of Emergency Meeting of the Country's Public Service Commission and other Recruitment Agencies, Lagos, February 1975

Report of the Mid West State Public Service Commission for the period January-December 1972, Benin City, 1973

Public Service Commission Selected Circulars, March 1964-April 1974, Benin City, 1974

Annual Volume of the Laws of Mid Western State of Nigeria, Benin, 1973

Mid Western State of Nigeria, Some Aspects of Public Administration in a Developing Economy, Benin, 1973

East Central State of Nigeria, Three Years After the Civil War, Official Document, No. 6 of 1974

ECS Civil Service Manpower and Staff Development, Enugu, March 1972, and March 1973

ECS of Nigeria, Progress Report 1970-72, Enugu, Official Document No. 3 of 1973

ECS of Nigeria Statistical Digest 1972 Enugu, Official Document No. 20 of 1974

Divisional Administration Edict 1971. ECS Extraordinary Gazette No. 33, Vol. 2, August 1971

ECS, Public Service Commission, Annual Report, 1973-74, Official Document No. 8 of 1974

INDEX

Action Group 12, 29, 32, 33, 34, 52, 58, 60, 62, 151
Administrative Class 79
Administrative Machines 1, 12
Administrative Positions 45
Akintola, Samuel 33, 60
Arochuku 17, 44
Aros 18
Asika 81
Authority 7, 8, 9, 10, 13
Awolowo 0, 2, 4, 29, 62,
Azikiwe, N 2, 4, 30
Ashby Commission on High Education 91

Balewa, Abubakar 33
Bendel Construction Company 132, 134
Bello, Ahmadu 2, 4, 32, 33, 57, 60
Biafra 62

Calabar 44
Centralized Chiefdom 20
Central Planning Office 99, 101, 102, 104, 105, 106, 107, 109
Central Political Authority 148
Civil Servants see Civil Service
Civil Service 3, 12, 13, 26, 31, 41, 42, 47, 48, 51, 53, 55-59, 61, 64, 68-70, 77, 79-81, 97, 114, 121, 123, 154-155
Cliffords Constitution 149, 150
Coersion 7, 8, 33, 147
Colonial Administration 45, 46, 87-88, 148
Colonial Authorities 44
Colonial Development Funds 89
Colonial Regimes 42
Common Services Organization 50
Constitution, Nigerian 11
Contractor Finance 74
Corruption 81, 82, 83
Counter Coup 3
Coups, Military 3, 8
Cultural Associations 24
Cultural Organizations 2

Cultural Pluralism 16

Economic Development 1, 11
Economic Activities 4
Economic Organization 16
Education Western 23, 24
Egba 19
Ekiti 19
Emir 2, 17, 44-45, 148
Ethnic Groups 2, 17, 18, 21-2, 25, 26, 153
Ethnicity and Discipline 79
Expatriate Firms 88
Extended Family 17

Federal Executive Council 110
Federal Housing Authority 126, 127, 128, 131, 137
Federalist Principle 41
FESTA see World Black Festival of Arts and Culture
Fulani 2, 17, 20

Gate-Keepers 44
God-fathers 80
Government White Paper.
Udoji, 76, 79
Gowon 34, 61, 62, 81, 127

Hausa 2, 16, 19, 21, 24, 25, 30, 31, 62, 153
Hausa Society 19
Hausa Status System 19
Hausa Traditional Political System 17
Housing Development Authority 134, 135, 137
Hutu 8
Ibadan 19
Ibibios 24, 25
Ideology 9
Ife 19
Igbo 2, 16, 17, 18, 20, 21, 22-26, 30-1, 55, 62, 153
Igbo Economic Institutions 17
Igbo Political Institutions 17, 19
Igbo Society 19
Igbo Status System 19

174

www.ingramcontent.com/pod-product-compliance
Lightning Source LLC
Chambersburg PA
CBHW021907020426
42334CB00013B/511

* 9 7 8 9 7 8 1 5 6 0 0 6 4 *